Praise for The Conflict of the Ages Series

" ... Great to teach about creation and that theory ... religious approach more then the scinetific but I want my children to know both and make up their minds."

" ... Exceptionally well researched and superbly informative ... "

" ... Should be required reading for every college bound teenager ... "

"I can't wait to dive into volume two."

The Conflict of the Ages
Part One Teacher Edition
The Scientific History of Origins

by

Michael J. and Mary C. Findley

The Conflict of the Ages Part One, Teacher Edition
1. The Scientific History of Origins

by Michael J. and Mary C. Findley

"Speaking the truth in love."

Table of Contents

Note to the Reader

Note to the Reader: Mouse over text for hyperlinks to references at the end of this work. If a quotation is included in a graphic, that graphic will contain a hyperlink. There are also hyperlinks from the reference back to the main text.

(Note: When clicking on a hyperlink, touch or place the mouse on or in a character, not in a space between letters or words, to ensure the hyperlink works correctly.)

This work includes three types of material:

A. Our Own Statements, Thoughts, and Opinions

B. Quotations from the Holy Scriptures

These will appear in Italic font. If no version is listed it is the King James Translation.

C. Quotes from Other Sources.

Fragment of Jubilees from Qumran
Public Domain image

Quotes from other sources vary wildly in accuracy and reliability. An example of highly reliable material outside of the Bible is the *Book of Jubilees*. The Coptic Church regards the *Book of Jubilees* as inspired Scripture. There are twenty-one copies of the *Book of Jubilees* among the Dead Sea Scrolls. The *Book of Jubilees* is not inspired. It contains errors. Note the testimony from Epiphaneus, a bishop of Salamis (A.D. 310-403?), referenced below.

> "Epiphaneus does not introduce the material from *Jubilees* as scripture, and *Jubilees* is not among the biblical books he names in his treatise *Measures and Weights;* but the information in the *Book of Jubilees* was reliable enough for him to use in refuting a sect that attributed a different origin and nature to Seth."
>
> "He also reproduces *Jubilees'* connection between the twenty-two works of creation until the Sabbath and the twenty-two generations until Jacob."

With Byzantine historians, "Josephus and *Jubilees* were regularly cited together, since, in the scope and the material treated, the two works were parallel."

Source for Jubilees Authority[a]

An example at the other extreme is the *Epic of Gilgamesh*. We refer to it because at the time of this writing it is considered to be the world's oldest written document. Its only true purpose was to deify man and support the local tyrant. It is mostly erroneous, sometimes dangerous, and is difficult to read and understand. Still, the *Epic of Gilgamesh* contains some useful information. There are multiple extant versions of the *Epic of Gilgamesh* with considerable variations. While there are fragments of the *Epic of Gilgamesh* dating back to the beginning of the second millennia, maybe even the third millennia, BC, the most complete extant copy is a Babylonian version found in 7th century BC library of the Assyrian king Ashurbanipal. This is the version we use. It is also the most common version, since it is the oldest complete version.

When Noah's family left the Ark they passed on the true history of mankind to their descendants. Every culture, therefore, was originally founded on accurate information. The various historical accounts included in this work still contain some accurate information. We begin each point with the information taught by the appropriate Scripture passages. That is followed by additional evidence to support the Scriptural teachings. This additional evidence includes various records as well as archeological and geological evidence.

Cover of the "Ancient book of Asher" from Biblefacts Annotated Edition

The *Book of Jasher* needs special explanation. One reviewer critiquing this work for publication stated that the "*Book of Jasher* is not authentic. What is being cited is an 18th century forgery". This reviewer's error concerning the *Book of Jasher*, is, sadly, widespread and accepted by many otherwise very well-educated believers. If you are concerned about this error, then please examine the article in the References, Footnotes, Expanded Study and Appendix Materials (near the end of the book) on the *Book of Jasher*.[b]

Many ancient Jewish sources are quoted, including Philo, Josephus, the *Sedar Olam,* the *Book of Jubilees, the Book of the Bee*, the *Cave of Treasures,* the first *Book of Enoch*, various Talmuds and Midrashes, in addition to the *Book of Jasher*. Many non-Jewish sources are also quoted. The Jewish books are from the Second Century AD or older. None of them are inspired by God and all contain errors. Sources quoted in these modules support positions in the Word of God. There is little value in extensive study of any of these works, but they are documented in case you wish to examine them. They are all based on older works and accurately record older Jewish traditions.

The Above Material Appears in the Student Text

I. Introduction

Preface to the Teacher

Preface to the Teacher

1. The *Conflict of the Ages* series is to aid in the partial fulfillment of academic requirements for history, philosophy, science, and literature, including vocabulary. It follows the chronology of World History.

2. The target audience is homeschool Middle/High School. The target reading level is 9th grade. Because it is a combination of vocabulary, literature, history, and science you, as the teacher, have opportunities as well as responsibilities. You are especially responsible for determining what is appropriate for your students. You may limit this material by either slowing the pace for your particular student or you may skip or eliminate material. You should not feel pressured to spend the same amount of time and energy on each section or even each student.

All students are not on the same level. As a teacher, you must be familiar enough with the material to know how much your students can handle. Homeschool, unlike a traditional classroom, can tailor both the methods and the amount of material to an individual student's needs.

3. The primary purpose is to equip students to face the established Secular Humanist culture. It is impossible to answer every possible invention of Secular Humanists. However, there is sufficient depth and scope to allow students and teachers to understand that answers do exist. Enough references are included that anyone who is interested can successfully research any problem they might encounter.

4) This is a reasonably comprehensive presentation of information encompassing the Creation through the Ice Age, including the Flood. Sometimes this need to be comprehensive requires presenting the same material from different perspectives.

5) This is essential information for a defense against indoctrination by the religion of Secular Humanism. This indoctrination process in western societies is done through the educational system, the workplace, entertainment, and through the legal system. The Secular Humanist indoctrination process has become so pervasive that it is likely found in the entire western culture as well as many cultures outside of the West.

6) The *Conflict of the Ages* is designed to be as inexpensive as possible. The ebook format meets this need very well. Our e-format and print books are available at major online retailers. Some ebook download sites set pricing according to file size and we keep within the minimum allowed. The books are available in print, mobi, and epub format. Epub is the most widely read and accepted format to many online retailers. These ebook formats limit the internal formatting. Options such as sidebars, multicolored text or backgrounds, parallel columns, and many other common magazine and textbook features are not available for the most basic ebook readers, so are not included in our textbook. Every effort has been made to make the books attractive and easy to follow, with plenty of graphics and illustrations.

The print books have minimal formatting changes necessary to convert from an ebook to a print format. Color graphics in the ebook versions will be black and white in print, again, to keep costs down.

The introductory material included in this Teacher's Edition is not included in the Student Editions. However, some of the necessary introductory material is included in the References, Footnotes, Expanded Study and Appendix Materials (near the end of the book). You, the teacher, need knowledge of the material, of the student, and the direction and guidance of the Holy Spirit.

A. What Is the History of Civilization?

The history of civilization is the record of man either yielding to God's will for His glory or struggling to rebel against God. "Nonreligious" history does not exist. All history is religious, especially secular history. We only choose which religion to follow. We either choose to follow the revealed religion of Jesus Christ or we rebel against the Creator. The forms of this rebellion vary greatly. At this time, the majority of Western cultures choose to rebel against God by practicing the religion of Secular Humanism.

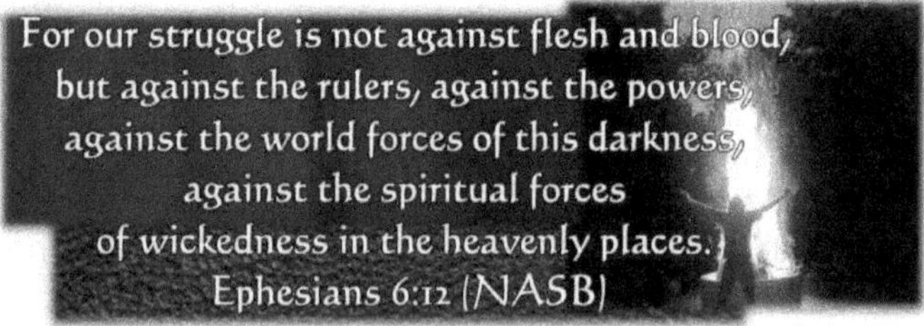

"For our struggle is not against flesh and blood, but

against the rulers, against the powers, against the world forces of this darkness, against the spiritual forces of wickedness in the heavenly places." Ephesians 6:12 (NASB)

Secular Humanism is America's Established Religion. All textbooks must conform to the Established Religion to get published by what are known as mainstream publishing houses. We who oppose this Establishment of Religion are Disestablishmentarians. Those in positions of political power, especially in academic positions of power, are fighting to keep their power and privilege. These are Antidisestablishmentarians; hence the title of our book.

Cover of Antidisestablishmentarianism from Findley Family Video Publications

Antidisestablishmentarianism began as the introduction to the *Conflict of the Ages* series, but grew to be a book in its own right.

The Preface and Introduction to *Antidisestablishmentarianism* are included in this book's References, Footnotes, Expanded Study and Appendix Materials. They are also on our blog, *Elk Jerky for the Soul,* (Accessible by going to the blog tab on our website, https://findleyfamilyvideopublications.com) available at no charge. Traditionally, a preface explains why a book is written. It lays out the foundations for the *Conflict of the Ages* series as well. We strongly recommend that you read this preface, even if you do not read the rest of *Antidisestablishmentarianism* or other parts of the *Conflict of the Ages* series.

The Magna Carta opens with the words, "In the first place we grant to God and confirm by this our present charter for ourselves and our heirs in perpetuity that the English Church is to be free and to have all its rights fully and its liberties entirely". The concept that the English Church is to be free became the basis for the first amendment to the US Constitution: "Congress shall make no law respecting an establishment of religion, or prohibiting the free exercise thereof..."

This amendment is today openly violated because Secular Humanism has become our established religion.

"The United States Supreme Court has held that secular humanism is a religion. Belief in evolution is a central tenet of that religion." (Supreme Court Justice Antonin Scalia in *Edwards v Aguillard, US Supreme Court,* 1987) Justice Scalia included this statement in his dissent. It is a simple statement of what should be a well-recognized fact of history.

B. The Tools of the Historian

Our responsibility is to limit the infinite. Buildings are better evidence than individual bricks. Cities are better evidence than individual buildings, and entire civilizations are better evidence than cities.

1. Education (The following quote is footnoted c in the introductory section of the endnotes.)

... Scientific history ... is that the method that we use ... something akin to the scientific method. It is based on at least three characteristics ....
The first is to establish that the evidence is reliable.
The second is making certain that the analysis being made is logical.
And third, the analysis must lead to a generalization
that is based on rational argument.
Romila Tharpar

"... Scientific history ... is that the method that we use is something akin to the scientific method. It is based on at least three characteristics ... The first is to establish that the evidence is reliable. The second is making certain that the analysis being made is logical. And third, the analysis must lead to a generalisation that is based on rational argument." Professor Romila Tharpar, *Frontline magazine Volume 18 - Issue 19, Sep. 15 - 28, 2001 India's National Magazine from the publishers of THE HINDU.*

The foundation of Scientific History is education. Education means that you do not have to personally experience something for it to be true. You can rely on the observation and experiences of others to learn things. You cannot personally experience everything that has ever taken place or been done. You do not need to personally experience poison, a fall from a cliff, or an explosion, to understand that each of these can be deadly.

For example, George Washington's inauguration took place on April 30, 1789. No one alive today was there, but no truly educated person questions that this event took place. It is documented and verified. We learned about George Washington's inauguration through education.

Yet for some inexplicable reason this understanding of the concept of education and how education works is ignored by the true believers in the new religion of "Science". Of course, Secular Humanism includes many more people than the true believers in Scientism. This new religion of "science" is simply one denomination of Secular Humanism.

Secular Humanism in general and Scientism specifically put faith and trust in education. Yet the very same process described by the word "education" describes the activities of a good eyewitness. The same Secular Humanists who put their faith and trust in "education", vehemently deny the exact same process when it describes an "eyewitness".

Here is just one example of this denial. Every year millions of scientific papers are written. We have to trust that these papers are honest, follow scientific methods, and prove what they intend to prove. We are not present at the experiments. These people are scientific eyewitnesses. No one who reads scientific papers has the resources, time or money to replicate every experiment described in every paper. We must trust the honesty of these papers for science to be true. These scientific eyewitnesses are providing us with an education.

Every educated person understands that scientific papers, teachers in a classroom, textbooks, encyclopedias, dictionaries, or any other sources can be deliberately forged or innocently contain errors. Yet they are still excellent eyewitnesses. They are even better when the reader has the skill and training to recognize and understand mistakes, errors, and forgeries.

It is also true that eyewitnesses at the scene of a crime are usually very poor witnesses. The problem is not the concept of an eyewitness, or education, but the quality or the education of the eyewitness. Just because the education and eyewitness processes are valid does not mean that all education is valid or all eyewitnesses are trustworthy.

2. Sources

It is critically important that scientific history knows the quality of the sources relied on. Yes, there are oral sources, but historically, oral sources have been as respected as reliable eyewitnesses or written documents. While there are some exceptions, in US courts, oral testimony is preferred over written testimony. Written documents can be "read in" at the time of the trial, but only under very limited circumstances. Eyewitnesses can be cross-examined, while written documents must be either accepted or rejected without the ability to further examine the written testimony.

Charlton Heston presents the Bible as part of the "oral tradition in storytelling" in his narration of the picturesque Bible video series *Charlton Heston Presents the Bible*, as if teachings passed on orally were understood to be less accurate or reliable and therefore merely legends and myths. In contrast to Charlton Heston's "oral tradition in storytelling", the Exodus of the children of Israel from Egypt is told in the Bible as a straightforward, factual, historical event.

Socrates, in Plato's Dialogue *Phaedrus*, addresses the subject of oral versus written history.

> "'Theuth [Thoth] ... was the inventor of many arts ... but his great discovery was the use of letters. ... Thammus [the god Ammon] was the king of ... Egypt; ...To him came Theuth ... desiring that the other Egyptians might be allowed to have the benefit of [his inventions]; ... when they came to letters, This, said Theuth, will make the Egyptians wiser and give them better memories; ... Thammus replied: ... you ... attribute to them a quality which they cannot have; for this ... will create forgetfulness in the learners' souls, ... they will trust to the external written characters ... This is an aid not to memory, but to reminiscence, ... not truth, but only the semblance of truth; they will be hearers

> of many things and will have learned nothing; they will appear to be omniscient and will generally know nothing; they will be tiresome company, having the show of wisdom without the reality."

Plutarch, in his discourse on the life of Lycurgus and his rule over Sparta (the Lacedaemonians) in ancient Greece, expresses the belief that oral tradition is a way of making the law more firmly fixed in the mind.

> "None of his laws were put into writing by Lycurgus, indeed, one of the so-called "rhetras" forbids it. For he thought that if the most important and binding principles which conduce to the prosperity and virtue of a city were implanted in the habits and training of its citizens, they would remain unchanged and secure, having a stronger bond than compulsion in the fixed purposes imparted to the young by education, which performs the office of a law-giver for every one of them."

There is considerable disagreement about whether the Scriptures were in some part orally communicated before being written down. The point is that even if they were it does not make them less authoritative or reliable. Socrates may not be entirely justified in discounting the value of written records but he reinforces the point that oral communication of history does not make it unreliable or inaccurate. Memorizing and passing on history demands great discipline and does not result in a form of the child's game "gossip".

3. Accuracy

The issue is the accuracy, truth, honesty, and importance or *significance* of the information. *If the information is correct, the method of transmission is not important.* So how can we know if the information is both accurate and significant? Historians usually begin by establishing a chronology. The mantra of many historians is "chronology is the backbone of history".

Stele of Hammurabi's Law Code

Stele of Hammurabi's Law Code image from Wikimedia Commons

Is this true? Is "chronology the backbone of history?" A simple look at the difficulties of dating the well-known stele of Hammurabi's Law Code teaches us dating is not as certain as secularists would have us believe. If chronology is fabricated then such a chronology is not the standard of accuracy on which to base everything else.

In A.D. 1901-1902 a French team excavating in Susa, one of the ancient capitals of Elam, then Persia, now modern Iran, discovered pieces of a basalt stele. It was completely reconstructed and now sits in the Louvre in Paris, France. The head of the French team, M. de Morgan, used the surroundings where it was found to date the stele, the now famous Law Code of Hammurabi, to around 1100-1200 BC.

Excavating in Nippur at the same time was an American/German team headed by the German-born American Hermann Hilprecht. Nippur is in ancient Mesopotamia, an area ruled over by the Assyrians, Babylonians, Persians, Greeks, and Ottoman Turks, and is now modern Iraq. They found a kings list with the name Hammurabi on it. This list made Hammurabi a ruler in the 24th century BC. Hermann Hilprecht immediately (January 1903) proclaimed in a lecture at the University of Pennsylvania that the Hammurabi stele was the oldest law code ever found.

A book entitled *The Oldest Code of Laws in the World by Hammurabi, King of Babylon*, was immediately published in early 1903 and is available as an ebook through *Project Gutenberg*. It proclaims that Hammurabi ruled from 2285-2242 B.C. The forward is by C.H.W. Johns, M.A., of Cambridge. The book was printed in Edinburgh.

Since 1903, several other Sumerian kings' lists were discovered. A rather brief but thorough article in the Roman Catholic online encyclopedia *New Advent* describes the major positions mainstream archaeologists take on the time Hammurabi actually ruled. Most 21st Century archaeologists hold to some type of a "middle" position, that Hammurabi ruled around 1700 B.C.

This very questionable date is the best archaeology can do. They honestly examine the evidence to the best of their abilities. But the evidence is always incomplete and human abilities are limited. The exact date Hammurabi ruled is far less important than the manner in which archaeologists arrive at their conclusions.

The true scientific approach is that One Who created the Universe was the only flawless observer. He has communicated accurately to us. God has left us with physical evidence to examine. That material evidence will lead us to honestly conclude that the earth is much less than one million years old. There never was a Jurassic or a Cambrian period.

While we will reference many articles and books which refute many false assumptions, this work will emphasize accurate historical records.

One well known source which needs special mention is *Wikipedia*. One reviewer wrote "*Wikipedia* is not a scholarly source, and it is always in a state of flux." That same reviewer also said, "Students who rely on your work for school projects will be penalized if they cite *Wiki*."

He is absolutely correct about the attitude of many (most?) professors grading papers at the university or college level. You should warn your students about this attitude and that they should be careful with their citations.

We cite one example of the kind of problems with *Wikipedia* in COA3, Point VI. Material Results of the Flood, D. Radiohalos, 3. The Uniformitarian Answer? This is a *Wikipedia* article which calls Creation Science a pseudoscience. We document how their false charge cannot stand.

It is also true that all scholarly sources are "always in a state of flux." The *Wikipedia* article we use as an example in the above link accurately quotes an incorrect peer-reviewed article. In the example we cite, *Wikipedia* chose to accurately quote an incorrect article because it stated what that author believed.

You are responsible to understand what is and what is not true. When you are educated well enough to understand the methods used to determine what is and what is not accurate, then *Wikipedia* will be a very valuable resource. It is filled with very simple, basic information and definitions which are accurate enough for most general use. Even though *Wikipedia* contains errors and changes, so do all sources. All major respected sources contain errors.

Wikipedia is a very good starting point with its citations. Even when you realize that the information and conclusions in the main article are inaccurate, you can read the source articles and begin a search using those sources. If you do not learn what you need to know from those sources, they should cite their sources and you can continue your search through those sources.

Whether, then, you eat or drink
or whatever you do, do all to the Glory of God.
(1 Corinthians 10:31).

"Whether, then, you eat or drink or whatever you do, do all to the Glory of God." (1 Corinthians 10:31 NASB).

Our touchstone of truth is the Word of God. Correlation of the literature, geology, physics, biology, archaeology, and art of all countries will be reduced to those elements which we understand to give the greatest possible glory to God or to point out the most significant rebellion against Him.

C. The Conflict of the Ages Series.

1. The book *Antidisestablishmentarianism* is the introduction to this series.

The main body of the work is divided into four sections:

a. *What Is an Establishment of Religion?*

b. *What Is Secular Humanism?*

c. *What Is Science?*

d. *What Are the Results of the Establishment of Secular Humanism?*

(The fourth section includes suggestions on what we should do about Secular Humanism.)

The four sections of *Antidisestablishmentarianism* are each available as a separate book. The section titles from the main book are the titles of the serial versions. It is simply the introduction to the *Conflict of the Ages* (COA) series. Each of the following work in the series is available as an individual book in the student edition.

2. COA part 1 covers origins. *(Conflict of the Ages Part One: The Scientific History of Origins)*

3. COA part 2 covers the origin of evil and the antediluvian world. (*Conflict of the Ages Part Two: The Origin of Evil in the World that Was)*

4. COA part 3 covers the Flood and the Ice Age. *(Conflict of the Ages Part Three: They Deliberately Forgot: The Flood and the Ice Age)*

5. Guidelines for all of the books in the *Conflict of the Ages* series.

a. Included sources are recognized by academic authorities as valuable and necessary for a complete study of World History. Many sources are compared with the Scriptures. This can build discernment about what to accept and reject.

Mythology (like the *Epic of Gilgamesh*) may not contain religious truth but gives insights into culture and lifestyles of the people of that time and even what the physical world was like.

Religion helped a ruler, as the representative or descendant of a god, unify authority. This is the earliest church-state union. In some cases grains of the original truth of the Scriptures (such as the flood epic) remained a part of the religion but in corrupted form.

Historical accounts (like Hesiod) seek to preserve a people's history and culture in the face of internal divisions or external corruptions or attacks. They may contain errors but sometimes include ancient sources no longer in existence today. They can add to the knowledge of the ancient world when compared with other sources. Other ancient documents, especially those of Jewish origin, combine religious teaching with history and other knowledge.

b. The writing style is what Microsoft Word calls "standard". The Flesch reading ease target is approximately 50%. The Flesch-Kincaid reading level is no more than 10th grade for the overall average of any individual module. For *COA1*, the Flesch reading ease is 54.6%, and the reading level is 9.7. For *COA2*, the Flesch reading ease is 56.2%, and the reading level is 9.8. For *COA3*, the Flesch reading ease is 48.4%, and the reading level is 10.8.

c. The amount of material has to be suitable for students to absorb. While we do not pretend that the material is easy, it is written on a level which, with due diligence, can be grasped by the average high school student.

d. Hyperlinks connect to more difficult books and articles outside of the main text.

There is a main text with hyperlinks to articles and books found in the References, Footnotes, Expanded Study and Appendix Materials and to reference works outside the main text. There is no attempt keep these expansion articles to the Flesch-Kincaid standards of the main text.

e. The Scriptures are the absolute authority. These other sources can contain valuable knowledge and studying those makes for a well-rounded education as well as fulfilling academic requirements. The key is not to allow secularist beliefs to confuse students into thinking that there are different kinds of truth. Segregating subjects encourages compartmentalizing information that should be taken and evaluated by one standard, God's Word.

f. This is essential information for defending yourself against those who attempt to indoctrinate you into their religion, the religion of Secular Humanism. This indoctrination process in Western Societies is done through the educational system, the workplace, entertainment, and through the legal system. This indoctrination process has become so pervasive that it is likely found in the entire western culture as well as many cultures outside of the West.

Our goal is not to answer every possible problem in detail, but to reveal to you and your students the correct questions and how to think the problem through to the correct conclusion.

Know this first of all, that in the last days mockers
will come with their mocking,
following after their own lusts, and saying,
"Where is the promise of His coming?
For ever since the fathers fell asleep,
all continues just as it was
from the beginning of creation."
For when they maintain this,
it escapes their notice that
by the word of God the heavens existed long ago
and the earth was formed out of water
and by water, through which the world at that time
was destroyed, being flooded with water.
2 Peter 3: 3-6

"Know this first of all, that in the last days mockers will come with their mocking, following after their own lusts, and saying, "Where is the promise of His coming? For ever since the fathers fell asleep, all continues just as it was from the beginning of creation." For when they maintain this, it escapes their notice that by the word of God the heavens existed long ago and the earth was formed out of water and by water, through which the world at that time was destroyed, being flooded with water." (2 Peter 3:3-6 NASB)

D. It Escapes Their Notice

The *Conflict of the Ages* Series is designed for believers. But the world is controlled by unbelievers who are experts at forcing their religion on others. Their religion appeals to human pride. They proudly classify anyone who refuses to accept their religion as ignorant. Point out that their belief system is a religion and usually they are outraged. They falsely claim that you do not know what they believe or what the word religion means.

Our culture indoctrinates into this religion from preschool. This established religion is founded on vast periods of time, often called deep time. People are indoctrinated to accept this as science. Deep time is not science. It is, rather, the foundation for the religious system of Secular Humanism. Though complete and detailed information can expose this religious belief system, we must understand that the god of this world has blinded the minds of the unbelieving (2 Corinthians 4:4 NASB). Evidence and information will not persuade these people. They are blinded so that they might not see the light of the gospel of the glory of Christ (2 Corinthians 4:4 NASB). Only God the Spirit can remove this blindness.

Nevertheless many even of the rulers
believed in Him, but because
of the Pharisees
they were not confessing Him,
for fear that they would be
put out of the synagogue;
for they loved the approval
of men rather than the approval of God.

John 12:42-43

Nevertheless many even of the rulers believed in Him, but because of the Pharisees they were not confessing Him, for fear that they would be put out of the synagogue; for they loved the approval of men rather than the approval of God. (John 12:42-43)

Mockers require acceptance of their religious mockery to obtain a PhD, to be offered a job, to hold any position of authority, and in many cases, to even earn enough money to make a living. Like the first century Jew facing the Pharisees of his day, people today fear to challenge this establishment of religion because they love the glory of men more than the glory of God.

Mockers dishonestly proclaim that refusal to believe in their religion is opposition to science. But Creation and the Flood are not issues of science. The scientific evidence supports the Word of God. To give an oversimplified explanation, science is how things work, while religion is why things work. Modern science has completely rejected this basic definition of science and elevated "Science" to an all-encompassing religion. Classical science is based on the orderly collection and observation of knowledge. Einstein's quote "God does not play dice with the universe" defends the foundations of classical science, Intelligent Design, and an orderly universe. Stephen Hawking used to attack this with the religious phrase, "Not only does God definitely play dice, but He sometimes confuses us by throwing them where they can't be seen."[c1]

The order of classical science is based on the order found in the Word of God. Isaac Newton's laws of physics (Note that Newton wrote more defending his beliefs in Christianity than he did about physics) and the genetics laws of the monk Gregor Mendel are examples of people professing faith in God who laid the foundation for entire branches of science (physics and genetics).

Yes, "God created the earth for His glory" is a religious statement. Just as religious is the statement that "the earth came into existence millions of years ago by random chance". It is a religious belief with no verifiable material evidence for support.

What we see in the world around us today is the material evidence for the Flood. This "general revelation" can be compared to the historical record. When compared to any other ancient religious document, the Word of God is the only historical document having a complete record in chronological order beginning with the creation of the universe. Other ancient documents, such as the Mesopotamian epics and the Qur'an, describe their versions of Creation and Flood in pieces interspersed throughout these writings. It is also likely that many of the events in these other documents happened near the end of the Ice Age, hundreds of years after the worldwide Flood. We are simply not capable of distinguishing, in many writings outside the Bible, the difference between a global Flood and massive local floods.

The physical evidence that remains of these floods is rocks. Rocks are often presented as evidence that the Earth is a certain age. However, rocks do not come with labels saying they formed gradually over millions of years. Neither do they have labels saying they were formed cataclysmically less than five thousand years ago.

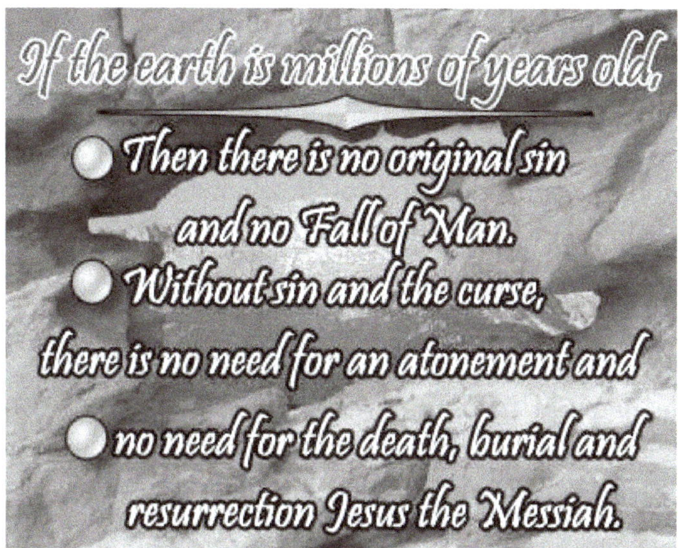

If the Earth is millions of years old, Then there is no original sin and no original sin and no Fall of Man; Without sin and and the curse, there is no need for an atonement and no need for the death, burial, and resurrection of Jesus the Messiah.
Window in rock image Public Domain from Pixabay

As Abraham told the rich man in Hades, "If they hear not Moses and the prophets, neither will they be persuaded, though one rose from the dead" (Luke 16:31). Jesus meant that rejection of the Old Testament Scriptures as historically and scientifically accurate and true leads to rejection of Him. *For had ye believed Moses, ye would have believed me: for he wrote of me. But if ye believe not his writings, how shall ye believe my words?* (John 5:46, 47) If you don't accept the literal accounts of Creation, the Fall, and the Flood, how can you accept the literal account of the death, burial, resurrection, and atonement of Jesus Christ?

This is not just an "interpretation" of the Bible in opposition to material evidence. See the appendix for "What Does the Scientific Evidence Prove?" which includes evidences for a young earth. This is Chapter Fourteen from *Antidisestablishmentarianism*. Secular

Humanists usually just ignore this evidence. Though most of these are what they dismiss as "the usual young Earth arguments", our works include them because they are factually correct. Getting a Secular Humanist to carefully examine even one of these points is, sadly, very difficult.

They almost always justify their positions with highly complex circular reasoning. They rely on their own authority (Citing education such as a PhD and years of experience in this field as authoritative). But they condemn Christians for relying on the authority of a two-thousand-plus-year-old book.

Dr. Larry Vardiman,[d] PhD in Atmospheric Sciences, spoke of meeting Carl Sagan. "He immediately began asking me a series of leading questions about how a well-trained scientist such as myself could have confidence in a book written by a bunch of ignorant sheep herders thousands of years before any real science had been discovered."

II. Foundational Assumptions

Why do you get up in the morning?

Do you go to work?

Do you go to school?

Do you fix your our own food?

Do you eat, bathe, study, work out, talk to friends, pray, sing?

Whatever decisions you make, you make because of assumptions. You stay in bed because you assume that it does not make any difference. You go to work or school because you assume that sometime in the future you will need money. Or perhaps you simply believe that you are doing what is right. These assumptions, or whatever assumptions guide our lives, are really what we believe. They are "why" we do what we do.

A. A System of Assumptions Is a Religion

Textbooks seldom inform the reader of their system of assumptions. Perhaps the authors are so thoroughly indoctrinated that they do not understand their own system of assumptions. One assumption leads to another assumption. You may choose to use the phrase "system of assumptions" or "belief system" but the most well-known term is a *religion*. Whatever term you use, they all have the same meaning.

1. Tools Used to Disguise Their Assumptions

When reading a textbook or discussing serious issues with Secular Humanists, always remember that the real issues are the religious assumptions the formulas are based on. Do not be misled by the use of:

a. Mathematical formulas,

b. Archaeological evidence, or

c. Physics to prove a point.

The mathematics, physics, or archaeology might be important and necessary points. But they also might cloud the real issue. The issue is not the language of mathematics, the use of formulas, or the kind of physical evidence. The correct use of a formula does not justify an incorrect underlying assumption. Always carefully examine their assumptions. These assumptions are why they believe what they believe.

2. An Example of How Assumptions Are Used: An "Assumed" Population Problem

This is easier to understand with an example. One possible example is the so-called "repopulation problem". Secular Humanists have invented a "repopulation problem" where no problem exists. They falsely claim that there was not enough time or the proper conditions did not exist for repopulating the earth after the flood. A look at the facts will expose the faulty foundational assumptions.

Noah lived for three hundred and fifty years after the Flood. His son Shem lived for six hundred years after the Flood. Though men likely died from accidents or murders during this time period, the natural death rate from old age for three hundred and forty years after the Flood was, statistically, zero. The first death the Bible records after the Flood was Peleg, three hundred forty years after the Flood. So when anyone claims repopulation after the Flood is a problem, they are using population formulas based on current population growth rates. They are using incorrect assumptions. The following is a list of incorrect assumptions for the assumed "repopulation problem".

a. They assume that existing known birth and death rates should be applied to the past.

The historical written record shows a statistically zero death rate combined with a much higher birth rate. Examples are:

- The number of children born to Abraham by Keturah and number of Jacob's children
- Noah died 58 years after Abraham was born.
- Shem died 50 years after Jacob was born.
- Jacob's first child was born when he was 84.
- Jacob died at 147 years old with a household of 70.

"The Number of children born to Abraham by Keturah and the number of Jacob's children; Noah died 58 years after Abraham was born; Shem died 50 years after Jacob was born; Jacob's first child was born when he was 84; Jacob died at 147 years old with a household of 70."

b. They assume a population of 27 million for the year 2000 BC.

They claim "archaeological evidence" for this number, but even a simple examination of the evidence shows an assumption of continuous growth over an assumed period of time.

1) One assumption (evolutionary time scale)

2) Is used with a second assumption (that population growth rate in the third century BC was the same as it is now)

3) As "proof" for a third assumption (world's population in 2000 BC).

c. They assume the harsh living conditions immediately after the Flood continued for hundreds of years.

They believe that these harsh conditions resulted in very low childbirth rates and high mortality rates. This assumption has no supporting evidence, is impossible to verify even if it were true, which it is not, and contradicts every written record of the time period. The written record of Scripture tells us that Noah did not open the door of the Ark and release the occupants until he had evidence of growing vegetation (the olive leaf the dove brought back). Noah also planted a vineyard after the Flood. The scientific evidence shows abundant vegetation at the end of the Ice Age. This evidence of abundant flora and fauna is preserved in much of the permafrost of Siberia and the Yukon. How long it took to develop the abundant vegetation is a completely unknown assumption. But secularists desperately need this third assumption to artificially suppress the population numbers in order create an artificial problem where no problem exists.

3. Facts compared with the population assumption

The real conditions for several decades after the Flood are in fact ideal for population blooms, especially with sea and plant life.

a. The slowly falling sea level

b. with high humidity,

c. warm temperatures, neither too hot nor too cold

d. abundant rainfall

e. lack of creatures to eat the vegetation (at first)

f. are optimal conditions for plant growth.

g. A far more reasonable assumption is that within a very few decades the available land would be covered in thick vegetation and animal populations would be exploding.

The hunter/gatherer culture, popularly depicted as a primitive, bare subsistence struggle for life, would more likely be a lifestyle based on extreme abundance and laziness. Food would be readily available with minimal effort.

4. Contradictions in the Bible is a false assumption

Always examine the assumptions of those doubting the Word of God. Those assumptions are their religious beliefs, even when they refuse to admit that they are religious. If these artificially-contrived "contradictions" in the Bible concern you, *Answers in Genesis* has two very good books answering these mythical contradictions, *Demolishing Supposed Bible Contradictions* *Volumes 1 & 2* by Ken Ham, Bodie Hodge, and Tim Chaffey.[e] If you just want articles proving the supposed contradictions in the Bible to be false, *Creation Ministries International* has a nice collection at *creation.com*.

Like every text ever written, this text, the *Conflict of the Ages 1*, is founded on assumptions. It is a simplified examination of the scientific records. The question-and-answer format is designed for homeschool use. Because we assume the Bible to be accurate and scientific, this material aligns with the scientific testimonies of the eyewitnesses to the historical records contained in the Word of God.

B. The Bible Is Historically Accurate.

Everyone builds his life on assumptions. Scientists assume that instruments are accurate. In this COA series, the word *assumption* is a synonym for belief. We assume, that is, believe, that the Word of God is true. If you would like to know more about the scientific basis for the assumption that the Word of God is true, Josh McDowell wrote a book explaining these assumptions, *New Evidence That Demands a Verdict*. Francis Schaffer's book, *The God Who Is There*, also does a good job of explaining why we believe that the Word of God is true. His series on civilization, *How Should We Then Live? The Rise and Decline of Western Thought and Culture* integrates art, literature, and languages, as we intend to do. We also have numerous short articles explaining our beliefs on our blog, http://findleyfamilyvideopublications.com/ where you can also find links to our other works.

The basic assumption that the Word of God is true leads to other assumptions. The Word of God includes accurate history and normal literature.

1. Historical-grammatical interpretation

   We take the historical-grammatical interpretation. "When the plain sense of Scripture makes common sense, seek no other sense; therefore, take every word at its primary, ordinary, usual, literal meaning unless the facts of the immediate context, studies in the light of related passages and axiomatic and fundamental truths, indicate clearly otherwise. God in revealing His Word neither intends nor permits the reader to be confused. He wants His children to understand." Dr. David L. Cooper.[f]

2 The Bible should be read like other literature.

We have examined the evidence and conclude that the facts teach that the Bible should be treated like any other literature in its proper historical and grammatical context. It claims to be the Word of God and it cannot be reasonably "interpreted" to be something else. It must be accepted or rejected as a whole.

3. Religion has a unity with all other academic fields

There is a unity of science, history, literature, mathematics, the arts, and the Scriptures. Divorcing the Bible from other subjects allows secularists to put it in a separate category from the "academic" studies. The Bible is scientifically and historically accurate. It also uses literary devices. Other ancient works contain similar poetic devices and figures of speech which can aid in understanding the Scriptures. The order of the universe, the methods God commands men to use for investigation, and the purpose of the universe are all found in the Word of God and are foundational to science. These concepts in the Word of God are the opposite of the concept that the universe is result of random chance and completely without any overriding purpose.

4. The Bible was written to be understood.

"Rightly Dividing the Word of Truth"[g]: from our blog

Public Domain period image from Shakespeare's Romeo and Juliet

Shakespeare put the words in Mercutio's mouth after he was stabbed in a swordfight, "No, 'tis not so deep as a well, nor so wide as a church-door; but 'tis enough, 'twill serve: ask for me to-morrow, and you shall find me a grave man." (*Romeo and Juliet*, Act 3, Scene 1.) Though Mercutio could still talk, like Adam and Eve, he knew that his wound was fatal. Though Romeo did not grasp the significance of this statement at first, Mercutio knew that he would be in the grave tomorrow.

Anyone who understands Shakespeare has little problem understanding Mercutio. Yet the same people who have no difficulty with Shakespeare suddenly find the Bible incomprehensible. I am told several times a day, by people who have no difficulty comprehending very difficult English literature, "You are not interpreting the Bible correctly." The real issue is not comprehension but a choice, a decision. They do not want to understand. They simply reject the clear meaning of the words of the Bible.

The Bible is a book of literature. It does not need to be interpreted. At least, it should not be interpreted in the sense that it does not mean what it says. They come back with, "So you believe the earth is flat when it says 'the four corners of the earth'?" *After this I saw four angels standing at the four corners of the earth, holding back the four winds of the earth, so that no wind would blow on the earth or on the sea or on any tree.* (Revelation 7:1) The Bible uses literary devices such as the four corners of the earth. As Mercutio used the double meaning of the word grave (serious and death) in Romeo and Juliet, so the Bible is filled with figures of speech.

Just like Shakespeare, or any other literature, the Bible is written to be understood. Since our culture is far removed from Hebrew, Greek, Roman, and even Egyptian, Babylonian, and Persian cultures, some things are difficult for us to understand.

Why did a wedding last seven days?

Why did Boaz's close relative take off his shoe as a sign of rejecting the marriage pledge?

Why would a wife give her husband a thousand pieces of silver?

The answers to these, and any other questions we might have about the Bible, are to be found in the Bible itself and understanding the culture in which they were written, not in fanciful personal opinions some glorify by calling them "interpretations" for the express purpose of discrediting the Word of God. For instance, when the vision of Jesus Christ in Revelation Chapter One mentions a sword coming out of the mouth of Jesus Christ, we already know that the sword of the Spirit is the Word of God and that God not only brought all things into existence by that Word but will also judge all things by that same Word.

C. Secular Humanism Is Founded on the Assumption (Belief, Choice) of "Deep Time."

The foundational assumption needed for this kind of unbelief, rejecting the science and history presented in the Bible, is a belief in deep time. This belief permits not only a rejection of a universe designed, created, and controlled by God, but also a belief in an entirely materialistic universe.

When we accept the Bible as the Word of God and rightly divide the Word of Truth, other assumptions follow. The Word of God describes in some detail how the world came into existence. Belief that God created the world in six days with each day having a single evening and morning is an assumption used throughout the *COA* series. The evidence for a young earth is the greatest material evidence that the Word of God is true and science falsely-so-called is a satanic lie. Since evolution is impossible in 6000 years, the evidence for a young earth and a catastrophic, worldwide flood must be lied about, disguised, and deliberately distorted. It is a religious bias, not a scientific disagreement. The Bible calls this attitude unbelief.

Evolution is impossible without vast amounts of time, which they call deep time. Without deep time, the only possible explanation for life is some form of God who created it. Also known as Intelligent Design, this can take the form of Deism, which seems to be the belief Albert Einstein took to the grave. It can also be some form of theistic evolution or it can be progressive creation, which believes that God directed evolution.

1. Deep time is founded on two basic beliefs.

a. The earth is millions or billions of years old.

b. Special or direct creation by God is not possible.

Unbelievers present many assumptions as evidence for the age of the earth and the universe. The following five are probably used more than anything else. They attempt to use two separate arguments; proving deep time and disproving Creation and the Flood.

Astronomy is not proof of "Deep Time"
The Geologic Column is not proof of "Deep Time"
Radiometric Dating is not proof of "Deep Time"
Dendrochronology is not proof of "Deep Time"
An Ice Age is not proof of "Deep Time"
Public domain image from Pixabay

Astronomy, radiometric dating, and the geologic column are their three major pillars presented as "proof" of vast ages for the earth. Astronomy is examined in more detail in the first module, *The Scientific History of Origins*.

Neither dendrochronology nor a series of ice ages are major pillars of deep time. However, they are commonly given as "evidence" that the Flood is a myth and never occurred. If God never judged the sin of men with a flood, then evolution by random chance is the most reasonable alternative.

Each of the following, except for astronomy, will be examined in detail in the third module, *They*

Deliberately Forgot: the Flood and the Ice Age. The following is a brief statement before looking in more detail at why these are assumptions and not evidence. The assumptions underpinning radiometric dating are more complicated, so the details of these assumptions are explained in the third module *They Deliberately Forgot: The Flood and the Ice Age*; Section VI, Material Results of the Flood.

Once again, the foundational assumption needed for this kind of unbelief, rejecting the science and history presented in the Bible, is a belief in deep time. None of these five assumptions presented by Secular Humanists are valid proof of deep time.

2. Astronomy

Deep time includes the belief that stars billions of light years distant are billions of years old. The only scientific way to arrive at such a conclusion is to use instruments to measure the distance. Today, the distance to the stars is measured by either stellar parallax for closer objects or by careful measurements of minute variations in the light for more distant objects where parallax measurements will not work. Stellar parallax carefully measures the position of stars and their relationship to one another. Six months later, when the earth is on the opposite side of the sun and the two measurements are separated by as great a distance as possible, a second set of measurements is taken. Extremely careful measurements are taken of the differences, which allow calculations to determine the exact position of the stars and other interstellar objects being measured.

Astronomers insist that these measurements are very accurate. It is very likely that the conclusions are very accurate, especially the measurements of nearer objects measured by stellar parallax. However, there is no way of verifying those distances and the measurements must be extremely precise with very sensitive instruments.

The important point is the claim that we are "looking back in time." The Scriptures teach that we can only look back a maximum of 6000 years, since that is the beginning of time. Because the concept and even the term deep time originated with "astronomical distances," we must confirm that these vast distances are accurate and how these distances, if accurate, translate into vast amounts of time. In this case confirmation does not mean other astronomers examining the same information with the same assumptions. Confirmation means examining astronomical distances using a different technique or tools. At this time, no other verification tools are known to exist.

After these warnings, we understand that a scientific examination of the evidence simply leaves us with the idea that billions of light-years are very likely true. But "probably true" still leaves the possibility open that astronomic distances might not be accurate.

The important point is expressed in the graphic below:

These vast distances are then assumed to equal vast amounts of time; the assumption is that there was no God to create the stars and put them in place; that assumption is then used as proof of "Deep Time."
Public Domain image of a nebula from Pixabay

To put it another way, the assumption that the stars were formed without a Creator, is used as proof there was no Creator. When simplified to the basic assumptions, the circular reasoning becomes very clear.

The term "death" of astronomical objects is also frequently given as some form of verification. The "death" of a star, or any other stellar object, is a manmade term. The death of a star or any other stellar object does not prove some type of mythical "life cycle" for stars, nor does the word death support any kind of age for the star. Neither the assumed "stellar life cycle" nor great distances prove great age for the universe.

When we observe more distant objects that are more than 6000 earth-years distant, the additional distance does not mean more time. Great distances are only that; great distances. They do not even imply great amounts of time. God created and placed these objects in space. While we cannot state with certainty the method God used, we can say that by the end of the fourth day of Creation the celestial objects and the photons of light between the object and the earth were in place. We are not looking billions or even millions of years back in time, as evolutionists believe. That belief is without any verifiable evidence.

3. The Geologic Column.

Exhibit at the Grand Canyon in Flagstaff, Arizona. The plaque reads "Grand Canyon Strata," as in, strata of the Geologic column. Wikimedia Commons

The phrase deep time is probably misused even more in connection with the "geologic column" than it is with astronomy. Very real strata from all over the earth are spliced together to create the geologic column. While the geologic column is easy to find on the Internet and is common in textbooks, it is a little more difficult to find in real life. Very few places on earth have as many exposed strata as the Grand Canyon. This is why the Grand Canyon is frequently referenced for strata of the geologic column. Even the many strata of Grand Canyon are only part of the supposed geologic column.

Careful examination of the strata of the Grand Canyon shows us upper strata containing fossils, then thick, angled strata nearly devoid of fossils on the bottom. These thick strata nearly devoid of fossils are angled downward and labeled Precambrian in the picture below. This clearly shows that these strata were created some time before the strata which are deposited horizontally. These horizontal strata make up the visible strata and include fossils.

a. Primary Strata

The thick strata nearly devoid of fossils were formed before life was created. Since there are almost no fossils in these layers, they were most likely created on the second or third day of creation. Nearly two hundred years ago, when geologic terminology was first crafted by creationist/catastrophists, this was called the Primary Strata.

b. Secondary Strata

The strata deposited as a result of the Flood were called the Secondary Strata. Secondary strata make up the majority of the strata we see.

c. Tertiary Strata

The strata deposited after the flood were called Tertiary. The first person to use the terms Primary, Secondary, and Tertiary to describe geologic strata was the Italian Giovanni Arduino (1714-95). Though he did not believe in a Flood as described in the Word of God, he did believe in a catastrophic division between Secondary and Tertiary strata. As the terms gained widespread acceptance, most were in agreement that a catastrophic event ended the Secondary strata and began Tertiary strata. Some believed that this catastrophe was the flood of Noah's day. Others believed in deep time and rejected the timing. Until about the time of Charles Lyell in the early 1800s, the divisions between Primary/Secondary strata and Secondary/Tertiary were almost always considered to be catastrophic. These original geologists used the word Tertiary to

> describe any strata "after the Flood." The Ice Age strata are included in the Tertiary. Though the term Tertiary is still used, uniformitarians do not realize that catastrophists first used the term Tertiary, which means "third stage".

We have no evidence of large strata being deposited after the original creation and before the Flood.

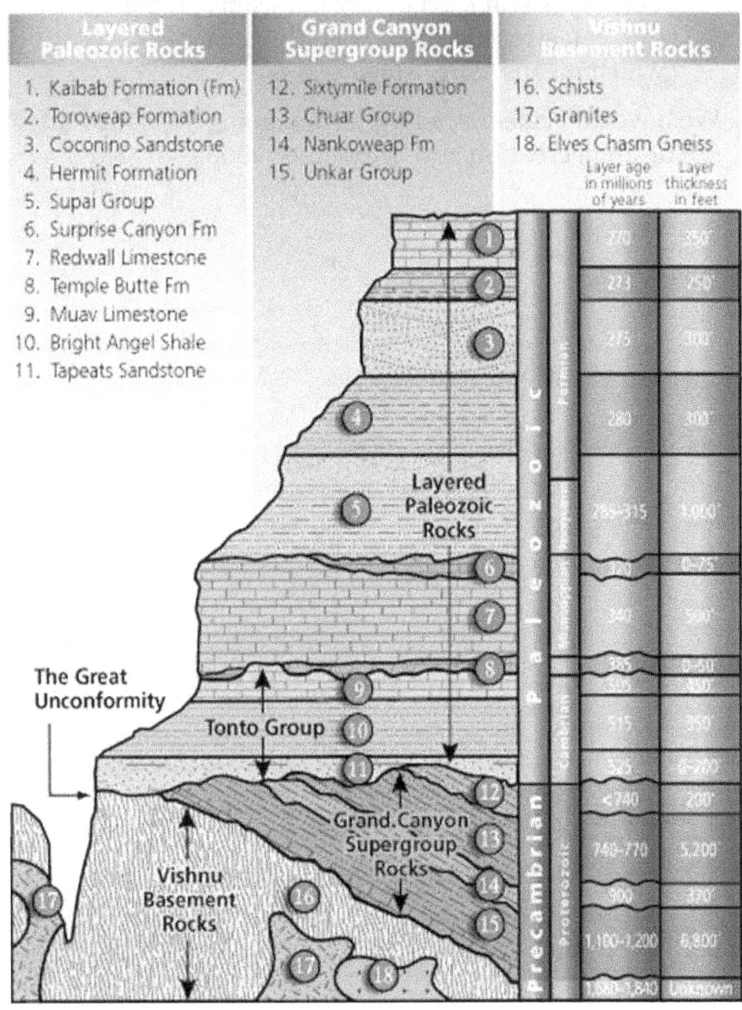

Diagram showing the placement, age and thickness of the rock units exposed in the Grand Canyon from Wikimedia Commons Public Domain

<u>The National Parks Service uses the acronym D.U.D.E.</u>[h] (Deposition, Uplift, Down-cutting, and Erosion) to

explain the formation of the Grand Canyon. The official National Parks Services use both their website and the USGS website to explain the formation of the Grand Canyon.

It will probably startle most committed uniformitarians to learn that creationists agree with D.U.D.E. We disagree with the amount of time involved, but we completely agree with the basic mechanics. The evidence we have, which includes the Word of God, informs us that the large strata which today have very few fossils were created on the first week of Creation. The strata containing fossils were laid down after Creation was finished. Some strata were laid down during the antediluvian period. But most strata containing fossils were deposited 1656 years after Creation during and after the Flood.

Even if you chose not to believe the chronology of a young earth, an honest examination of the geologic column must admit that the possibility of a young earth exists. None of the observed strata demand the assumption of deep time. There are no rocks anywhere on earth with tags revealing when they were deposited.

4. The Third Evidence: Radiometric Dating.

Though there are many types of radiometric dating, every method which claims to be able to test samples and arrive at ages in the millions of years relies on three basic assumptions.

a. No daughter material in the original sample

First and most important is the assumption that the sample being tested began its existence with no daughter material. Daughter material is the result of the decay of a radioactive isotope from parent material. In a decay chain, the original parent material decays into a daughter isotope. The original daughter isotope now becomes a parent isotope which will decay into yet another different isotope. That isotope will then decay to another isotope. The chain will continue until the daughter material is stable, that is, not radioactive.

b. Nothing contaminated the sample

The second assumption is nothing contaminated the sample during its existence. The uniformitarians correctly point out that samples from the same strata all over the world test the same so any possible contamination would have to be worldwide.

c. No change in the rate of decay

The third assumption used to be considered inviolate, that nothing can alter the rate of radioactive decay. Not only has the rate of decay proved to be changeable, but honest scientists today are searching for the amount of change. The change in radioactive decay rates is now assumed to be a fact. The disagreement now is that uniformitarian assumptions call for small changes which produce small overall changes. The evidence shows massive amounts of nuclear decay during the flood.

5. Dendrochronology.

Bristlecone Pine Tree free image from Kozzi

Dendrochronology[i] (tree-ring dating) is promoted as a solid dating system back about nine thousand years, making the Flood impossible. This belief is based on the Bristlecone pine, which grows in the western United States. A sample from one particular tree in the eastern mountains of California was taken in 1957. With the assumption that each tree ring represents one, and only one, year, the tree was dated, in 1957, to be 4,789 years old. That is 4789 BP (Before Present) or 2832 BC, which is hundreds of years before the Flood. Core samples from other dead Bristlecone Pines are compared with the living core sample to establish what secularists believe to be a chronology of almost nine thousand years.

Since Bristlecone Pines have been observed for over one hundred years without any variation in the one ring for one-year pattern, it is assumed that there never was any variation in the one ring per year pattern. These same people assume that the last glacial period ended 10,000 years ago. So they believe that the last 9000 years were geologically stable.

There are two important considerations necessary to understand this.

> When the dove returned to Noah in the ark, it had an olive branch in its mouth. Not only had vegetation returned to the earth, but also a tree had sprouted leaves. The Bristlecone Pine today is found between 9,800 and 11,000 feet. It is possible, though highly unlikely, that this old Bristlecone Pine tree survived the Flood.
>
> It is also true that a tree ring is not a period of time. It is a period of growth. When moisture is present, rapid growth occurs, followed by a period of dormancy. Dendrochronology relies on only one major growth/dormancy cycle per year. So establishing dates with trees rings is only possible in a stable climate. Even with a stable climate, something can interfere with a growth cycle. So dendrochronology, even under ideal conditions, is only an approximation, though it can be a very good approximation. When the tree rings are calibrated against another known standard, dendrochronology can be very useful.

Written documents are the most likely calibration method. Written documents record the date Mt. Vesuvius erupted. The A.D. 79 eruption which buried the city of Pompeii was recorded in writing by Pliny the Younger in a letter to Tacitus. Evidence of the eruption is visible in the tree rings, so those tree rings can be calibrated against the A.D. 79 eruption of Vesuvius. The written record is compared to the tree rings to produce a very accurate dendrochronology around the first century in Italy. This dendrochronology is useful for dating the entire Roman Empire for hundreds of years both before and after the eruption of Mount Vesuvius. This same eruption also helps us understand fossil creation.

The A.D. 79 eruption of Mount Vesuvius also fossilized bread and garbage in Pompeii. The people and animals found buried in Pompeii are plaster and resin casts, not fossils. Resin and plaster was poured into the cavities people and animals left. The only known natural processes for turning living organisms into fossils require:

high heat,

the absence of oxygen,

a source of minerals to transfer to the skeleton of the organism.

Rapid burial by means of volcanic activity can meet all of these conditions. Scientifically, volcanic eruptions are the only known method of large-scale fossilization, including petrifying wood. Billions of organisms were turned into fossils during the Flood. We do not know if these fossils were formed over a period of years, during the first forty days, or perhaps on just one day of the Flood.

Mount Vesuvius as seen from Pompeii. Photo by Morn the Gorn from Wikimedia Commons

Without something to calibrate the tree rings against, dendrochronology is, like all other forms of dating, little more than circular reasoning.

a. Assume a tree ring represents only one year.

Tree ring dates, especially trees older than written records, are based on the assumption that, with very minor exceptions, tree rings always represent one and only one year.

b. Assume past conditions similar to present conditions.

The assumption is made that the conditions in the past which formed tree rings are similar to conditions today.

c. Assume a 9000-year continuous, uniform history assuming assumptions a and b to be correct.

This assumption is then used to prove that assumptions A and B are correct. That is, that conditions in the past were the same as they are today.

The approximately 9000 years represented by tree rings of Bristle Cone Pines can be verified by examination of the existing samples. That leads to the assumption that the conditions of the past are the same as current conditions. There is no way of knowing if the conditions in the past only allowed for just one annual tree ring. In fact, the early part of the Bristle Cone Pine's existence was during the Ice Age, when conditions were radically different from what they are today. During the melting of the ice, especially in the summer, it was very likely that there were many growth/hibernation cycles per year.

d. Assume that there was no Flood

They also assume that there was no Flood. They also assume that no tree could survive the Flood, even though it is possible that at least one olive tree survived the Flood.

e. Ice Ages alter tree ring patterns

Uniformitarians understand that the annual growth/dormancy cycles would be altered during an ice age. They just assume that the Ice Age ended before the oldest Bristlecone Pine began growing.

f. Post-flood trees living through an Ice Age is the most reasonable explanation.

The most likely assumption is that the Flood destroyed all trees and the Bristlecone Pine trees we see today are post-flood and lived through some dramatic climate changes. The Pre-Ice Age, Ice Age and immediate Post-Ice Age could have caused more rapid ring formation.

6. Ice Ages

The mainstream position today believes in a series of ice ages ending around 10,000 years ago. We must understand this is only one hypothesis of many. While there is abundant evidence of ice retreating and advancing, the mechanisms or causes which could have triggered many ice ages have proved to be problematic. Guesses, which are presented as fact, include but are not limited to the following:

a. Fluctuating Solar Radiation

fluctuations in the amount of incoming solar radiation[j]

b. Milankovitch Cycles

"A new twist in the most recent ice age cycle and demonstrate once again the rapidity with which large ice sheets can come and go."the so-called Milankovitch cycles.[k]

c. Combination of many factors

"What causes an ice age[l] and glacial-interglacial cycles? Many factors contribute to climate variations, including changes in ocean and atmosphere circulation patterns, varying concentrations of atmospheric carbon dioxide, and even volcanic eruptions."

d. Scientists are not sure

"Scientists aren't sure[m] what causes ice ages, or what combination of events might trigger another one."

e. Causes of ice ages not understood

This is common knowledge. "What causes ice ages is not completely understood." BBC /Ice Ages/ Science[n]

This is just a brief list of some of the more reasonable assumptions, which are always presented as fact. The last two positions

Scientists are not sure, and
the causes of ice ages are not understood

are the only scientific facts in this list. A more realistic hypothesis says that immediately after the Flood, the warm oceans, cool atmosphere and volcanic ash blocking the sun combined to make enormous snowfalls, creating new glaciers in just a few years. These conditions likely caused glaciers to advance and retreat rapidly. Perhaps the creation of a new continent ended an ice age in one place, Europe for one possible example, as it created a new ice age on a newly formed continent, America.

f. Rapid Catastrophic Canyon Formation

As the Ice Age began to end, ice dams created enormous lakes at this time all across the world, such as the one known as Missoula[o] in North America. As the volcanic ash dissipated and allowed more sunlight to penetrate, ice and snow melted, swelling the lakes.

Foaming sea. Public Domain Image from Pixabay

The official website of the Montana Natural History Center records the standard uniformitarian position on the Missoula Ice Dam. A "finger from the glacial ice sheet moved south through the Purcell Trench in northern Idaho, near present day Lake Pend Oreille, damming the Clark Fork River creating Glacial Lake Missoula.

"The water began to build up behind the 2,500-foot ice dam [and] filled the valleys to the east with water, creating a glacial lake the size of Lake Erie and Lake Ontario combined. The water continued to rise until it reached its maximum height at an elevation of 4,200 feet. As the water rose, the pressure against the ice dam increased, ultimately causing the dam to fail catastrophically. The failure occurred when the water reached a depth of 2000 feet. The water pressure caused the glacier to become buoyant, and water began to escape beneath the ice dam by carving sub-glacial tunnels at an exponential rate.

"It is estimated that the maximum rate of flow was equal to 9.46 cubic miles per hour (386 million cubic feet per second). This rate is 60 times the flow of the Amazon River, the largest river in the world today. At this rate, the lake probably drained in a few days to a week. Water

> moving at speeds between 30 and 50 miles per hour raced across eastern Washington.
>
> "The floodwaters from Glacial Lake Missoula moved through eastern Washington on a 430-mile journey to the Pacific Ocean, forever changing the landscape by stripping away topsoil and picking apart the bedrock. The floodwater carved an immense channel system across eastern Washington."

This secular geologic website is not significantly different from our position. That is, the Columbia River/Snake River gorge systems in the present state of Washington were formed rapidly through catastrophes, not through long-term erosion.

This is what the evidence says. Whether you choose to believe that this catastrophic canyon formation took place less than 4000 years ago or 15,000 years ago is a religious choice. There is no verifiable scientific evidence to support the belief (assumption) in the position that this ice dam formed and broke several times over thousands of years. See especially this information on Lake Titicaca in the "What Does the Scientific Evidence Prove?" portion of the appendix.

The sedimentary strata had to be deposited during and after the Flood. The continents then uplifted

> 1) at the end of the Flood (or shortly after the end of the flood) when water receded,
> 2) several hundred years after the Flood during the time of Peleg when God divided mankind based on language,
> 3) or perhaps in stages throughout this time period.

During the Ice Age, perhaps at the very beginning as the sea level dropped, volcanic eruptions petrified the trees. At some time during the Ice Age, ice dams formed. It is also very likely the uplifting occurred in stages over hundreds or even thousands of years. These eruptions/uplifts could also have caused the almost 13,000 foot elevation of Lake Titicaca on the border of modern Bolivia and Peru. Lake Titicaca has a city with a harbor. This harbor seems to have connected to the sea at one time.

Geologic strata along with the evidences for the Ice Age indicate catastrophic formation of the earth's major geologic features. This contrasts sharply with the main pillar of Secular Humanism, the concept of deep time. When examined in total, the evidence shows that Secular Humanism's tenet, uniformitarianism, has foundations built on assumptions resulting in highly complex circular reasoning.

The *Conflict of the Ages* series examines the available information in a scientific format, using the Word of God as our foundation, but drawing on other resources.

This is the end of the teacher-only section. The teacher will see some duplication in the following material, as it is presented for students. Several articles are also included in the appendix materials for both teachers and students. These can be the basis for optional assignments, if you determine that you have enough time and you want your students to cover the material.

This is the end of the teacher-only section. The

teacher will see some duplication in the following material, as it is presented for students. These can be the basis for optional assignments, if you determine that you have enough time and you want your students to cover the material.

The Conflict of the Ages: Part One
The Scientific History of Origins

"There is a fundamental difference between religion,
which is based on authority, and science,
which is based on observation and reason.
Science will win, because it works."
Stephen Hawking

For we wrestle not against flesh and blood,
but against principalities, against powers,
against the rulers of the darkness of this world,
against spiritual wickedness in high places.
Ephesians 6:12

"There is a fundamental difference between religion, which is based on authority, and science, which is based on observation and reason. Science will win, because it works." Stephen Hawking

For we wrestle not against flesh and blood, but against principalities, against powers, against the rulers of the darkness of this world, against spiritual wickedness in high places. (Ephesians 6:12 KJV)

See endnotes for source of Hawking quote[1].

Our Assumptions on Origins

Unlike secular textbooks, our foundations, our assumptions, are clearly laid out. Everything is based on assumptions. Many fail to list or even understand their assumptions. It is dishonest and an attempt to deceive when assumptions are not disclosed. Being dishonest by failing to disclose your assumptions is a lie. "The Big

Lie,"[2] *die Grosse Luge,* was the foundation of the Nazi propaganda machine. "The great mass of people will more easily fall victim to a big lie than to a small one."

To keep you, the reader from being any kind of victim, we make our assumptions very clear and easy to understand.

A. There Is No Difference Between Religious and Scientific Truth.

There are not different kinds of truth or even different views or perspectives on truth. Dr. Mendel Sachs,[3] Professor Emeritus at the State University of New York at Buffalo, says this on his website:

> "There has been much discussion, over the ages, on the possible interaction of the bases of science and religion. It has been my proposition that such interaction is illusory, primarily because the logics of these two disciplines are out of context. That is to say, religious truth and scientific truth have different meanings."

Stephen Jay Gould[4] had another way of expressing this concept. He preached "Non-overlapping Magisteria," that science and religion govern separate aspects of society and can co-exist as long as they keep separate. Yet in his 1997 article with that title, he systematically attacks Pope John Paul II's 1996 statement on evolution as confusing and troubling. He calls Scientific Creationism, the belief that the Bible is to be taken literally, a position uniquely American and held by almost nobody, as if nobody ever believed the Bible to be true except this tiny, ridiculous faction.

If the Scriptures are not true, how can they be even useful moral and philosophical guides? The truth is that secularists want people to realize that having two kinds of truth makes no sense. Most Secular Humanists insist they are their own moral guides, and they don't need religious truth at all. They pretend to allow for these "separate truths" so that religion can be segregated more and more from people's "regular" lives. They hope that religion will keep being pushed aside until it isn't given any place in society. One day they expect that people will come to accept their teaching as the only truth.

The fact is that both Sachs' and Gould's positions say the same thing, and they are both false. There is no difference or separation between religious truth and scientific truth. Truth is truth. And the Scriptures do accurately report first-person observations and scientific facts.

B. The History of Mankind Progressing from Primitive to Civilized Does Not Fit the Evidence

Even many Secular Humanists understand that the current "mainstream" view of history, the progression from primitive to civilized to technological, makes no sense. Everywhere we can see examples of ancient technology. There is so much evidence of advanced early man that Secular Humanists must explain this advanced technology is some way. While there are a wide range of answers given, they all fall into three basic categories. Besides listing the type of argument, we also list a major proponent of each position. We also list simply ignoring the evidence, perhaps hoping that it will go away, as a position.

1. There is no explanation for ancient technology. The technology does not fit any existing theories, yet it exists.

Graham Hancock and people like him are more reasonable, though still not accurate. They also view the ancient artifacts as technological marvels and sometimes allow for the possibility of extraterrestrials. But they are for the most part content to find the ancient evidence for advanced technology without drawing dogmatic conclusions. Hancock has traveled the world, researching and documenting advanced ancient civilizations, and has written many books, such as *Fingerprints of the Gods*,[5] to point out that something is wrong with the secularist position that man's development began primitive and advanced to the complex through time. The following quote is from *Fingerprints of the Gods*.

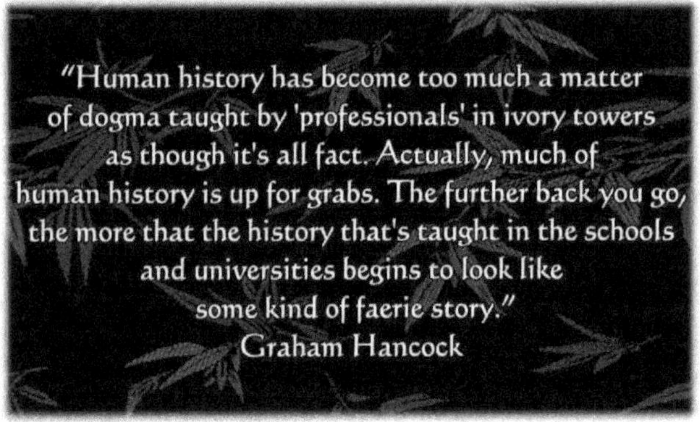

"Human history has become too much a matter of dogma taught by 'professionals" in ivory towers as though it's all fact. Actually, much of human history is up for grabs. The further back you go, the more that the history that's taught in the schools and universities begins to look like some kind of faerie story." Graham Hancock

Hancock is saying that we should not blindly accept "experts" who ignore clear evidence. He almost comes out and says that these people are inventing fictional explanations. He has a point. Secularists have to ignore many facts and pieces of evidence, such as those Hancock and others have uncovered, to hold on to their "simple to complex" ideas about origins and advancement in science and history.

2. Extraterrestrials gave advanced technology to primitive humans

Some believe that ancient technology came from extraterrestrials who guided mankind and were mistaken for gods.

Modern authors (such as Erich Von Däniken[6] in his books *Gold of the Gods* and *Chariots of the Gods?)* accept the timeline of the mainstream religion of Secular Humanism, but clearly see that the technology of ancient humans does not fit with their presuppositions. So Erich Von Däniken and his followers believe that some type of extraterrestrials gave technology to ancient primitive humans. They see hundreds of religions and differing accounts of key events. They don't dismiss all religions as delusional like other secularists. But they still come to a conclusion that excludes any possibility that the Scriptures are accurate.

> "If the Almighty Controller of the Universe was worried about what we believe about religion, then the Eternal Being would reveal Himself and clearly enlighten the world on the true nature of reality and religion. The fact that there is so much massive confusion about religion on our planet gives credence to the possibility that human religions may not be divinely inspired.
>
> "Instead, our religious beliefs might have been created by devious extraterrestrial alien tricksters, who actively seek deception."

The Bible calls these tricksters "demons," "unclean spirits," or "evil spirits."

The Bible calls these tricksters "demons," "unclean spirits," or "evil spirits."

Von Däniken has misidentified the beings responsible for deceiving mankind and leading us to create conflicting and wildly varying religions. By claiming that God did not clearly explain Himself in His Word, by rejecting the Scriptures as truth, he has fallen into the same trap as those he claims were deceived by aliens.

3. Simply Ignore the Advanced Ancient Technology

If you can get a secularist to clearly state his position on origins, even he may tell you that the universe is not eternal, but began in an explosion of matter billions of years ago. This is often called the "Big Bang". He will make no attempt to explain where this matter came from. The Big Bang theory is explained in detail in Stephen Hawking's book *A Brief History of Time*.[7] This theory is the most commonly held position of the Established Religion of western culture, Secular Humanism.

As Stephen Hawking said in the quote at the beginning of this study, religion is based on authority and science is based on observation and reason. The problem with Stephen Hawking, the High Priest of Physics, and Richard Dawkins, The High Priest of Biology, is that they also represent a religion, speaking authoritatively, without evidence. It ignores the observations and reason opposing their religion. It is a religion opposed to the Bible.

Iron pillar Qutub Minar Delhi, India. The iron has not rusted even after 2000 years. Photographer Dennis Jarvis from Halifax, Canada. Wikimedia Commons.

4. The Physical Information in the Bible Is Correct.

Men like Immanuel Velikovsky[8] irritate other Secular Humanists even more. Absolutely vilified by mainstream archaeology, Immanuel Velikovsky was an agnostic Jew and a psychiatrist who did extensive research demonstrating that mainstream dating schemes do not work. When Velikovsky speaks of "collective memory" in the quote below, he means he has studied written works, artifacts, and records from ancient cultures. He claims that most secularists have ignored clear evidence to promote their theories about Earth's age and their false chronology of historical events.

> "I came upon the idea that traditions and legends and memories of generic origin can be treated in the same way in which we treat in psychoanalysis the early memories of a single individual. I spent ten years on this work. I

> found that the collective memory of mankind spoke of a series of global catastrophes that occurred in historical times. I believed that I could even identify the exact times and the very agents of the great upheavals of the more recent past. The conclusions at which I arrived compelled me to cross the frontiers into various fields of science, archaeology, geology, and astronomy."[8]

Velikovsky was a committed Secular Humanist. Still, his book *Ages in Chaos* uses the Hebrew Old Testament as the standard to date events throughout the Middle East. Archaeologists cannot honestly explain the problems he exposes in mainstream chronologies. But his solutions have just as many, if not more, problems in presenting a true picture of history. His major failing is that he rejects the supernatural and attempts to give materialistic explanations for everything in the Old Testament.

> "The biblical story of the last plague has a distinctly supernatural quality in that all the firstborn and only the firstborn were killed on the night of the plagues. An earthquake that destroys only the firstborn is inconceivable, because events can never attain that degree of coincidence. No credit should be given to such a record. Either the story of the last plague, in its canonized form, is a fiction, or it conceals a corruption of the text."[9]

Immanuel Velikovsky Photographer: Donna Foster Roizen. Copyright holder: Frederic Jueneman. Wikimedia Commons.

Velikovsky attempts to discredit or dismiss chunks of the biblical record because he doesn't want to acknowledge God's direct working through supernatural events. Like the others mentioned earlier, he has found some evidence that secularism doesn't have the answers, but he refuses to accept the truth about where the answers can really be found.

How Did the Universe Begin?

III. How Did The Universe Begin?

The Bible is the book of true science. Yes, the Bible is also a book of religion, because it is the authority, but it is also the foundation of science. No matter what you believe about the Bible or science, there are only three possible positions to hold concerning the beginning of the universe.

Origin of the Universe: Unknowable and Unimportant

A. Origin of the Universe: Unknowable and Unimportant

The first position on origins, held by the vast majority of people, is that it is neither possible to know about the beginning of the universe, nor is the beginning of the universe important. They are Epicureans, seeking to make the best life possible here and now and having no concern for beginnings or endings of the universe. They belong to the "eat, drink and be merry, for tomorrow we die" school of thought. Or lack of thought, which is the best way to describe the average modern Epicurean.

B. Origin of the Universe: Entirely Material

The second position states that the beginning of the universe can be discovered from observations of the world around us. This is the position of Stephen Hawking, Richard Dawkins, and any academic professional who ever hopes to have a career and be repeatedly published. This is an entirely religious position, without a shred of science. Not one of the pieces of evidence that man can examine has a label to tell us how it arrived in the universe.

In the following excerpt, Dr. Duane Gish quotes scientist J.D. Bernal, who is presenting the viewpoint of another scientist, Dr. Mora, so the notation in the appendix includes references to Gish's article and J.D. Bernal's reference as well.

Dr. Duane Gish explains that,

> "The first thing that may be said about theories on the origin of life is that none satisfy the criteria of a scientific theory. There were no human observers of the origin of life, and it is impossible to reenact the process. If such a process did occur, it could have left no fossil record or history. There is no way to observe or test any postulated evolutionary origin of life. All such theories are mere postulates; all related laboratory experiments are mere exercises in organic chemistry. This has been acknowledged even by a number of prominent evolutionists. Thus, Bernal, in a discussion of a paper by Mora, states ' ... Dr. Mora has shown that the principles of experimental science do not apply to discussions on the origin of life, and indeed cannot apply to any problem of origin.'"[10]

Dr. Gish is saying that no one can examine evidence and prove the origin of the Earth. He lists the common scientific practices for gaining knowledge and says they don't apply to origins. It's very simple and straightforward to understand that nobody can scientifically "prove" how the universe came into being. Even though many secularists agree that this is true, others just won't accept that. Science even claims to have built an instrument for observing how the universe came into existence.

The Large Hadron Collider is said to exist for almost no other reason than to discover how the universe came into existence. If that is its only function, then it is a temple and not a scientific instrument. It is an enormous "leap of faith" to believe that examining the energy and matter which make up the present universe can reveal to us how it came into existence. Yet that is exactly what Stephen Hawking has put his faith in. That is the definition of a religion. In this case it is the religion that calls itself Secular Humanism. And like all religions, belief in Secular Humanism requires faith in the authority of those in positions of leadership. It is so sad that a religion whose followers call themselves skeptics primarily support their beliefs with mockery and lawsuits.

C. God Created the Universe Outside of the Material

The third position concerning origins is scientific. A Person who observed the birth of the universe recorded His observations and gave those scientific records to us. The concept of God as a scientist is very much at odds with the religion of Secular Humanism, but taking this position fulfills the requirements of basic scientific inquiry. All you have to do is admit the testimony of a first-person observer of when the universe began. Just as men can reject any scientific evidence, so they can reject the scientific record of the only Observer of the birth of the universe. In the Book of Jubilees, II:1, it says, "And the angel of the presence spake to Moses according to the word of the Lord, saying: Write the complete history of the creation, how in six days the Lord God finished all His works and all that He created..."[11]

"After trying to shatter the historicity and validity of the Scripture, I came to the conclusion that it is historically trustworthy. If one discards the Bible as being unreliable, then one must discard almost all literature of antiquity." Josh McDowell's quote above is sourced as endnote[12].

How Can We Know About Origins?

IV. How Can We Know About Origins?

According to the record of the eyewitness to the origin of the universe, *"The things which are seen were not made of things which do appear"* (Hebrews 11:3). This means that the entire universe, time, matter, and energy, came into existence from outside of the universe.

"On the seventh day God ended his work which he had made" (Genesis 2:2). God ceased the activities described in Hebrews 11:3. After the original creation, events that followed made changes in the way things worked. The Fall, sin entering into the universe, and the Flood, all changed the earth through processes which do not exist today. These changes mean that the observation of the present universe will not reveal to us anything about origins or the creation of the universe. A careful scientific examination of the evidence reveals that the earth is only a few thousand years old. Our curriculum books all contain Chapter Fourteen of *Antidisestablishmentarianism*, included in the References, Footnotes, Expanded Study and Appendix Materials of this book. This chapter is simply more than two dozen evidences of a young earth.

Accepting the Bible and the records in the Bible is religious. So is rejecting them. *Antidisestablishmentarianism* explains this religious bias in detail.

Michael Ruse, in the quote below, admits that evolution is a religion.

> "Evolution is promoted by its practitioners as more than mere science. Evolution is promulgated as an ideology, a secular religion: a full-fledged alternative to Christianity, with meaning and morality. I am an ardent evolutionist and an ex-Christian, but I must admit that in this one complaint: and Mr. [sic] Gish is but one of many to make it: the literalists are absolutely right. Evolution is a religion. This was true of evolution in the beginning, and it is true of evolution still today.
> "... Evolution therefore came into being as a kind of secular ideology, an explicit substitute for Christianity." [13]

Richard Dawkins, in *The Greatest Show on Earth,* exposed his own bias in the quote below.

> "Evolution is a fact, and [my] book will demonstrate it. No reputable scientist disputes it, and no unbiased reader will close the book doubting it."[14]

As we said, the standards we use are no more religious than the average textbook or "scientific" work. Our three guiding, foundational standards are:

A. The Bible Is Authoritative.

For example, when the Bible says *"and the evening and the morning were the first* (and 2nd thru 7th) *day"* it means just what it says: one complete revolution of the earth, what we know today as a 24-hour period.

Other Written Records Outside of the Bible

B. Other Written Records Outside of the Bible.

Each of these documents has varying degrees of accuracy. They are capable of error, and must be held up to the standard of the Word of God.

Under the category of other written records are oral traditions which are now written down. Oral traditions are often discounted by secularists as less reliable or valuable. But the discipline of memorizing and passing on records by word of mouth is not a game of "Gossip". Ancient oral traditions rely on groups of people, often entire civilizations. This is a more reliable method than just having an individual, such as a king, as the maker and keeper of ancient written records. Socrates, in Plato's Dialogue *Phaedrus,* discusses written versus oral tradition.

Finally,

Physical Evidence Easily and Often Manipulated

C. Physical Evidence Is Easily and Often Manipulated.

Physical evidence is also capable of a wide range of interpretations. Though physical evidence is important, it is also the least reliable.

We do not normally waste time of showing why something is in error. When facts are available, we present them and proceed from that point. This is a work of history that relies on the Bible, world literature, and scientific observations. We make one exception with the origin of the universe. Since fanciful myths are presented as scientific facts for the origin of the universe and these myths are the foundation of moral relativism, we include a brief refutation.

V. Before Time: Eternity Past

"For had ye believed Moses, ye would have believed me (Jesus): for he wrote of me. But if ye believe not his writings, how shall ye believe my words?"
(John 5:46, 47)

"Abraham saith unto him, They have Moses and the prophets; let them hear them. And (the rich man) said, Nay, father Abraham: but if one went unto them from the dead, they will repent. And (Abraham) said unto him, If they hear not Moses and the prophets, neither will they be persuaded, though one rose from the dead."
(Luke 16:29-31)

"By faith we understand that the worlds were prepared by the word of God, so that what is seen was not made out of things which are visible."
(Hebrews 11:3) NASB

A. Time Was Created With the Universe.

"By faith we understand that time was created by the word of God, so that what is seen was

> *made from things that are invisible."* (Hebrews 11:3 ISV)

"Then assuredly the world was made, not in time, but simultaneously with time."[15] (from Augustine's *City of God)*

"Let them therefore see that there could be not time without a created world."[16] (from Augustine's *Confessions)*

Saint Augustine in His study by Sandro Botticelli, 1480. Chiesa di Ognissanti, Florence, Italy. Image from Wikimedia Commons

Time begins with creation. Before creation, there was no time. Before there was time there was the Trinity. Perhaps there were other created spiritual beings, but we do not know that.

B. The Creator Is Jesus the Messiah, the 2nd Person of the Trinity.

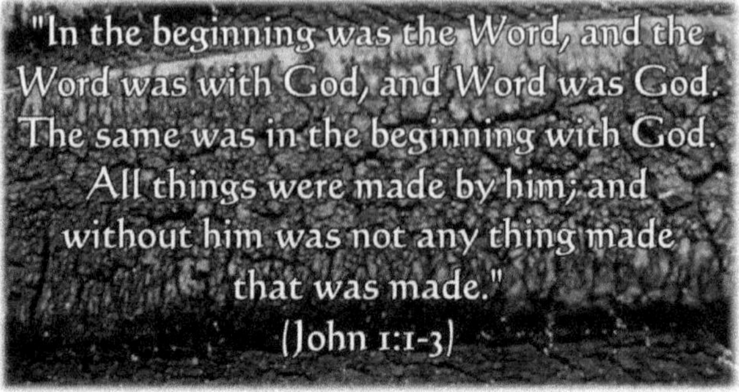

In the Beginning was the Word, and the Word was with God, and the Word was God. The same was in the beginning with God. All things were made by Him and without Him was not anything made that was made.(John 1:1-3 KJV)

"The Word," *Logos,* Jesus Christ, the second Person of the Godhead, is singular. The Hebrew word *Adonai,* usually translated Lord, is singular. The Hebrew word *Jehovah,* usually translated LORD, is singular. The Hebrew word *Elohim,* usually translated God, is plural.

"Hear, O Israel: The LORD our God is one LORD" (Deuteronomy 6:4). This statement uses the singular, plural, singular formula. This combination of Father, Son, and Holy Spirit as three distinct, separate persons yet one God is what we call the Trinity. This is not a book of Systematic Theology attempting to explain the Trinity. This is just a simple statement of the facts. Before there was time or a material universe, there was one God, the Father, Son, and Holy Spirit. We use the words Trinity and Eternity Past to explain in imperfect language what the Scriptures teach about God.

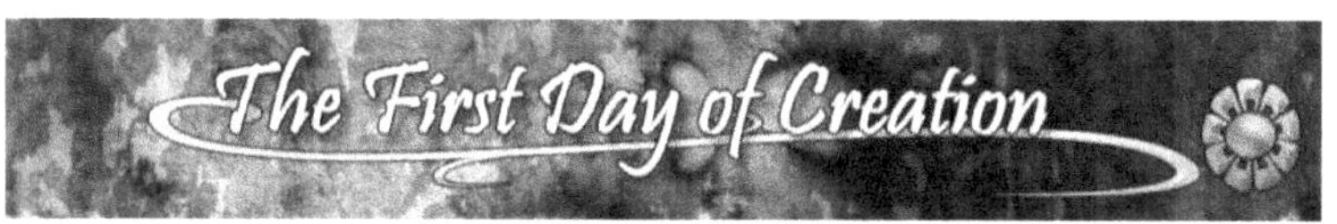

VI. The First Day of Creation

A. The Heavens

The first act of creation was to make “the heavens,” a place to put everything else. What Genesis 1:1 calls the heavens, we generally call “space” or “outer space”.

1. Secular Misconceptions

At this point Secular Humanists use the language of mathematics to express the belief that all energy and matter began as a single point, called a singularity. The language of mathematics is, however, completely unable to explain where this massed energy came from. Without any evidence, they propose that from this singularity an explosion took place which is popularly known as “the Big Bang,” the beginning of the universe.

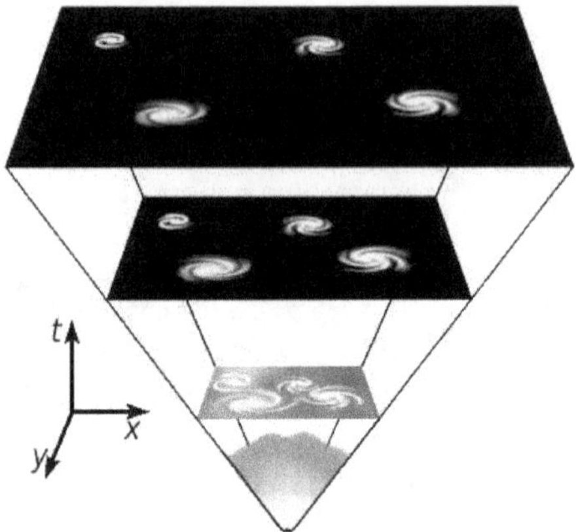

Slices of expansion of universe without an initial singularity Released into the Public Domain by Gnixon Wikimedia Commons

Physicists dogmatically assert that the Big Bang is a scientific theory, not a religious belief. Depending on the person making such a claim, they are either deceived or dishonest. Since the Big Bang is the foundation for Secular Humanism and Secular Humanism is America's Establishment of Religion, this false religion needs a careful examination.

Physicists use their religious bias to draw incorrect conclusions from certain facts which can be observed about the material universe. An objective examination of the facts is difficult because Secular Humanists rely on authoritative religious pronouncements which hide the actual scientific information. Since the "Big Bang" theory of the origin of the universe is based on relativity, we strongly recommend that you take a brief look at relativity to understand the problems with this theory of origins. Please see in the appendix the two short articles introducing the concept of relativity.

Combining the mathematics of physics with the religious belief that the examination of the material universe can reveal the origin of the universe produces several probable answers. The first is that the universe is expanding and will continue to expand until it comes to an eventual "heat death" with every atom motionless and a temperature near absolute zero. Second, the universe will stop expanding and then it will collapse back into another single point called the "Big Crunch". Third, the universe is infinite and will always expand in similar fashion. Though there are many, many other positions and many, many variations on these positions, the important fact is that they are all religious beliefs which can never be proved. We can observe and measure the universe and some observations fit some models better than others. There is no materialistic scientific data on origins.

2. Created by God *ex nihilo* (Latin "out of nothing")

> *In the beginning was the Word, and the Word was with God, and the Word was God. The same was in the beginning with God. All things were made by him; and without him was not any thing made that was made.*
> (John 1:1-3)
>
> *"God, who at sundry times and in divers manners spake in time past unto the fathers by the prophets, Hath in these last days spoken unto us by his Son, whom he hath appointed heir of all things, by whom also he made the worlds; Who being the brightness of his glory, and the express image of his person, and upholding all things by the word of his power."*
> (Hebrews 1:1-3)
>
> *"By faith we understand that time was created by the word of God, so that what is seen was made from things that are invisible."*
> (Hebrews 11:3 ISV)
>
> *"In the beginning God created the heaven and the earth. And the earth was without form, and*

void; and darkness was upon the face of the deep. And the Spirit of God moved upon the face of the waters."
(Genesis 1:1-3)

First Act of Creation
Formless Water

B. The First Act of Creation Was Formless Water.

At the start of time God created out of nothing a formless, empty waste, often referred to outside the Bible as *chaos*. It was not created with form then became formless, but began without form. The darkness is not just an absence of light, but has the double meaning of absence of order. We think of "the face of the deep" as the surface of an ocean. While it can mean that, it can also mean the boundary edge of moisture. The deep described in Genesis, along with *out of water and in water* from 2 Peter 3:5, means that the entire original universe, all matter, began as water. The deep does not refer to ice, but it might mean vapor as "in the year and in the day of the clouds."[17]

In both Hebrew and Greek, just one word can be translated into English as "Spirit," "breath" or "wind," depending on the context. Also, the word translated "moved" in the KJV also means fluttered, moved or hovered over.

In both Hebrew and Greek, just one word can be translated into English as "spirit," "breath," or "wind," depending on context. Also, the word translated "moved" in the KJV also means fluttered, moved, or hovered over.

1. Everything Material Was Formed from Water

A possible interpretation of these three verses is that the original creation was moisture (clouds) with the Spirit (wind, breath) of God on the outer boundary compressing this moisture until it became liquid water where gravitational forces caused further collapse until it ignited in thermonuclear fusion. The resulting universal explosion might have been similar to the proposed Big Bang.

> *"For the invisible things of him from the creation of the world are clearly seen, being understood by the things that are made, even his eternal power and Godhead; so that they are without excuse"*
> (Romans 1:20).

> *"He is the image of the invisible God, the first-born of all creation. For by Him all things were created, both in the heavens and on the earth, visible and invisible, whether thrones or dominions or rulers or authorities-all things have been created by Him and for Him. And He is before all things and in Him all things hold together"*
> (Colossians 1:15-17, NASB)

2. Similarities to the Biblical record in other sources

a. *The Cave of Treasures*

The Cave of Treasures is an ancient book which gives the traditional Christian and Jewish position, though there are many variations. God created everything, spiritual as well as material, on the first day. Here is one possibility as described below.

> "In the beginning, on the First Day, which was the holy First Day of the Week, the chief and Firstborn of all the days, God created the heavens, and the earth, and the water, and the

air, the fire, and the hosts which are invisible (that is to say, the Angels, Archangels, Thrones, Lords, Principalities, Powers, Cherubim, and Seraphim), and all the ranks and companies of Spiritual beings, and the Light, and the Night, and the Day-time, and the gentle winds, and the strong winds (i.e. storms). All these were created on the First Day. And on the First Day of the Week the Spirit of holiness, one of the Persons of the Trinity, hovered over the waters and through the hovering thereof over the face of the waters, the waters were blessed so that they might become producers of offspring, and they became hot, and the whole nature of the waters glowed with heat, and the leaven of creation was united to them."[18]

Page from the Syriac Cave of Treasures from http://www.patheos.com/blogs/anxiousbench/2013/10/the-cave-of-treasures/

Descriptions using this type of language are found throughout the Bible, and these same descriptions occur in the many ancient cultures all over the world. While these obviously rely on traditions which might be in error, notice the similarities as well as the differences.

b. The *Book of Jubilees* II: 2-3[19]

"For on the first day He created the heavens which are above and the earth and the waters and all the spirits which serve before Him: the angels of the presence, and the angels of sanctification, and the angels [of the spirit of fire and the angels] of the spirit of the winds, and the angels of the spirit of the clouds, and of the darkness, and of snow and of hail and of hoar frost, and the angels of the voices and of the thunder and of the lightning, and the angels of the spirits of cold and of heat, and of winter and of spring and of autumn and of summer, and of all the spirits of His creatures which are in the heavens and on the earth, (He created) the abysses and the darkness, eventide (and night), and the light, dawn and day, which He hath prepared in the knowledge of His heart. And thereupon we saw His works, and praised Him, and lauded before Him on account of all His works; for seven great works did He create on the first day."[19]

c. Polynesian Creation Myth

The following quotes are from a Polynesian creation myth.

Te Kore "The Void" (endnote also sources text in graphic below.)

In Whai-tua [space] two existences without shape were formed: Maku ('Moisture'), a male, and Mahora-nui-a-rangi ('Great Expanse of Heaven'), a female; and from these sprang Rangi-potiki ('The Heavens'), who took to wife Papa ('Earth') and begat the gods.[20]

Te Kore "The Void"
Te Kore-tua-tahi — "The First Void"
Te Kore-tua-rua — "The Second Void"
Te Kore-nui — "The Vast Void
Te Kore-roa — "The Far-Extending Void"
Te Kore-para — "The Sere Void"
Te Kore-whiwhia - - "The Unpossessing Void"
Te Kore-rawea — "The Delightful Void"
Te Kore-te-tamaua —"The Void Fast Bound"
Te Po — "The Night"
Te Po-teki — "The Hanging Night"
Te Po-terea — "The Drifting Night"
Te Po-whawha — "The Moaning Night"
Hine-maki-moe — "The Daughter of Troubled Sleep"
Te Po — "The Night"
Te Ata — "The Dawn"
Te Ao-tu-roa — "The Abiding Day"
Te Ao-marama — "The Bright Day"
Whai-tua — "Space."

Graphic shows a sampling of elements of the Polynesian creation myth, including terms for different ideas about "night," "the void," "sleep," "dawn," "day," and "space."

d. Samoan Creation Myth

"The god Tangaloa dwelt in the Expanse; he made all things; he alone was [there]; not any sky, not any country; he only went to and fro in the Expanse; there was also no sea, and no earth."[21]

"But they deliberately forget that long ago by God's word the heavens existed and the earth was formed out of water and by water" (2 Peter 3:5, NIV)

"The LORD possessed me [wisdom] in the beginning of his way, before his works of old. I was set up from everlasting, from the beginning, or ever the earth was. When there were no depths, I was brought forth; when there were no fountains abounding with water. Before the mountains were settled, before the hills was I brought forth: While as yet he had not made the earth, nor the fields, nor the highest part of the dust of the world. When he prepared the heavens, I was there: when he set a compass upon the face of the depth: When he established the clouds above: when he strengthened the fountains of the deep: When he gave to the sea his decree, that the waters should not pass his commandment: when he appointed the foundations of the earth" (Proverbs 8:22-29)

"For he founded it [the earth]
upon the seas
and established it
upon the waters"
(Psalm 24:2, NIV)

"For He founded it (the Earth) upon the seas and established it upon the waters." (Psalm 24:2, NIV)

e. Babylon myth recorded by Berosus "For the whole universe consisting of moisture ..." "There was a time in which there existed nothing but darkness and an abyss of waters ..."[22]

"To him that by wisdom made the heavens: for his mercy endureth for ever. To him that stretched out the earth above the waters: for his mercy endureth for ever." (Psalm 136:5, 6)

"To Him who made the heavens with skill, For His lovingkindness is everlasting; To Him who spread out the earth above the waters." (Psalm 136:5, 6, NASB)

f. *Popol Vuh* Mayan

"In the year and in the day of the clouds, before ever were years or days, the world lay in darkness. All things were orderless, and water covered the slime and ooze that the earth then was."[23]

"And the earth was without form, and void; and darkness was upon the face of the deep. And the spirit of God moved upon the face of the waters" (Genesis 1:2)

g. *Metamorphosis* Ovid (Latin)

"Before the seas, and this terrestrial ball,
And Heav'n's high canopy, that covers all,
One was the face of Nature;
If a face: Rather a rude and indigested mass:
A lifeless lump, unfashion'd, and unfram'd,
Of jarring seeds; and justly Chaos nam'd.
No sun was lighted up, the world to view;
No moon did yet her blunted horns renew:
Nor yet was Earth suspended in the sky,

Nor pois'd, did on her own foundations lye:
Nor seas about the shores their arms had thrown;
But earth, and air, and water, were in one.
Thus air was void of light, and earth unstable,
And water's dark abyss unnavigable.
No certain form on any was imprest;
All were confus'd, and each disturb'd the rest.
For hot and cold were in one body fixt;
And soft with hard, and light with heavy mixt."[24]

h. *Antiquities of the Jews* Josephus

"But when the earth did not come into sight, but was covered with thick darkness, and a wind moved upon its surface, God commanded that there should be light."[25]

i. *Popol Vuh* Mayan

"Over a universe wrapped in the gloom of a dense and primeval night passed the god Hurakan, the mighty wind. He called out 'Earth,' and the solid land appeared."[26]

j. *Theogony* Hesiod (Greek)

"Verily at the first Chaos came to be, but next wide-bosomed Earth, the ever-sure foundations of all the deathless ones who hold the peaks of snowy Olympus, and dim Tartarus in the depth of the wide-pathed Earth, and Eros (Love), fairest among the deathless gods, who unnerves the limbs and overcomes the mind and wise counsels of all gods and all men within them. From Chaos came forth Erebus and black Night; but of Night were born Aether and Day, whom she conceived and bare from union in love with Erebus. And Earth first bare starry Heaven, equal to herself, to cover her on every side, and to be an ever-sure abiding-place for the blessed gods."[27]

k. Babylon myth recorded by Berosus

"This Belus, *by whom they signify Jupiter*, divided the darkness, and separated the Heavens from the Earth, and reduced the universe to order."[28]

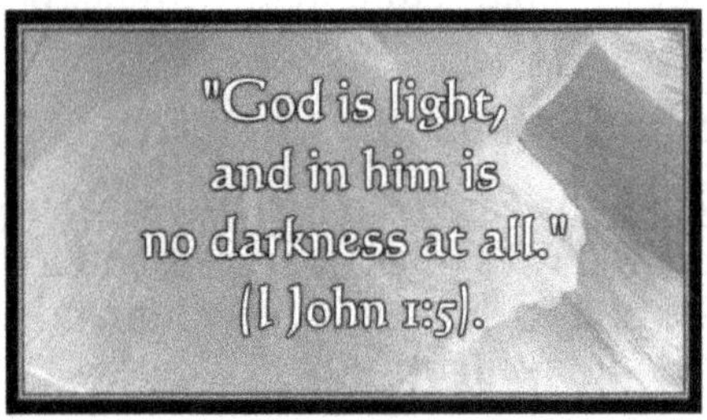

"God is light, and in Him is no darkness at all." (1 John 1:5)

l. *Narration 28 Bundahis* Persian

"Of Aûharmazd's creatures of the world, the first was the sky; the second, water; the third, earth; the fourth, plants; the fifth, animals; the sixth, mankind."[29]

m. *Enuma Elish*, Babylonian creation myth

1. When in the height heaven was not named,
2. And the earth beneath did not yet bear a name,
3. And the primeval Apsû, who begat them,
4. And chaos, Tiamat, the mother of them both,
5. Their waters were mingled together,
6. And no field was formed, no marsh was to be seen;
7. When of the gods none had been called into being,
8. And none bore a name, and no destinies [were ordained];

9. Then were created the gods in the midst of [heaven].[30]

n. *The History of Creation A* (Egyptian)

[These are] the words which the god Neb-er-tcher spake after he had come into being: "I am he who came into being in the form of the god Khepera, and I am the creator of that which came into being, that is to say, I am the creator of everything which came into being: now the things which I created, and which came forth out of my mouth after that I had come into being myself were exceedingly many. The sky (or heaven) had not come into being, the earth did not exist . . . from being one god I became three gods, and I came into being in the earth. Then Shu and Tefnut rejoiced from out of the inert watery mass wherein they were, and they brought to me my Eye (i.e., the sun).[31]

o. Phoenician Creation Myth

"But when this wind became enamoured of its own first principles (the Chaos), and an intimate union took place, that connection was called Pothos: and it was the beginning of the creation of all things. And it (the Chaos) know not its own production; but from its embrace with the wind was generated Mot; which some call Ilus (Mud), but others the putrefaction of a watery mixture. And from this sprung all the seed of the creation, and the generation of the universe."[32]

p. Polynesian Creation Myth[33]

"From the conception the increase
From the increase the swelling
From the swelling the thought
From the thought the remembrance
From the remembrance the consciousness, the

desire.
The word became fruitful:
It dwelt with the feeble glimmering
It brought forth night;
The great night, the long night,
The lowest night, the loftiest night,
The thick night, the night to be felt,
The night touched, the night unseen.
The night following on,
The night ending in death.
From the nothing, the begetting,"
From the nothing the increase
From the nothing the abundance,
The power of increasing, the living breath;"
It dwelt with the empty space,
It produced the atmosphere which is above us.
The atmosphere which floats above the earth,
The great firmament above us,
The spreadout space dwelt with the early dawn,
Then the moon sprang forth;
The atmosphere above dwelt with the glowing sky,
Forthwith was produced the sun,
They were thrown up above as the chief eyes of Heaven:
Then the Heavens became light, the early dawn, the early day,
The mid-day. The blaze of day from the sky.
The sky which floats above the earth
Dwelt with Hawaiki."[33]

These ancient documents, each the record of creation from different cultures, contain obvious errors, but show how the memory of the original creation is preserved throughout the entire earth. A modern physicist, Dr. Russell Humphreys, beginning with the authority of the Word of God, also concludes that the original creation was water. He then develops a theory of one possible way God could have created the universe.

q. *Starlight and Time*, Dr. Russell Humphreys

"God creates a large 3-D space and within it a ball of liquid water, the "deep." The ball is greater than two light-years in diameter, large enough to contain all the mass of the universe. Because of the great concentration of matter, this ball of water is deep within a black hole, whose event horizon is more than half a billion light-years away. The earth at this point is merely a formless, undefined region of water at the center of the deep, empty of inhabitant or feature... "

PhotoImpact Image of "the liquid ball" by Mary C. Findley

"The gravitational force on the deep is very strong ... This force compresses the deep very rapidly toward the center, making it extremely hot and dense. The heat rips apart the water molecules, atoms, even the nuclei into elementary particles. Thermonuclear fusion reactions begin, forming heavier nuclei from lighter ones and liberating huge amounts of energy. As a consequence, an intense light illuminates the interior, breaking through to the surface and ending the darkness there."[34]

r. Whai-tua Maori of New Zealand[35]

"Io dwelt within the breathing-space of immensity.
The Universe was in darkness, with water everywhere,
There was no glimmer of dawn, no clearness, no light.
And he began by saying these words, That He might cease remaining inactive:
'Darkness! Become a light-possessing darkness.'
And at once light appeared.
[He] then repeated those self-same words in this manner,
That He might cease remaining inactive:
'Light! Become a darkness-possessing light.'
And again an intense darkness supervened,
And a third time He spake, saying:
'Let there be one darkness above,
Let there be one darkness below (alternate),
Let there be a darkness unto Tupua,
Let there be a darkness unto Tawhito,
It is a darkness overcome and dispelled.
Let there be one light above,
Let there be one light below (alternate),
Let there be a light unto Tupua,
Let there be a light unto Tawhito,
A dominion of light,
A bright light.'
And now a great light prevailed.
[Io] then looked to the waters, which compassed him about,
And spake a fourth time, saying:
'Ye waters of Tai-kama be ye separate
Heaven, be formed' The sky became suspended.
'Bring-forth, thou, Tupua-horo-riuku.'

And at once the moving earth lay stretched abroad."[35]

s. <u>Plato's</u> "Timaeus" in Augustine's *City of God*

"For in the Timæus, when writing on the formation of the world, he [Plato] says that God first united earth and fire..."[36]

t. <u>Phoenician creation</u> myth

"And when the air began to send forth light, by its fiery influence on the sea and earth, winds were produced, and clouds, and very great defluxions and torrents of the heavenly waters. And when they were thus separated, and carried out of their proper places by the sun, and all met again in the air, and were dashed against each other, thunder and lightings were the result:" [It is possible that this might refer to the beginning of the flood of Noah's Day.][37]

"And God said, 'Let there be light:' and there was light. And God saw the light, that it was good: and God divided the light from the darkness. And God called the light Day, and the darkness he called Night. And the evening and the morning were the first day" (Genesis 1:3-5).

3. Everything is from Earth's point of view.

Everything written in the Word of God and all of these other documents are from the point of view of Earth. To use Albert Einstein's vocabulary when he wrote on relativity; the *Co-ordinate System* is earth. Light was created and there was an evening and morning, the first day. Since God was working, that is, putting in energy and matter, in ways different from what we observe today, He could have miraculously caused an evening and morning. But more likely, He set the earth in motion, rotating it. The phrase "and God saw that it was good" refers to the light before there was a sun. It also seems that on the end of the first day there was only one light source in entire universe visible on earth. While there is no amount of time mentioned, the phrase "And the evening and the morning were the first day," indicates one revolution of the earth. That would be either a twenty-four hour period or something close to a twenty-four period. Also, evening was the first time indicator mentioned. So the first day started with darkness, then light until evening, night, morning and another period of daylight.

VII. The Second Day of Creation

Expanse Separating Water Is Created

A. The Expanse Separating the Water Is Created.

"Then God said, 'Let there be an expanse in the midst of the waters, and let it separate the waters from the waters.' And God made the expanse, and separated the waters which were below the expanse from the waters which were above the expanse; and it was so. And God called the expanse heaven. And there was evening and there was morning, a second day" (Genesis 1:6-8 NASB).

"The heavens are telling of the glory of God;
And the expanse is declaring the work of hands" (Psalm 19:1, NASB).

"Praise the LORD!
Praise God in His sanctuary;
Praise Him in His mighty expanse"
(Psalm 150:1, NASB).

"It is He who sits above the vault of the earth,
And its inhabitants are like grasshoppers,
Who stretches out the heavens like a curtain

And spreads them out like a tent to dwell in" (Isaiah 40:22, NASB).

"Thus says the LORD, your Redeemer, and the one who formed you from the womb,
'I, the LORD, am the maker of all things,
Stretching out the heavens by Myself,
And spreading out the earth all alone"
(Isaiah 44:24).

"The LORD, which stretcheth forth the heavens, and layeth the foundation of the earth, and formeth the spirit of man within him" (Zechariah 12:1).

B. Similarities to the Biblical Record in Other Sources.

1. *Antiquities of the Jews* Josephus

"On the second day, he placed the heaven over the whole world, and separated it from the other parts, and he determined it should stand by itself. He also placed a crystalline [firmament] round it, and put it together in a manner agreeable to the earth, and fitted it for giving moisture and rain, and for affording the advantage of dews."[38]

2. *The Book of Chilam Balam of Chumayel* Mayan[39]

"On 1 Chuen he raised himself to his divinity, after he had made heaven and earth.
On 2 Eb he made the first stairway. It descended from the midst of the heavens, in the midst of the water, when there were neither earth, rocks nor trees.
On 3 Ben he made all things, as many as there

are, the things of the heavens, the things of the sea and the things of the earth.
On 4 Ix sky and earth were tilted.
On 5 Men he made everything.
On 6 Cib the first candle was made; it became light when there was neither sun nor moon."[39]

3. *Popol Vuh* Mayan[40]

"This is the account of how all was in suspense, all calm, in silence; all motionless, still, and the expanse of the sky was empty. This is the first account, the first narrative. There was neither man, nor animal, birds, fishes, crabs, trees, stones, caves, ravines, grasses, nor forests; there was only the sky. The surface of the earth had not appeared. There was only the calm sea and the great expanse of the sky."

"There was nothing brought together, nothing which could make a noise, nor anything which might move, or tremble, or could make noise in the sky. There was nothing standing; only the calm water, the placid sea, alone and tranquil. Nothing existed. There was only immobility and silence in the darkness, in the night.

"Only the creator, the Maker, Tepeu, Gucumatz, the Forefathers, were in the water surrounded with light. They were hidden under green and blue feathers, and were therefore called Gucumatz. By nature they were the great sages and great thinkers. In this manner the sky existed and also the heart of Heaven, which is the name of God thus He is called.

"Then came the word. Tepeu and came together in the darkness, in the night, and Tepeu and Gucumatz talked together. They talked then, discussing and deliberating; they agreed, they united their words and their thoughts. Then while they meditated, it became clear to them that when dawn would break, man must appear. Then they planned the creation, and the growth of the trees and the thickets and the birth of life and the creation of man.

"Thus it was arranged in the darkness and in the night by the Heart of Heaven who is called Huracan. The first is called Caculha Huracan. The second is ChipiCaculha. The third is Raxa-Caculha. And these three are the Heart of Heaven. Then Tepeu and Gucumatz came together; then they conferred about life and light, what they would do so that there would be light and dawn, who it would be who would provide food and sustenance.

Watery emptiness image from IMSI Hijack Collection

"'Thus let it be done! Let the emptiness be filled! Let the water recede and make a void, let the earth appear and become solid; let it be done.' Thus they spoke. 'Let there be light, let there be dawn in the sky and on the earth! There shall be neither glory nor grandeur in our creation and formation until the human being is made, man is formed.'

"So they spoke. Then the earth was created by them. So it was, in truth, that they created the earth. "Earth! They said, and instantly it was made. Like the mist, like a cloud and like a cloud of dust was the creation, when the mountains appeared from the water; and instantly the mountains grew."[40]

4. *Hurúing Wuhti and the Sun* Hopi

"A very long time ago there was nothing but water. In the east Hurúing Wuhti, the deity of all hard substances, lived in the ocean."[41]

5. *Origin de los Indias* Mixtec

"In the year and in the day of the clouds before ever were years or days, the world lay in darkness. All things were orderless, and a water covered the slime and ooze that the earth then was."[42]

C. Three Heavens

At the end of the second day there are three heavens. The order is optional. (first and third can be reversed) The first heaven is the dwelling of God, often called God's Throne. God has not chosen to reveal much information about this heaven. We do not know how big it is, but it is the dwelling of "thousands upon thousands and ten thousands times ten thousand." It existed before time and is not material.

The second heaven is what we call space or outer space. It is the material universe beyond the earth's atmosphere. It is the home of the sun, moon and stars, though none of these existed at the end of the second day. It is possible that the second heaven did not exist at all before the fourth day.

The third heaven is what we call the atmosphere, where birds and airplanes fly.

The word translated “firmament” (KJV), what we call an expanse, could refer to either the second or third heaven. The fowl created on the fifth day to fly “above the earth in the open firmament of heaven” actually flew “on the face of the firmament”, that is, the side turned toward the earth.

The question is: are the waters above the firmament (expanse) between the second and third heavens, creating a water canopy around the earth, or are the waters placed at the end of “heaven two”, the edge of the universe? While this second interpretation seems to agree with the text better, we must understand that this is only the second day of creation and the sun, moon, planets and stars have not been created yet. Perhaps at this point the expanse was the atmosphere and the entire rest of the universe was water, or at least some form of water. This at least implies that the sun, moon, planets, and stars were originally water.

This is real and material, not spiritual or allegorical. Still with no sun, moon or stars there was an evening and a morning for the second day. There was some form of light. And that light provided enough energy to supply the needs of plants (created on the third day) until the creation of the sun. The 24-hour day sequence starts in the evening, not the morning.

This is the only day where God does not make the statement that His work was good.

VIII. The Third Day of Creation

A. Dry Land Appears

"And God said, 'Let the waters under the heaven be gathered together unto one place, and let the dry land appear:' And it was so. And God called the dry land Earth; and the gathering together of the waters called he Seas: and God saw that it was good"
(Genesis 1:9,10).

This is the first mention of anything material besides water and expanse. This implies that there is one land mass surrounded by water. The earth also might have been a different size, perhaps smaller? If the total volume of water was significantly less, the earth's gravitational field might have been slightly weaker.

B. Similarities to the Biblical Record in Other Sources.

1. Metamorphosis Ovid (Latin)

"But God, or Nature, while they thus contend,
To these intestine discords put an end:
Then earth from air, and seas from earth were drive'n,
And grosser air sunk from aethereal Heav'n.
Thus disembroil'd, they take their proper place;
The next of kin, contiguously embrace;
And foes are sunder'd, by a larger space.
The force of fire ascended first on high,
And took its dwelling in the vaulted sky:
Then air succeed, in lightness next to fire;
Whose atoms from unactive earth retire.
Earth sinks beneath, and draws a num'rous throng
Of pondrous, thick, unwieldy seeds along.
About her coasts, unruly waters roar;
And rising, on a ridge, insult the shore.
Thus when the God, whatever God was he,
Had form'd the whole, and made the parts agree,
That no unequal portions might be found,
He moulded Earth into a spacious round."[43]

2. *The Seven Tablets of Creation* (Babylonian) Another version of the creation of the world by Marduk.[44]

1.The holy house, the house of the gods, in the holy place had not yet been made;
2. No reed had sprung up, no tree had been created.
3. No brick had been laid, no building had been set up;
4. No house had been erected, no city had been built;
5. No city had been made, no creature had been created.
6. Nippur had not been made, E-kur had not been built;

7. Erech had not been created, E-ana had not been built;
8. The Deep had not been created, Eridu had not been built;
9. Of the holy house, the house of the gods, the habitation had not been made.
10. All lands were sea.
11. At that time there was a movement in the sea,
12. Then was Eridu made, and E-sagil was built,
13. E-sagil, where in the midst of the Deep the god Lugal-dul-azaga dwelleth;
14. The city of Babylon was built, and E-sagil was finished.
15. The gods, the Anunnaki, he created at one time.[44]

"And God said, Let the earth bring forth grass, the herb yielding seed, and the fruit tree yielding fruit after his kind, whose seed was in itself, after his kind: and God saw that it was good. And the evening and the morning were the third day" (Genesis 1:11-13).

"And God said, 'Let the earth bring forth grass, the herb yielding seed, and the fruit tree yielding fruit after his kind' whose seed was in in itself, after his kind: and God saw that it was good. And the evening and the morning were the third day." (Genesis 1:11-13)

3. *Antiquities of the Jews* Josephus

"On the third day he appointed the dry land to appear, with the sea itself round about it; and on the very same day he made the plants and the seeds to spring out of the earth."[45]

4. *Annals of the World* Ussher

"(Tuesday, October 25) When these waters below ran together into one place, the dry land appeared. From this collection of the waters God made a sea, sending out from here the rivers, which were to return there again. Ecc. 1:7 He caused the earth to bud and bring forth all kinds of herbs and plants with seeds and fruits."[46]

C. God Creates Plants.

At this time there were no stars, no sun, no moon. This is the creation of plant life from the microbe to the largest tree. The plants are also divided into categories of food. Grass is for animals such as horses and cattle, though certain plants for human food might fall into this category. The herb yielding seed, such as grains and vegetables will also include spices. The third and final category, the fruit tree, seems to be the primary food for Adam and Eve. Perhaps mankind in the sinless state was designed to only enjoy fruit and not even need fruit to survive.

You might notice that plants need light for photosynthesis, yet there was no sun. The general light created on the first day was enough light for the plants until the sun was created less than twenty four hours later. Since the plants had to wait until the next day for the sun, this is another proof that the days were a single rotation of the earth and not ages. There is no way of knowing how much or what kind of light the earth had prior to the creation of the sun. But whatever light God provided, it is doubtful that worldwide plant life would have survived for millions of years without the sun.

The Fourth Day of Creation

IX. The Fourth Day of Creation

The Celestial Objects Coalesced and Put in Place

A. The Celestial Objects Coalesced and Put in Place

"And God said, Let there be lights in the firmament of the heaven to divide the day from the night; and let them be for signs, and for seasons, and for days, and years; and let them be for lights in the firmament of the heaven to give light upon the earth: and it was so. And God made two great lights; the greater light to rule the day, and the lesser light to rule the night: he made the stars also. And God set them in the firmament of the heaven to give light upon the earth, and to rule over the day and over the night, and to divide the light from the darkness: and God saw that it was good And the evening and the morning were the fourth day"
(Genesis 1:14-19).

B. Similarities to the Biblical Record in Other Sources.

1. *Metamorphosis* Ovid (Latin)

"High o'er the clouds, and empty realms of wind,
The God a clearer space for Heav'n design'd;
Where fields of light, and liquid aether flow;
Purg'd from the pondrous dregs of Earth below.
Scarce had the Pow'r distinguish'd these,
when streight the stars, no longer overlaid with weight, Exert their heads, from underneath the mass;
and upward shoot, and kindle as they pass,
and with diffusive light adorn their heav'nly place.
Then, every void of Nature to supply,
with forms of Gods he fills the vacant sky."[47]

2. *Antiquities of the Jews* Josephus

"On the fourth day he adorned the heaven with the sun, the moon, and the other stars, and appointed them their motions and courses, that the vicissitudes of the seasons might be clearly signified."[48]

3. *Annals of the World* Ussher

"On the fourth day (Wednesday, October 26th) the sun, the moon and the rest of the stars were created."[49]

4. *The Poetic Edda* (Norse)[50]

"Of old was the age when Ymir lived; Sea nor cool waves nor sand there were; Earth had not been, nor heaven above, But a yawning gap, and grass nowhere. Then Bur's sons lifted the level land, Mithgarth the mighty there they made; the sun from the south warmed the stones of earth, and green was the ground with growing leeks. The sun, the sister of the moon, from the south her right hand cast over heaven's rim; no knowledge she had where her home should be, the moon know not what might was his, the stars know not where their stations were. Then sought the gods their assembly-seats, the holy ones, and council held; names then gave they to noon and twilight, morning they named, and the waning moon, night and evening, the years to number."[50]

Earth from space with bright reflection Public Domain image from Pixabay

5. *Pahlavi Texts* Zoroastrian (Persian) "On the formation of the luminaries".[51]

Aûharmazd produced illumination between sky and the earth, the constellation stars and those also not the constellations, then the moon, and afterwards the sun..."

6. *The Prose Edda of Snorri Sturlson* (Norse)

"The sun know not where she had housing; The moon know not what Might he had; The stars know not where stood their places. Thus was it ere the earth was fashioned."[52]

7. *The Babylonian Legends of Creation* Berosus

"Belus formed also the stars, and the sun, and the moon, and the five planets."[53]

C. The Purpose of Celestial Objects

God's creative acts on the fourth day of creation clearly put the earth at the center of the universe. This does not mean the sun revolves around the earth. The earth is the center of importance, not the center of physical movements The earth revolving around the sun does not make the sun more important in God's plan. The divine purpose for everything is to glorify God. The way the sun, moon, stars, planets and other heavenly bodies glorify God is to provide light on earth. They divide day from night and act as timepieces. God chose to do this by rotating the earth on its axis and revolving the earth around the sun. The purpose of these movements, even the existence of these celestial objects is for men on earth. The entire material universe exists for man and the decisions men make. The religious belief that mankind is an insignificant animal on an insignificant planet in an insignificant place in the universe, is contrary to the regular movements of the sun, moon, stars, planets and other celestial objects.

The word "rule" for the sun and moon seems to us to be the wrong word. How can an inanimate material object in any sense of the word "rule" anything? The most sensible answer is that the sun, moon, and stars are to rule in the sense of regulate. The sun regulates the day and night. The moon and stars regulate seasons, months and years. We are responsible to obey this rule, that is, understand what the day is, what the months, years, and seasons are.

The words sun and moon do not occur until more than 2000 years later, yet they are clearly the greater and lesser lights. It is very likely they were quite different from the sun and moon we know today; different enough that had we been there on the fourth day of creation, we might not even recognize them. Also, the sun, moon, and stars are in the firmament, set in the expanse.

D. Possible Methods God Might Have Used.

If we view the fourth day as an astrophysicist, the explosion of the first day has cooled to the point of coalescing. From the point of view of someone on earth, stars, galaxies, planets and all other celestial objects were formed at the same time on the fourth day. Also on the fourth day God worked. God input matter and energy into the universe. He also supernaturally changed the existing matter and energy. This means that we are unable to measure the processes God used on any of the days of creation with processes we observe today.

The secular humanist Stephen Hawking points out in his book *A Brief History Of Time* that even if we just use the principles ruling the universe today, gravity affects time. The fourth day of Creation was the greatest possible expansion of the universe. According to the theory of general relativity, weightless or nearly weightless material, such as light photons traveling outside of a gravitational field, such as between stars or between galaxies, would travel for much longer periods of time and therefore greater distances as measured from earth. These light photons cannot travel faster than light, but time is very different to the observer on earth and the light photon with almost no gravity to slow it down. So one hour on earth could be many years to that light photon. It is theoretically possible that light could travel many, many light years while an observer on earth would only notice a short period of time. If we accept this theory, the fourth day of creation was when God stretched out the heavens.

It is also possible that God simply moved the stars, interstellar gases, comets, planets, asteroids, galaxies and all parts of the universe mass distances in one day. This rapid expansion is sometimes simply referred to as miraculous. Usually it is tied to time dilation.[54] That is, as mentioned in the previous paragraph, while the speed of light is a constant, time is not a constant.

So God could have coalesced the stars and planets in their existing location (approximately, taking the movements we measure today into account). Or God could have coalesced the stars and planets much closer to the earth on the fourth day of creation. He could afterward, combined with time dilation, have caused them to move into their (approximate) positions where we view them today.

The important point is, whatever method God used, by the end of the fourth day of creation week, the sun, moon and stars were visible from earth. So at that time, the fourth day of creation, the photons of light existed between the stars and earth.

The Fifth Day of Creation

X. The Fifth Day of Creation

God Creates Swarms of Life in the Oceans and Air

A. God Creates Swarms of Life in the Oceans and Air.

"And God said, Let the waters bring forth abundantly the moving creature that hath life, and fowl that may fly above the earth in the open firmament of heaven. And God created great whales, and every living creature that moveth, which the waters brought forth abundantly, after the kind, and every winged fowl after his kind: and God saw that it was good. And God blessed them, saying, Be fruitful, and multiply, and fill the waters in the seas, and let fowl multiply in the earth. And the evening and the morning were the fifth day" (Genesis 1:20-23).

Similarities to the Biblical Record in Other Sources

B. Similarities to the Biblical Record in Other Sources.

1. From Keil and Delitzsch OT Commentary

"God said: Let the waters swarm with swarms, with living beings, and let birds fly above the earth in the face (the front, i.e. the side turned towards the earth) of the firmament."[55]

2. *Annals of the World* Ussher

"On the fifth day (Thursday, October 27th) fish and flying birds were created and commanded to multiply and fill the sea and the earth."[56]

3. *Antiquities of the Jews* Josephus

"And on the fifth day he produced the living creatures, both those that swim, and those that fly; the former in the sea, the latter in the air: he also sorted them as to society and mixture, for procreation, and that their kinds might increase and multiply."[57]

4. *Metamorphosis* Ovid (Latin)

"Then, every void of Nature to supply,
With forms of Gods he fills the vacant sky:
New herds of beasts he sends, the plains to share:
New colonies of birds, to people air:
And to their oozy beds, the finny fish repair."[58]

5. from *Keil and Delitzsch OT Commentary*

"It is not stated that only a single pair was created of each kind; on the contrary, the words, "let the waters swarm with living beings," seem rather to indicate that the animals were created, not only in a rich variety of genera and species, but in large numbers of individuals."[59]

God's Purpose for Creating Swarms of Animals

C. God's Purpose for Creating Swarms of Animals.

Almost none of the ancient records outside the Bible divide the creation of animals into two separate days. "Let the waters bring forth abundantly" (KJV) can be translated "Let the waters swarm with swarms." In the old "which came first the chicken or the egg?" argument, God originally created swarms of creatures living in water. There is no mention of a division of salt and fresh water in the original creation. The phrase "after their kind" describes the boundary God placed on the animal world, as He had on the plant world. The word *kind* is not the same as *species*. For example, all dogs are the same kind and all horses are the same kind, though our artificial taxonomies divide these kinds into lower subcategories. If creatures can naturally interbreed then they are the same kind. The barrier which God set up is the natural limits to interbreeding. There is adaptation and change within a kind, within the boundary God ordained. A dog or a horse might be bred to be large and strong or quite small. It might have long hair, short hair or no hair. But a dog never was and never will be a horse.

A *kind* as found in the Bible, should be roughly the same as species. The problem is defining the word *species*. Many species, especially in captivity, can interbreed, which means that they are the same kind. This problem is in great part a result of professional pressure and the personal prestige to find and name new species. Another problem is the discovery of animals in remote locations. The discoverers are completely unaware of the relationship with distant similar creatures so it is classified as a different species. For example, there are 41 known species of cats (felids) today. That is certainly a larger number than the Biblical *kinds* of cats. Many of these different species of felids (cats) have successfully interbred in captivity. For example, there are twelve subspecies of lions and nine subspecies of tigers, yet lions and tigers can interbreed and might be only one *kind*.

Family of swans Image from IMSI Hijack

Creatures were procreating before sin entered into the world. If death is a result of sin, then how could these creatures procreate when they would soon overwhelm the earth? Without death to keep the populations of swarming creatures in check and only minimal original populations, the oceans would eventually be completely filled. God's command that the flying and swimming swarms should *"Be fruitful and multiply, and fill the waters in the seas, and let fowl multiply in the earth."* can only come to one of two conclusions. First, the animal kingdom had death before the fall because death is essential to control populations. This cannot be reconciled with a world that was created good. Second, the animal kingdom had a purpose never realized that would either control population growth or God had a plan that was never realized to enlarge the places where animals and people could live.

The Sixth Day of Creation

XI. The Sixth Day of Creation

A. God Creates Land Animals and Man.

"And God said, Let the earth bring forth the living creature after his kind, cattle, and creeping thing, and beast of the earth after his kind: and it was so. And God made the beast of the earth after his kind, and cattle after their kind, and every thing that creepeth upon the earth after his kind: and God saw that it was good. And God said, Let us make man in our image, after our likeness: and let them have dominion over the fish of the sea, and over the fowl of the air, and over the cattle, and over all the earth, and over every creeping thing that creepeth upon the earth. So God created man in his own image, in the image of God created he him; male and female created he them. And God blessed them, and God said unto them, Be fruitful, and multiply, and replenish the earth, and subdue it: and have dominion over the fish of the sea, and over the fowl of the air, and over every living thing that moveth upon the earth. And God said, Behold, I have given you

every herb bearing seed, which is upon the face of all the earth, and every tree, in the which is the fruit of a tree yielding seed; to you it shall be for meat. And to every beast of the earth, and to every fowl of the air, and to every thing that creepeth upon the earth, wherein there is life, I have given every green herb for meat: and it was so. And God saw every thing that he had made, and, behold, it was very good. And the evening and the morning were the sixth day"
(Genesis 1:24-31).

Then God said, "Let the earth bring forth living creatures after their kind: cattle and creeping things and beasts of the earth after their kind"; and it was so. God made the beasts of the earth after their kind, and the cattle after their kind, and everything that creeps on the ground after its kind; and God saw that it was good.

Then God said, "Let Us make man in Our image, according to Our likeness; and let them rule over the fish of the sea and over the birds of the sky and over the cattle and over all the earth, and over every creeping thing that creeps on the earth." God created man in His own image, in the image of God He created him; male and female He created them. God blessed them; and God said to them, "Be fruitful and multiply, and fill the earth, and subdue it; and rule over the fish of the sea and over the birds of the sky and over every living thing that moves on the earth." Then God said, "Behold, I have given you every plant yielding seed that is on the surface of all the earth, and every tree which has fruit yielding seed; it shall be food for you; and to every beast of the earth and to every bird of the sky and to every thing that moves on the earth which has life, I have given every green plant for food"; and it was so. God saw all that He had made, and behold, it was very good. And there was evening and there was morning, the sixth day. Genesis 1:24-31 NASB

Similarities to the Biblical Record in Other Sources

B. Similarities to the Biblical Record in Other Sources.

1. *Dreamtime* Australian Aborigine

"The (Sun) Mother ventured into a very deep cave, spreading her light around her. Her heat melted the ice and the rivers and streams of the world were created. Then she created fish and small snakes, lizards and frogs. Next she awoke the spirits of the birds and animals and they burst into the sunshine in a glorious array of colors. Seeing this the Father of All Spirits was pleased with the Sun Mother's work."[60]

Diorama of Water Buffalo and Crocodile from Cabella's. photo taken by the authors.

2. *Antiquities of the Jews* Josephus

"On the sixth day he created the four-footed beasts, and made them male and female: on the same day he also formed man. Accordingly Moses says, That in just six days the world, and all that is therein, was made. And that the seventh day was a rest, and a release from the labor of such operations; whence it is that we Celebrate a rest from our labors on that day, and call it the Sabbath, which word denotes rest in the Hebrew tongue."[61]

3. *Metamorphosis* Ovid (Latin)

"A creature of a more exalted kind
Was wanting yet, and then was Man design'd:
Conscious of thought, of more capacious breast,
For empire form'd, and fit to rule the rest:
Whether with particles of heav'nly fire
The God of Nature did his soul inspire,
Or Earth, but new divided from the sky,
And pliant, still retain'd th'aetherial."[62]

4. *Antiquities of the Jews* Josephus

"God took dust from the ground, and formed man and inserted in him a spirit and a soul."[63]

5. *Antiquities of the Jews* Josephus

"God also presented the living creatures when he had made them, according to their kinds, both male and female, to Adam, who gave them those names by which they are still called."[64]

6. *Metamorphosis* Ovid (Latin)

"From such rude principles our form began;
And earth was metamorphos'd into Man."[65]

7. *Antiquities of the Jews* Josephus

"But when he saw that Adam had no female companion, no society, for there was no such created, and that he wondered at the other animals which were male and female, he laid him asleep, and took away one of his ribs, and out of it formed the woman; whereupon Adam knew her when she was brought to him, and acknowledged that she was made out of himself. Now a woman is called in the Hebrew tongue Issa; but the name of this woman was Eve, which signifies the mother of all living."[66]

8. *Antiquities of the Jews* Josephus

"God planted a paradise in the East, flourishing with all sorts of trees; and that among them was the tree of life, and another of knowledge, whereby was to be known what was good and evil; and that when he brought Adam and his wife into this garden, he commanded them to take care of the plants. Now the garden was watered by one river, which ran round about the whole earth and was parted into four parts."

C. Man Created in the Image of God.

This is the most examined passage in the entire Bible. Not only individual comments but also entire series are written about our creation, fall and sin nature.

Though it is not so obvious in the English, the word for God here is the Hebrew plural, *Elohim*. The ancient Church Fathers unanimously agreed that this referred to the Trinity. Adam was created in the image and similitude of God. Since God does not have a body like we do (though He may choose to appear in a body) this refers to Adam's spirit and soul. Animals cannot build cities, organize into orchestras, design bridges, write books on the motions of the planets, make movies, design fashions, weld automobiles, understand chemistry to make jet fuel, pray, sing, or glorify God. These represent the image and similitude of God. The concept of likeness to God does not refer to physical shape.

Another way man is like God is in the responsibility to manage the Earth. God put the Earth, including every living creature, under the authority of Adam. But this responsibility must glorify God. It includes understanding how the physical universe operates and doing what is best for others, not just yourself.

D. What Is Death?

Since there was no death before the Fall of man we must understand; "What is death?" Plants were created to be food. When Adam ate a piece of fruit did he kill the cells of the fruit? When a sheep eats a blade of grass, roots and all, did it kill that blade of grass? Is an exploding star "dying?"

Humans do not have the answers to these and many more similar questions. Rather than frustrating ourselves even more, we will stay with the information we have. For a human being, death is separation for God. The body dies when it is separated from the soul.

Though humans can breed "new" types of animals, the original creation contained all the genetic material there ever was or ever will be. Genetic material can be recombined to expose recessive or damaged genes. This recombination can expose never seen before traits, such as red hair or albinism, even though the genetic information was there all along.

"Thus the heavens and the earth were finished, and all the host of them." (Genesis 2: 1-2 KJV)

2 And on the seventh day God ended his work which he had made; and he rested on the seventh day from all his work which he had made.

God ceased working, that is, inputting energy and matter into the universe. Without sin or death the universe was not deteriorating as it is now. All of the other physical laws that we know and understand today, except those modified by the curse of the Fall were in place by this time.

E. The *Toldot* of the Heavens and of the Earth.

Genesis 2:4 *"These are the generations of the heavens and of the earth when they were created."* (KJV) *"This is the account of the heavens and the earth when they were created" (NASB) "This is the book of the generation of heaven and earth, that came into being, the day God made the heaven and the earth"* (English translation of LXX). *"These are the toldot of HaShomayim and of Ha'Aretz when they were created, in the Yom that Hashem Elohim made Eretz v'Shomayim."*[67] (Orthodox Jewish Bible) *Toldot* is the transliteration of the Hebrew instead of translating it *generations*. It is the formal record God gave mankind of the creation of the heavens and the earth. It is the Law, a legal document. It is also an authoritative scientific document. If you do not believe, that is understand and choose to accept, this record of Creation, then how can you believe, that is understand and choose to accept, anything the Bible teaches about anything else, including Salvation?

Condition of the Earth on the Seventh Day

XII. Condition of the Earth on the Seventh Day

The Ground Was Prepared for Man

A. The Ground Was Prepared for Man.

> *"And every plant of the field before it was in the earth, and every herb of the field before it grew: for the LORD God had not caused it to rain upon the earth, and there was not a man to till the ground. But there went up a mist from the earth, and watered the whole face of the ground"* (Genesis 2:5-6).

This can either mean that God only created seeds which had not yet sprouted or more likely, the plants suitable for food were not organized into what we might think of as fields of a farm because there were no men to do the work. Without either rain or men to organize and irrigate, the fertile soil had too little moisture. So the earth as a whole on the seventh day was fertile yet barren. The mist (perhaps *"an underground stream would rise from the earth and water the surface of the ground."* Genesis 2:6 ISV) was enough to sustain plant life, but the Earth needed a man to organize and plant. Once again, God emphasized man's responsibility.

The absence of rain tells us that the conditions on earth were vastly different than they are now. The new soil was covered with a heavy mist, probably every morning, and possibly groundwater, but the ground was not tilled or harvested yet. With proper farming, the mist or groundwater would be enough to allow plants to grow. The important point is the high humidity level. The original earth, at least around Eden, did not have completely arid deserts.

If this only describes conditions around Eden, then the Antediluvian world might have had rain in other places.

B. The Entire Universe Was Created for Man.

The emphasis of the Bible is that the universe was created for man. Man was also created for the material world.

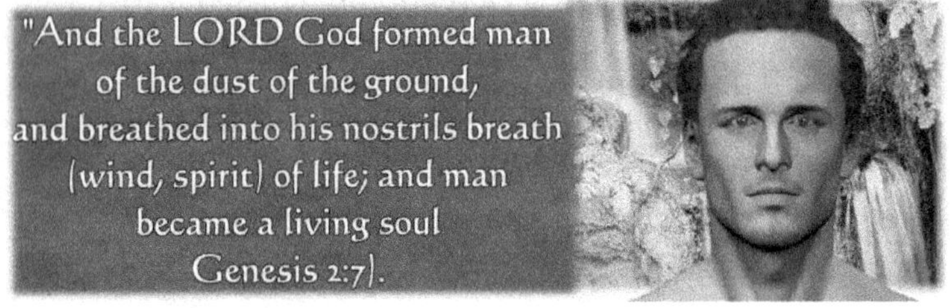

"And the Lord God formed man of the dust of the ground, and breathed into his nostrils the breath of life; and man became a living soul." (Genesis 2:7 KJV) Image of Adam in Eden created by authors using Daz 3D character.

Animals, birds, fish, reptiles and mammals, were created in large groups. Adam was created as an individual. We are not told how God made the animals. We do know that the entire creation of every kind of animal, from the tiniest single celled microbe to the great blue whale, the largest creature to every live, took place in less than 48 hours.

> *"And the LORD God planted a garden eastward in Eden; and there he put the man whom he had formed. And out of the ground made the LORD God to grow every tree that is pleasant to the sight, and good for food; the tree of life also in the midst of the garden, and the tree of knowledge of good and evil"* (Genesis 2:8).

C. The Hedged Place in Eden Was Created for Man.

After the creation of animals and man was completed, God made a "hedged place," translated "garden" in English. The LXX translates the "hedged place" as "paradise." Probably a better English translation today would be a "park" unless we think of it as a very large English style garden. The park was "eastward" "in" Eden. With the entire earth a single landmass, perhaps all the arable land was called Eden. Perhaps the words Eden and eastward were from the point of view of Moses, the author of the Pentateuch. If that is true, then eastward is likely to be what we think of as China or the Orient.

"And a river went out of Eden
to water the garden; and from thence it
was parted and became into four heads"
(Genesis 2:10).

"And a river went out of Eden to water the garden; and from thence it was parted, and became into four heads." (Genesis

2:10) Image of footprints at water's edge Public Domain from Pixabay.

For one river to water the whole earth, there had to be only one continent. Modern geologists call this original continent *Pangea*. God simply called it land. Part of that mass of dry land God called Eden. Inside Eden somewhere God made a garden. The Garden of Eden was only one part of Eden.

This also means that Eden was the highest point on earth, or at least the highest point that was watered, since water flows downhill.

D. Woman Was Created for Man.

The creation of Eve from a piece of Adam's rib is usually accepted without close examination or rejected as mythology out of hand. A scientific examination of the evidence would discover that even today, medical procedures can remove pieces of a human rib and afterward that rib will regrow. [68] This is normal. The procedure must be performed carefully.

Summary of The Scientific History of Origins

XIII. Summary of The Scientific History of Origins

A. Summary of Creation

God existed before time. God created time as one dimension of a four dimensional material universe. We know nothing about creatures such as angels which might have existed before the first of act of creation of the material universe. If spiritual beings did not exist before the first day of creation, then God created all spiritual beings and the universe as we know it in six days, as viewed from the co-ordinate system of earth. God worked (input creative energy) for six days then rested. From the standpoint of energy, God created all the order and physical laws that exist in that one week. He also created all life, spiritual as well as material, in that week. Some spiritual beings might have been created before the creation of the universe. All genetic material and all genetic possibilities were created at the beginning.

God created the laws of what Albert Einstein calls general relativity. It is possible, even likely, that the entire universe was created at the same time but the earth is only six thousand years old while the distant stars might be billions of years old. This is difficult to grasp, but it fits the facts, at least as we understand the facts today. The great variable is time itself. The speed of light seems to be the universal constant God created.

The original creation seems to have been moisture, a cloud. The Spirit (breath, wind) of God contained the cloud and forced individual droplets to coalesce, creating gravity, which formed liquid water. The next step in creation was light and heat, then rotation, then land, then plants, then stars, then the sun and moon, then animal and human life.

Since water flows downhill, the Garden in Eden was the highest (watered) place on earth. The earth had to be one continent, since only one river watered the entire earth.

Summary of Suggested Teaching Methods

B. Summary of Suggested Teaching Methods

Though we understand the concept of a Scope and Sequence, we do not believe this to be the best approach for homeschool or individual instruction. We are also aware that many parents/teachers want a complete, correlated set of lesson plans, questions made into quizzes, tests, and projects, and everything divided into preset teaching units. There are two problems with this approach.

1. Teaching the Test

The first problem is the trap that many students and, sadly, many teachers, fall into. They are busy, so the information in the questions, quizzes, tests, and projects becomes important and truly learning other information is less important or unimportant. This is extremely sad because what a person believes about origins is a topic students will encounter all their lives. This trap is called “teaching the test” or “teaching to the test”. The only information that is important or even covered at all is the information the teacher knows will be on the test.

2. Level of the Material Is Not Student Appropriate.

The second problem is the material appropriate for the maturity level of the student. One student might handle the basic material very well, but be completely unable to grasp the reference material in the References, Footnotes, Expanded Study and Appendix Materials. Another more advanced student might find the same material just a jumping off point. For one example, he might become interested in understand the differences between General and Special Relativity and use the short articles as a place to start serious research and study.

So our questions might be very challenging to some students, while others will likely be able to answer these basic questions quickly. Since the References, Footnotes, Expanded Study and Appendix Materials make up much of this book, we intend for parent/teachers to decide how much of this material individual students can handle.

End of Main Text

XIV. Review Questions

TEACHERS/PARENTS: You have complete and final authority. You can choose the amount of detail you expect for an answer. You may choose to use some of these questions, you may choose to use all of them or you may choose to add more of your own. You may even decide to alter what you believe a correct answer is. You can change the way you administer the questions. You can make them multiple choice, True/False, sort answer or even essay. It is your decision.

1. What do the Scriptures say we struggle against?

Spiritual forces of wickedness

2. History of Civilization is the record of man's taking two positions toward God. What are they?

a. yielding to God's will or b. rebelling against Him

3. What religion is today's primary form of rebellion against God in Western cultures?

Secular Humanism

4. Why is the book *Antidisestablishmentarianism* important for understanding the purpose behind this series?

It explains what we believe and why

5. What does the Magna Carta say about the church?

It is to be free and have its rights entire (not controlled by government)

6. What document was based on this principle?

The first amendment to the US Constitution

7. How has the first amendment been violated?

Secular Humanism has become the controlling force in government and education. Textbooks must conform to evolutionary dogma to be published.

8. State briefly how Scientific history is similar to the scientific method.

It requires reliable evidence, logical analysis, and a rational generalization.

9. How is education valuable?

It relies on verified, documented evidence to learn the experiences of others, since it is impossible for one person to experience, document, and verify everything personally.

10. What is the important thing about sources, whether they are oral or written communications?

They must be reliable and verifiable.

11. What must be true if chronology is the backbone of history?

You must have an accurate timeline, and God is the only true witness to all of history.

12. What are the two most important things we will focus on for all the areas studied in this series?

a. Giving God the greatest glory and b. pointing out the most significant rebellion.

13. What is the one thing all produced works are based on?

The assumptions of the creator of the work.

14. Refusing to inform readers of the assumptions on which your work is based makes you guilty of what?

Telling a great lie.

15. Sachs and Gould both deny what truth?

They manufacture a nonexistent separation between religious and scientific truth. Truth is truth.

16. If the Scriptures are not historically and scientifically accurate, what else must we conclude about them?

They are useless as moral and philosophical guides.

17. Many secularists agree with Bible believers about what concerning the mainstream view of history?

It makes no sense in the light of ancient document records and archaeological finds of ancient technology and civilizations around the world.

18. What is true of all theories about the origin of life?

There were no human observers, and none of the processes can be reenacted.

19. What are the three possible positions on the beginning of the universe?

a. impossible to know how it began
b. it can be discovered from observation of the world around us
c. God as an accurate, scientific observer recorded events and passed on the records to us.

20. Name at least two secularists who disagree with mainstream accounts of history.

Three possible answers are:
a. Erich Von Däniken
b. Graham Hancock
c. Immanuel Velikovsky.

21. What device has the stated purpose of discovering

how the universe came into existence?

The Large Hadron Collider

22. By accepting the third view of the origin of the universe, that of God as Creator and Observer, what must we conclude?

Time, matter, and energy came from outside the universe

23. Briefly summarize the three foundational standards of this work.

a. The Bible is reliable and true
b. other ancient records are less reliable and must be held to the Bible's standard of truth
c. Physical evidence can be manipulated and is subject to interpretation

24. Why is it necessary to present the facts concerning the origins of the universe?

The secular mythologies about origins (including the Big Bang, deep time, and evolution) are presented as fact and are the basis for society's moral relativism, so these untruths must be refuted.

25. Write a brief essay summarizing the facts presented concerning God, Creation, and Time.

The teacher may decide to split this assignment into a choice of three assignments, dealing with God, or Creation, or Time as separate topics. In any case, students should include at least mention of the following: Jesus Christ not only upheld the authority of the Old Testament but also confirmed its testimony to His own nature as part of the Trinity. He placed the truth and power of the Scriptures above supernatural events (miracles including resurrection from the dead) and human experience (people's telling about and reacting to things they say happened to them personally). The Bible taken as a whole teaches that

God, in the form of the Trinity, existed before any Creation, and that Creation was a result of God's direct act, not from previously existing matter or energy. Other ancient testimony confirms that time began with creation and did not exist before it. Therefore God existed before time, created it, and exists outside it.

26. What is a "singularity" in the context of this study?

The belief that all energy and matter began converged at a single point.

27. "Heat Death", "Big Crunch", and "infinite" refer to what?

Various theories about the future of the universe

28. Briefly explain in your own words a biblically-based theory similar to the "Big Bang".

The "deep" may have been clouds which the Holy Spirit compressed into liquid water. Gravitational collapse resulted in thermonuclear fusion and an explosion.

29. List three common elements of creation accounts from many ancient writings.

References to clouds, water, moisture, darkness giving way to light, heat or energy, and an "expanse" (space)

30. What is the most likely explanation for the phrase "evening and morning"?

God set the earth in motion to rotate on the first day, creating the 24-hour period or something close to it from the beginning.

31. Briefly list and describe the three heavens.

a. God's dwelling, non-material, vast in size, existing before time and not affected by it.
b. the material universe, or outer space.
c. the atmosphere or "air".

32. What had not yet been created by the end of the third day, causing some to doubt the 24-hour day interpretation?

The sun, moon, and stars were not yet created.

33. What three categories of plants were created, with some overlap between categories?

a. grasses/animal food b. grains and vegetables/human food c. fruit tree/specifically designated for Adam and Eve

34. What is strange about the creation of plants on the third day?

No sun for photosynthesis. (But the student should realize that there was light, created on the first day, and though God does not tell us the source, it was enough light for the plants until the next day of creation.

35. What is clear from the events of the fourth day of creation?

God made the earth to be the center of the universe, put man on it, and did this for His glory, meaning that the purpose of man is to glorify God in this perfectly-aligned universe created for his habitation.

36. What is probably the real meaning of the word “rule” as it relates to the planets?

Regulate days, months, years, and seasons.

37. Write a brief essay discussing the astrophysical aspects of the fourth day.

Answers may vary but should include some of the following: God’s creative work is not comparable to the natural processes we can observe today, so we cannot measure or quantify how the universe was actually created and spread out. Most of that work, however, was done on this day, from the perspective of someone on earth. Light, energy, and even matter could travel at a different rate across the universe from what earthly observers would define as a "passage of time". One hour on earth could be years to a traveling photon, for example. God could also have immediately moved things great distances in that day.

38. How is the word "kind" different from the word "species"?

Kind is a simple division between creatures that can and cannot interbreed. Species is part of a manmade system of taxonomy developed by man to subdivide kinds.

39. What might explain how population growth of animals was controlled before the fall?

Death is one explanation, but this seems contradictory to scriptures that say everything was "very good", and also that death was a result of the fall and did not exist before it. The other theory is that God may have had a plan we do not know about (because the fall did occur and death is now the means of population control) to expand the habitation in which the creation could live.

40. Write a brief essay on what it means that man was made in the image of God.

Answers may vary but should include the following: The word for God here is plural and refers to the Trinity. Man shares God's creative and inventive nature, unlike the animals, and resembles Him in his soul and spirit. Man shares God's management responsibility for the creation and must glorify God in how he carries out this responsibility, exploring and understanding as much as he can and being unselfish. It is not necessary to be concerned about the definition of "death" as it relates to plant life or inanimate things, but only spiritual death. Man does not have power to create new genetic information. All was present originally, but mutations or recessive traits might be exposed.

41. What is the meaning of "work" as it relates to God and His acts of creation?

Putting matter and energy into the universe. Teachers should also be certain students understand that it probably also includes enacting the physical laws we know of today that govern matter, energy and the universe. The word for "generation" in Genesis 2:4, according to the Septuagint, may refer to a legal or scientific record of God's work, that is, the written account in the Scriptures.

42. List three ways in which the earth at the end of creation may have been different from what we know today.

a. Probably no organization of field versus forest b. no rain or multiple sources of water (possibly daily mist and one river with four branches, versus irrigation ditches or canals, and many ponds, lakes or rivers) c. high humidity, no arid deserts, high concentration of fertile soil d. A single land mass and relatively moderate high and low areas. e. Large numbers of plants and animals, but only one man.

43. Briefly explain the difference between "Eden" and "the garden".

Eden appears to have been a fairly large region, possible all the land on the new created earth that could be cultivated or inhabited. The garden was located "eastward, in Eden". The Scriptures indicate that it was a smaller, in the eastern part of the larger Eden, and that it was walled or enclosed in some way, separated from the rest of Eden.

44. What is significant about Adam's rib being used to form Eve from a scientific view?

A portion of a rib can be surgically removed today and the tissue inside the body will regrow it.

XV. Vocabulary

NOTE: These are suggestions only.

The teacher should adjust the number of words to suit student needs.

Students should spell correctly and know the proper definition in context for the word the teacher selects.

As the teacher, you may use any method you believe is best for your students. We have found the following suggestions to be helpful.

1) Require the student to write his answers on a piece of paper. This provides the opportunity to develop handwriting skills as well as answer the question correctly.

2) More frequent, smaller assignments seem to allow students a better grasp of the material.

3) Tests, however, are necessary at regular intervals to validate the teaching method. We recommend at least one test per month, using different methods such as fill in the blank and matching. However, requiring an essay using the words properly is a valid test method. It also allows you, the teacher, to see if the student grasps the material.

4) We recommend a quiz of five words daily which includes both spelling and comprehension. Reading the words and definitions out loud aids in learning.
5) Ask the student write an original sentence using some the vocabulary words in the proper context. This should not take more than 5 minutes.
6) Make the vocabulary list the student is responsible for cumulative.
7) Only add 1 to 3 words per day to the list. Ten new words per week seems like a small number, but at that rate, the total will still be over 300 words per year. Advanced students can handle many more, but remember that you will be responsible for grading those words in a final examination at the end of the school year.

A small number of these words are no longer in the main text. After the vocabulary section was written, the entire book was rewritten. Some of the words are included in the Introduction at the beginning of the teacher's manual but deleted from the student editions. A very few words included in this list were deleted entirely from the revised version.

Total words: 183

1. retrieval

"No part of this publication may be reproduced in whole or in part, or stored in any retrieval system, or transmitted in any form by any means, electronic, mechanical, photocopying, recording, or otherwise, without permission of the publisher."

means of storing and accessing information

2. Hammurabi (context sentence follows number 3 below)

3. stele

"Images in this text come from the following sources: Hammurabi stele image from Wikimedia Commons"

Hammurabi: Ancient king credited with establishing a code of laws, identified by various Assyrian Kings' Lists and the stele pictured in the text

Stele: pillar-like stone with carvings depicting historical events or records in ancient civilizations

4. English Composition

"Dr. Ray St. John, in freshman English Composition at Bob Jones University, taught that a student's first research paper tended to be something along the lines of, "the universe and everything in it."

A course, usually taught in college, including the study of grammar, language usage, and writing in structured forms.

5. postdoctoral

"These reference links will usually be more difficult reading material, sometimes on a postdoctoral level."

studies taking place after a student has obtained a doctoral level degree; very advanced or difficult reading

6. literature

"Third, when the course reaches book or module 4, it divides into separate history and literature tracks. There will be only one reference works list. It is identical for the history and the literature tracks."

study of writings from various cultures, countries, and time periods with the purpose of better comprehending the content, use of figurative language, vocabulary, and other elements

7. Annotated bibliography

"This annotated bibliography will be continually expanding, never complete."

listing of sources or relevant references including explanations or commentary in the form of notes

8. prologue

"Our Prologue to this entire series, the book *Antidisestablishmentarianism,* explains what we believe and why in detail."

part of written work that explains its purpose, scope, and content

9. antidisestablishmentarianism

"Our Prologue to this entire series, the book *Antidisestablishmentarianism,* explains what we believe and why in detail."

In the 1800s churches which tried to break away from the Church of England were called disestablishmentarians. The people who fought against the disestablishment of those churches within the Church of England in the 1800s were called Antidisestablishmentarians. In this book we identify Secular Humanism as the established religion of America. Those who seek to end its influence in government, education, and other aspects of society are disestablishmentarians, and the Secular Humanists are antidisestablishmentarians because they seek to retain control in society.

10. Magna Carta

"The *Magna Carta* opens with the words, 'In the first place we grant to God and confirm by this our present charter for ourselves and our heirs in perpetuity that the English Church is to be free and to have all its rights fully and its liberties entirely'."

document of historical England signed by the nobility in 1215 affirming the rights of Englishmen in society

11. amendment

"The concept that *the English Church is to be free* became the basis for the first amendment of US Constitution 'Congress shall make no law respecting an establishment of religion, or prohibiting the free exercise thereof...'"

material added to the Constitution to clarify, expand upon, or add to principles and practices of government

12. secular (context sentence follows number 14 below)

13. humanism

14. Secular Humanism

"This amendment has been openly violated because Secular Humanism has become the warp and woof of federal government practice and therefore it is our established *religion."*

Secular: claiming to be philosophically devoid of religious nature or content

Humanism: claiming to seek the betterment of mankind

Secular Humanism: opposing religious practice differing from its own, relying on belief in evolution and uniformitarianism and condemning belief in any spiritual power

15. Establishment of Religion, Established Religion

"Since secular humanism became America's Established Religion, all textbooks must conform to the Established Religion to get published. Those who oppose this Establishment of Religion are Disestablishmentarians."

religious belief and practice operating jointly with government, sharing control over the people and usually over each other

16. academic

"Those in positions of political power, especially in academic positions of power, are fighting to keep their power and privilege."

related to education and teaching

17. introduction

"*Antidisestablishmentarianism* the book began as the introduction to this work, but grew to be a book in its own right."

part of a written work that explains or lays groundwork for understanding the main part of the work

18. preface

"The Preface of that book is included in this book and is also on our blog. We strongly recommend that you read this preface, even if you do not read the rest of *Antidisestablishmentarianism* or other parts of *The Conflict of the Ages* series. Traditionally, a preface explains *why* a book is written."

part of a written work that explains the reasons for writing it

19. science

"What Is Science?"

the orderly collection and observation of knowledge; discovering how things work

20. deductive reasoning

"Deductive reasoning might make good detective work (and it might not), but these are rarely of much use to the historian."

starts out with a general statement, or hypothesis, and examines the possibilities to reach a specific, logical conclusion. The scientific method uses deduction to test hypotheses and theories. In deductive reasoning, if something is true of a class of things in general, it is also true for all members of that class.

21. inductive reasoning (context sentence follows number 22 below)

22. evidence

"The historian tends to be more inductive, relying on major pieces of evidence."

inductive reasoning: Making broad generalizations from specific observations.

Evidence: the available body of facts or information indicating whether a belief or proposition is true or valid.

23. documented (context sentence follows number 24 below)

24. verify

"It is documented and verified."

Documented: the statement and substantial proofs of its accuracy are easily available

Verified: subjected to a process of discovering and confirming its truth

25. education

"Education means that you do not have to personally experience something for it to be true. You can rely on the observation and experiences of others to learn things."

imparting information, culturally important knowledge, skills, and principles for living through various teaching methods

26. critical

"It is critically important that scientific history knows the quality of the sources relied on."

vitally important; absolutely necessary

27. oral sources

"Yes, there are oral sources, but historically, oral sources have been respected as reliable eyewitnesses. In US courts, oral testimony is actually preferred over written testimony."

testimony or historical records initially transmitted by speech rather than writing

28. narration (context sentence follows number 31 below)

29. picturesque

30. legend

31. myth

"Charlton Heston, in his narration of the picturesque Bible video series, presents the Bible as part of the 'oral tradition in storytelling' as if teachings passed on orally were understood to be less accurate or reliable and therefore merely legends and myths."

Narration: relating or telling information in a straightforward method

Picturesque: creating charming, pleasing, or entertaining mental or visual images

Legend: stories told about the past that may or may not be true; often including details that seem exaggerated or hard to believe

Myth: story about spiritual or religious characters or events told as part of the culture and past of a people but judged non-historical by scholars or anthropologists

32. dialogue

"Socrates, in Plato's Dialogue *Phaedrus*, addresses the subject of oral versus written history."

A form of teaching involving a principle speaker engaging one or more other persons in a discussion to get a single point across. In Socratic dialogues the teacher primarily engages one person, though others may be present and interacting, and attempts to cause that person to think seriously about (and usually re-evaluate) his position on the matter under discussion.

33. attribute

"Thamus replied: '... you ... attribute to them a quality which they cannot have; for this ... will create forgetfulness in the learners' souls, ... they will trust to the external written characters ...'"

claim that something has a certain property, ability, or nature

34. express

Plutarch, in his discourse on the life of Lycurgus and his rule in ancient Greece, expresses the belief that oral tradition is a way of making the law more firmly fixed in the mind.

speak or write about an opinion, belief, or teaching

35. compulsion

"For he thought that if the most important and binding principles which conduce to the prosperity and virtue of a city were implanted in the habits and training of its citizens, they would remain unchanged and secure, having a stronger bond than compulsion in the fixed purposes imparted to the young by education, which performs the office of a law-giver for every one of them."

force someone to do, think, or believe something

36. considerable (context sentence follows number 38 below)

37. disagreement

38. communicate

"There is considerable disagreement about whether the Scriptures were in some part orally communicated before being written down."

Considerable: large in quantity, volume, or number

Disagreement: contrary beliefs about a topic

Communicate: express to others with the goal of making them understand

39. authoritative (context sentence follows number 40 below)

40. reliable

"The point is that even if they were it does not make them less authoritative or reliable."

Authoritative: based on evidence from a very credible or believable source

Reliable: trustworthy, dependable

41. reinforce

"Socrates may not be entirely justified in discounting the value of written records but he reinforces the point that oral communication of history does not make it unreliable or inaccurate."

add supporting evidence to help confirm truth

42. accuracy

"The issue is the accuracy, truth, honesty, and importance or significance of the information."

correctness or reliability

43. Information

"Still, the *Epic of Gilgamesh* contains some useful information."

Important knowledge; a source of learning

44. Transmission

"If the information is correct, the method of transmission is not important."

How something is communicated; passing information from one person to another

45. chronology

"Some people say that 'chronology is the backbone of history'."

correct historical order of events

46. observer

"The true scientific approach is that One Who created the Universe was the only flawless observer."

person who was present when something occurred, witnessed it taking place, and accurately reported what happened

47. touchstone

"Our touchstone of truth is the Word of God."

method or test for identifying something

48. correlation (context sentence follows number 49 below)

49. significant

"Correlation of the literature, geology, physics, biology, archaeology, and art of all countries will be reduced to those elements which we understand to give the greatest possible glory to God or to point out the most significant rebellion against Him."

Correlation: organizing to show important common elements and relationships

Significant: important to be aware of

50. assumption

"Unlike secular textbooks, our foundations, our assumptions, are clearly laid out in the beginning. All written ideas, all books, all videos, and all blogs are based on assumptions."

things accepted as true, upon which subsequent teaching material is based

51. perspective

"There are not different kinds of truth or even different views or perspectives on truth."

based on a person's point of view

52. interaction

"There has been much discussion, over the ages, on the possible interaction of the bases of science and religion."

how knowledge about one subject affects the treatment of another subject, or how they affect each other

53. proposition

"It has been my proposition that such interaction is illusory, primarily because the logics of these two disciplines are out of context."

a strong suggestion or recommendation intended to encourage or produce a particular action

54. Magisteria

"Stephen Jay Gould had another way of expressing this concept. He preached "Non-overlapping *Magisteria,"* that science and religion govern separate aspects of society and can co-exist as long as they keep separate."

areas of teaching or study; educational fields

55. ridiculous (context sentence follows number 56 below)

56. faction

"He calls Scientific Creationism, the belief that the Bible is to be taken literally, a position uniquely American and held by almost nobody, as if nobody ever believed the Bible to be true except this tiny, ridiculous faction."

a small, vocal group with a position differing from a more widely-held position

57. philosophical

'If the Scriptures are not true, how can they be even useful moral and philosophical guides?"

examine knowledge and belief to determine what should be taught and learned and how to accomplish those goals

58. segregated

"They pretend to allow for these 'separate truths' so that religion can be segregated more and more from people's '"regular' lives."

keeping things completely separated; not allowing any interaction or overlap

59. separation

There is no difference or separation between religious truth and scientific truth. Truth is truth.

dividing things into distinct areas

60. progression

"Even many Secular Humanists understand that the current 'mainstream' view of history, the progression from primitive to civilized to technological, makes no sense.

Going from something lesser or simpler to something greater or more complex

61. ancient (context sentence follows number 63 below)

62. technology

63. extraterrestrial

"Everywhere we can see examples of ancient technology. There is so much evidence of advanced early man that some believe that ancient technology came from extraterrestrials who guided mankind and were mistaken for gods."

Ancient: occurring very early in the world's history

Technology: inventions, tools, methods of construction, and devices that improve human ability to live, work, and accomplish what they need to do

Extraterrestrial: originating off the earth

64. mainstream (context sentence follows number 65 below)

65. presupposition

"Modern authors such as Erich Von Däniken in his books *Gold of the Gods* and *Chariots of the Gods?* accept the timeline of the mainstream religion of Secular Humanism, but clearly see that the technology of ancient humans does not fit with their presuppositions."

Mainstream: majority positions or those with strongest support and public acknowledgment

Presupposition: things accepted or taken for granted before a study begins

66. primitive

"So Erich Von Däniken and his followers believe that some type of extraterrestrials gave technology to ancient primitive humans."

perceived to be at an earlier stage of development; having fewer examples of technological or cultural development

67. delusional

"They don't dismiss all religions as delusional like other secularists."

resulting from a defective mentality; relying on false beliefs or erroneous information

68. devious (context sentence follows number 69 below)

69. deception

"Instead, our religious beliefs might have been created by devious extraterrestrial alien tricksters, who actively seek deception."

Devious: deceitful or inclined to dishonest behavior

Deception: seeking to mislead or lie

70. reasonable

"Graham Hancock and people like him are more reasonable, though still not completely accurate."

holding views that are based on examining and presenting evidence and exercising good judgment

71. dogmatic

"But they are for the most part content to find the ancient evidence for advanced technology without drawing dogmatic conclusions."

insisting that a position is the only truth and everyone must agree with it

72. development

"Hancock has traveled the world, researching and documenting advanced ancient civilizations, and has written many books, such as *Fingerprints of the Gods,* to point out that something is wrong with the secularist position that man's development went in a straight line from primitive to complex through time."

how changes occur in something from its beginning to the present time

73. origins (context sentence follows number 74 below)

74. advancement

"Secularists have to ignore many facts and pieces of evidence, such as those Hancock and others have uncovered, to hold on to their 'simple to complex' ideas about origins and advancement in science and history."

Origins: where things began or came from; sources

Advancement: gaining in aspects of technology, culture, or civilization

75. vilify (context sentence follows number 80 below)

76. archaeology

77. agnostic

78. psychiatrist

79. scheme

80. extensive

"Absolutely vilified by mainstream archaeology, Immanuel Velikovsky was an agnostic Jew and a psychiatrist who did extensive research demonstrating that mainstream dating schemes do not work."

Vilify: seek to destroy the credibility and reputation of a person

Archaeology: study of physical remains of man's living conditions from ancient times

Agnostic: questioning or doubting the existence of God

Psychiatrist: a medical doctor who studies and attempts to treat mental disease or defect

Scheme: a method or system for gathering and presenting information

Extensive: large, broad, and substantial in nature

81. collective

"When Velikovsky speaks of 'collective memory' in the quote below, he means he has studied written works and records from ancient cultures.

"'I found that the collective memory of mankind spoke of a series of global catastrophes that occurred in historical times.'"

gathering many individual pieces of evidence and coming to conclusions about things they have in common

82. upheaval

"I believed that I could even identify the exact times and the very agents of the great upheavals of the more recent past."

raising up of parts of the earth; formation of elevated geological features

83. compel

"The conclusions at which I arrived compelled me to cross the frontiers into various fields of science, archaeology, geology, and astronomy."

to force something to happen that wasn't originally intended

84. committed

"Velikovsky was a committed Secular Humanist."

convinced of the rightness of a position and determined to continue holding to it

85. chronologies

"Archaeologists cannot honestly explain the problems he exposes in mainstream chronologies."

determinations of dates when things occurred; order of events from earliest to latest

86. inconceivable (context sentence follows number 87 below)

87. coincidence

"An earthquake that destroys only the firstborn is inconceivable, because events can never attain that degree of coincidence."

Inconceivable: no reason to believe it; impossible

Coincidence: events that happen at the same time but have no relationship, common cause, or cause-and-effect

88. plague (context sentence follows number 90 below)

89. canonize

90. corruption

"Either the story of the last plague, in its canonized form, is a fiction, or it conceals a corruption of the text."

Plague: disease causing widespread and usually sudden death

Canonize: included as part of the sacred Scripture; acknowledged as part of a holy writing

Corruption: error, mistake, something wrong

91. discredit (context sentence follows number 93 below)

92. dismiss

93. acknowledge

"Velikovsky attempts to discredit or dismiss chunks of the biblical record because he doesn't want to acknowledge God's direct working through supernatural events."

Discredit: prove false or not worthy of attention

Dismiss: say that something should not be considered or noticed

Acknowledge: give attention to as important or significant

94. observation

"As Stephen Hawking said in the quote at the beginning of this study, religion is based on authority and science is based on observation and reason."

careful study to learn all important information about something

95. Epicureans

"They are Epicureans, seeking to make the best life possible here and now and having no concern for beginnings or endings of the universe. They belong to the 'eat, drink and be merry, for tomorrow we die' school of thought."

Epicureanism is the teaching that existence is based on materialism. Practitioners reject anything spiritual in nature and especially divine intervention (such as creation by God and God's interest in the world or man). They seek to live modestly and to gain knowledge of how the world works and the limits of one's desires. Tranquility, freedom from fear, and absence of bodily pain produce true happiness.

96. criteria (context sentence follows number 97 below)

97. theory

"The first thing that may be said about theories on the origin of life is that none satisfy the criteria of a scientific theory."

Criteria: set of standards by which to evaluate something

Theory: an idea that a scientist desires to prove is factual

98. reenact

"There were no human observers of the origin of life, and it is impossible to reenact the process."

essentially duplicate the conditions and processes by which something occurred

99. Postulate (context sentence follows number 100 below)

100. organic chemistry

"There is no way to observe or test any postulated evolutionary origin of life. All such theories are mere postulates; all related laboratory experiments are mere exercises in organic chemistry."

Postulate: presents to be accepted as fact or taken for granted

organic chemistry: originally limited to substances found only in living organisms, dealing with the compounds of carbon.

101. prominent

"This has been acknowledged even by a number of prominent evolutionists."

well-known, respected, high among the ranks of a field

102. principle

"Dr. Mora has shown that the principles of experimental science do not apply to discussions on the origin of life, and indeed cannot apply to any problem of origin."

a fundamental, primary, or general law or truth from which others are derived

103. instrument (context sentence follows number 104 below)

104. existence

"Science even claims to have built an instrument for observing how the universe came into existence."

Instrument: tool or device which performs various functions such as exploration, testing, measuring, or observational functions

Existence: a state of being real, tangible, observable, in some sense

105. requirement

"The concept of God as a scientist is very much at odds with the religion of Secular Humanism, but taking this position fulfills the requirements of basic scientific inquiry."

something necessary, without which other things cannot occur

106. testimony

"All you have to do is admit the testimony of a first-person observer of when the universe began."

information given by a competent eyewitness about an event

107. processes

"The Fall, sin entering into the universe, and the flood, all changed the earth through processes which do not exist today."

methods by which events occur

108. promulgated (context sentence follows number 110 below)

109. ideology

110. alternative

"Evolution is promulgated as an ideology, a secular religion: a full-fledged alternative to Christianity, with meaning and morality."

Promulgated: publicly teach and promote; set forth

Ideology: set of beliefs that guide thinking, behavior, and practices

Alternative: choice between two mutually exclusive possibilities

111. Complaint (context sentence follows number 112 below)

112. literalist

"I am an ardent evolutionist and an ex-Christian, but I must admit that in this one complaint: and Mr. [sic] Gish is but one of many to make it: the literalists are absolutely right."

Complaint: expression of disagreement or dissent

Literalist: person who takes the Bible and its historical record to be true without special interpretation or spiritualizing its meaning

113. reputable (context sentence follows number 114 below)

114. unbiased

"'No reputable scientist disputes it, and no unbiased reader will close the book doubting it.'" (Richard Dawkins quote)

Reputable: worthy of honor and respect

Unbiased: having no prejudices or restraints against an idea

115. manipulated

"Physical evidence is easily and often manipulated."

altered or modified to suit an agenda

116. interpretation

"Physical evidence is also capable of a wide range of interpretations."

explanation for something's nature or substance

117. mention (context sentence follows number 119 below)

118. discount

119. traditions

"As we mentioned earlier, oral traditions are often discounted by secularists as less reliable or valuable."

Mention: bring up a subject to speak about it

Discount: claim something is not true, valuable, or reliable

Traditions: customs or common practices based on a culture or religion

120. available (context sentence follows number 121 below)

122. proceed

"When facts are available, we present them and proceed from that point."

Available: in existence and useable

Proceed: go forward; make progress

123. refutation

"Since fanciful myths are presented as scientific facts for the origin of the universe and these myths are the foundation of moral relativism, we include a brief refutation."

arguments and/or evidence designed to refute falsehoods

124. simultaneously

"Then assuredly the world was made, not in time, but simultaneously with time." (from Augustine's *City of God)*

at the same moment

125. combination

"This combination of Father, Son, and Holy Spirit as three distinct, separate persons yet one God is what we call the Trinity."

things that are put together

126. systematic

"This is not a book of Systematic Theology attempting to explain the Trinity."

teaching in a step-by-step process based on specific categories of information

127. singularity

"At this point Secular Humanists use the language of mathematics to express the belief that all energy and matter began as a single point, called a singularity."

A point of infinite density and infinitesimal volume, at which space and time become infinitely distorted according to the theory of General Relativity. According to the big bang theory, a gravitational singularity existed at the beginning of the universe. Singularities are also believed to exist at the center of black holes.

128. pronouncement

"An objective examination of the facts is difficult because Secular Humanists rely on authoritative religious pronouncements which hide the actual scientific information."

public statement intended to be accepted as truth

129. relativity

"Since the 'Big Bang' theory of the origin of the universe is based on relativity, we strongly recommend that you take a brief look at relativity to understand the problems with this theory of origins. We have two short articles on relativity in the appendixes."

either of two theories developed by Albert Einstein, the special theory of relativity, which requires that the laws of physics shall be the same as seen by any two different observers in uniform relative motion, and the general theory of relativity which considers observers with relative acceleration and leads to a theory of gravitation

130. probable

"The mathematics of Physics combined with the religious belief that the examination of the material universe can reveal the origin of the universe produces several probable answers."

likely to be true but not yet proven

131. infinite

"Third, the universe is infinite and will always expand something like it is now."

having no beginning or ending; boundless

132. compress (context sentence follows number 133)

133. ignite

"A possible interpretation of these three verses is that the original creation was moisture (clouds) with the Spirit (wind, breath) of God on the outer boundary compressing this moisture until it became liquid water where gravitational forces caused further collapse until it ignites in thermonuclear fusion."

Compress: applying force to reduce volume

Ignite: burst into flames; superheat

134. description

"Descriptions like these are found throughout the Bible, and these same descriptions occur in the many ancient cultures all over the world."

list of characteristics intended to make the appearance or nature of something clear

135. Polynesian

"The following quotes from a Polynesian creation myth."

people originating from or living in Oceana with a heritage of Malaysian, Maori, Hawaiian, or other people groups

136. abyss

"'There was a time in which there existed nothing but darkness and an abyss of waters ...' (from the Babylonian creation myth recorded by Berosus)"

extremely deep, wide, or extensive area such as a pit, canyon, or simply a huge empty or void area

137. mingled

"Their waters were mingled together."

mixed, combined

138. inert

"'Then Shu and Tefnut rejoiced from out of the inert watery mass wherein they were, and they brought to me my Eye' (i.e., the sun)."

unmoving; lacking energy or life; still

139. enamored

"'But when this wind became enamoured of its own first principles (the Chaos), and an intimate union took place, that connexion was called Pothos: and it was the beginning of the creation of all things. And it (the Chaos) knew not its own production;' ..."

in love with

140. putrefaction

"'From its embrace with the wind was generated Mot; which some call Ilus (Mud), but others the putrefaction of a watery mixture. And from this sprung all the seed of the creation, and the generation of the universe'."

rotting, composting, or fermentation

141. consciousness

"From the thought the remembrance
From the remembrance the consciousness, the desire."

awareness; being alert or mentally active

142. concentration (context sentence follows number 143 below)

143. event-horizon

"Because of the great concentration of matter, this ball of water is deep within a black hole, whose event horizon is more than half a billion light-years away."

Concentration: densely-packed; close together

event-horizon: The region, usually described as spherical, marking the outer boundary of a black hole, inside which the gravitational force is strong enough to prevent matter or radiation from escaping.

144. indicates

"'And the evening and the morning were the first day,' indicates one revolution of the earth."

to briefly state or express

145. immobility

"'There was only immobility and silence in the darkness, in the night'."

no movement; complete stillness

146. deliberate

"'They talked then, discussing and deliberating; they agreed, they united their words and their thoughts'."

weighing options or evidence and attempting to come to a decision

147. confer

"'Then Tepeu and Gucumatz came together; then they conferred about life and light, what they would do so that there would be light and dawn, who it would be who would provide food and sustenance'."

speak together to try to arrive at a mutually-agreeable decision

148. photosynthesis

"You might notice that plants need light for photosynthesis, yet there was no sun."

The process in green plants and certain other organisms by which carbohydrates are synthesized from carbon dioxide and water using light as an energy source. Most forms of photosynthesis release oxygen as a byproduct.

149. axis (context sentence follows number 151 below)

150. rotate

151. revolve

"God chose to do this by rotating the earth on its axis and revolving the earth around the sun."

Axis: a straight line about which a body or geometric object rotates or may be conceived to rotate

Rotate: a planet turning in a circle around the center axis

Revolve: to orbit or move in a circular path around a central point, such as a planet around its sun

152. celestial

"The purpose of these movements, even the existence of these celestial objects is for men on earth."

related to or found in the sky, space or heavens

153. insignificant

"The religious belief that mankind is an insignificant animal on an insignificant planet in an insignificant place in the universe, is contrary to the regular movements of the sun, moon, stars, planets and other celestial objects."

not important; having no impact; without purpose

154. inanimate

"How can an inanimate material object in any sense of the word 'rule' anything?"

without life or movement

155. responsible

"We are responsible to obey this rule, that is, understand what the day is, what the months, years and seasons are."

personally accountable for; charged with acting a certain way because of something

156. coalescing

"If we view the fourth day as an astrophysicist, the explosion of the first day has cooled to the point of coalescing."

coming together into a whole; cooling into a more solid form; unifying in structure or substance

157. photon (context sentence follows number 158 below)

158. gravitational

"According to the theory of general relativity, weightless or nearly weightless material, such as light photons traveling outside of a gravitational field, such as between stars or between galaxies, would travel for much longer periods of time and therefore greater distances as measured from earth.”

Photon: The quantum of electromagnetic energy, regarded as a discrete particle having zero mass, no electric charge, and an indefinitely long lifetime.

Gravitational: the natural phenomenon of attraction between physical objects with mass or energy

159. interstellar

“It is also possible that God simply moved the stars, interstellar gases, comets, planets, asteroids, galaxies and all parts of the universe mass distances in one day.”

existing between stars

160. interbreed

“If creatures can naturally interbreed then they are the same kind.”

conceive and produce fertile offspring (young that can mature and produce offspring of their own)

161. adaptation (context sentence follows number 162 below)

162. ordain

“There is adaptation and change within a kind, within the boundary God ordained.”

Adaptation: change in physical characteristics to help the organism better survive in a new or changing environment

Ordain: deliberately established or set up ahead of time for a purpose

163. species

“The word *kind* is not the same as *species*.”

The lowest, most specific type of an organism based on taxonomy or the classification of distinguishing characteristics of living things

164. taxonomy

"For example, all dogs are the same kind and all horses are the same kind, though our artificial taxonomies divide these kinds into lower subcategories."

a method of distinguishing characteristics of organisms

165. overwhelm

"If death is a result of sin, then how could these creatures procreate when they would soon overwhelm the earth?"

become too great in number, influence, or power for the environment to sustain their life

166. swarming

"Without death to keep the populations of swarming creatures in check and only minimal original populations, the estimates are that the oceans would be completely filled in less than 50 years."

large, constantly moving and co-operative groups such as bees or schools of fish

167. venture

"'The (Sun) Mother ventured into a very deep cave, spreading her light around her'."

move forward into a place that is unusual for the organism to visit or inhabit

168. conscious (context sentence follows number 169 below)

169. capacious

"'Conscious of thought, of more capacious breast,
For empire form'd, and fit to rule the rest:'"

Conscious: aware; not mindless; having intelligence or the ability to think

Capacious: possessing greater ability or higher level of formation to contain something

170. unanimous

"The ancient Church Fathers unanimously agreed that this referred to the Trinity."

Unanimous: no dissenting opinion; all of the same mind; belief, or conclusion

171. represent

"These represent the image and similitude of God."

stand as a clear example of; show what something is like

172. concept

"The concept of likeness to God does not refer to physical shape."

Something that exists in thought; a mental perception or idea

173. authority

"God put the Earth, including every living creature, under the authority of Adam."

in charge of; having power over and responsibility for

174. genetic

"Though humans can breed 'new' types of animals, the original creation contained all the genetic material there ever was or ever will be. Genetic material can be recombined to expose recessive or damaged genes."

most basic and original material in a living thing; that which determines or is used to produce all possible characteristics of an organism

175. albinism

"This recombination can expose never seen before traits, such as red hair or albinism, even though the genetic information was there all along."

lack of pigment in an organism; produces whitish skin and hair and colorless eyes (the apparent pink or red color of an albino's eyes is the blood vessels showing through the transparent iris)

176. cease (context sentence follows number 178 below)

177. input

"God ceased working, that is, inputting energy and matter into the universe."

Cease: to stop or discontinue; to end

Input: that which is added to something

178. deteriorate

"Without sin or death the universe was not deteriorating as it is now."

decaying, dying, or breaking down

179. transliteration

"This is the transliteration of the Hebrew instead of translating it *generation.*"

converting a word from one language into the corresponding characters in the new language; not translating (using a word of equivalent meaning)

180. examination

"The creation of Eve from a piece of Adam's rib is usually accepted without close examination or rejected as mythology out of hand."

careful study and investigation to learn all about something

181. variable

"The great variable is time itself."

something that can change; not constant; not to be relied upon as remaining the same

182. continent

"The earth had to be one continent, since only one river watered the entire earth."

land mass surrounded by or divided from another area of land by water (or a division of one very large land mass into separate areas for geopolitical reasons)

183. population

"What might explain how population growth of animals was controlled before the fall?"

number or quantity of organisms

References, Footnotes, Expanded Study, and Appendix Materials

XVI. References, Footnotes, Expanded Study, and Appendix Materials

A. References to Outside Sources

Special Note: Wikipedia is easily the most common online source. One of our reviewers said, "*Wikipedia* is not a scholarly source, and it is always in a state of flux. So I strongly recommend against citing. Students who rely on your work for school projects will be penalized if they cite *Wiki*."

While this is true, it is only one side of the coin. *Wikipedia* is first and foremost an encyclopedia and an encyclopedia is a poor source for citing in a paper. But encyclopedias are an excellent place to begin your research. Here is what one well-respected secular source, *livescience,* said about *Wikipedia.*

> "In 2005, the peer-reviewed journal *Nature* asked scientists to compare *Wikipedia's* scientific articles to those in *Encyclopaedia Britannica* "the most scholarly of encyclopedias," according to its own Wiki page. The comparison resulted in a tie; both references contained four serious errors among

the 42 articles analyzed by experts.

And last year, a study published in the *Journal of Clinical Oncology* found that *Wikipedia* had the same level of accuracy and depth in its articles about 10 types of cancer as the *Physician Data Query*, a professionally-edited database maintained by the National Cancer Institute.

The self-described "free encyclopedia that anyone can edit" has fared similarly well in most other studies comparing its accuracy to conventional encyclopedias, including studies by *The Guardian, PC Pro, Library Journal, the Canadian Library Association*, and several peer-reviewed academic studies.

Still, because anyone can edit *Wikipedia* entries, they "can easily be undermined through malice or ignorance," noted *BBC* technology commentator Bill Thompson.

http://www.livescience.com/32950-how-accurate-is-wikipedia.html

1. Notes to the Reader

a The Book of Jubilees (link to the text note "Source of Jubilees Authority") translated by R. H. Charles, published by the Society for Promoting Christian Knowledge, London, 1917.
(Note: To return to the text, just click the link in the "footnote/reference above.)
http://wesley.nnu.edu/index.php?id=2127
The *Book of Jubilees* from "The Apocrypha and Pseudepigrapha of the Old Testament" R.H. Charles Oxford: Clarendon Press, 1913

b More Information on the *Book of Jasher*
Also called *Sepher HaYasher* Referenced Joshua 10:13, 2 Samuel 1:18, and 2 Timothy 3:8 (The reference to Jannes

and Jambres as Egyptians who withstood Moses is also made in the *Book of Jasher*)
Ancient Book of Jasher A New Annotated Edition

Also called Sepher HaYasher Referenced in Joshua 10:13; 2 Samuel 1:18; and 2 Timothy 3:8. Copyright Ken Johnson 2013 Biblefacts Edition.
https://vbook.pub/documents/ancient-book-of-jasher-johnson-ken-9odn5r1pygwy
Also;

Salt Lake City, J.H. Parry and Company, 1887.
http://www.sacred-texts.com/chr/apo/jasher/

We intentionally provide multiple sources for The *Book Jasher*. See the *Jewish Encyclopedia* 1906 edition http://www.jewishencyclopedia.com/articles/8526-jasher-book-of for a history of various editions of The *Book of Jasher*. Ken Johnson takes the position that it is the actual book referenced in the OT, whereas the Jewish Encyclopedia accepts it simply as ancient Jewish tradition to which the name "*Book of Jasher*" was later appended. This latter is the position of the *Conflict of the Ages* series in referencing the *Book of Jasher*.

The *Book of Jasher* is quoted in many ancient sources. It is not inspired and contains errors, so it must be read with caution. It contains ancient Jewish traditions on the same order as Josephus' *Antiquities of the Jews*, the *Sedar Olam, the Cave of Treasures, The Book of the Bee,* and the *Book of Jubilees*. It is probably more reliable than the *Talmuds, the Book of Enoch,* or the *Midrash,* because it is older. It is almost certainly not the *Book of Jasher* quoted in the Old Testament.

The following is from the introduction of Ken Johnson's 2013 edition of the *Book of Jasher*.

> **How can we be sure this is the real *Jasher* and not a forgery from the Middle Ages?**

There have been at least two forgeries. One is an ethical treatise from the Middle Ages and does not exist in English currently, as far as I know. It is somewhat Gnostic in style beginning with a section on the mystery of creation. A second forgery was published in AD 1829, supposedly translated by Flaccus Albinus Alcuinus. These two are nowhere near the caliber of this *Book of Jasher* and both are missing the information that Scripture tells us is in the real *Book of Jasher*. This is the only *Jasher* that corresponds to what Scripture says it contains. Much of the extra information contained in *Jasher* can also be found in the Babylonian Talmud, the Mishna, and Ginzberg's *Legends of the Jews*. There are numerous quotes showing Rabbi Eliazar used this *Book of Jasher* extensively in the first century AD. The Mishna was completed about AD 200, and the Talmud about AD 800. We can know for a fact that the Mishna and Talmud used this *Book of Jasher* as a source document and not the other way around. Also, since the Ancient Seder Olam was written in about AD 169 and references Jasher, we know the *Book of Jasher* was used by other historians in the second century AD.

"Now as Jannes and Jambres withstood Moses, so do these also resist the truth: men of corrupt minds, reprobate concerning the faith. But they shall proceed no further: for their folly shall be manifest unto all men, as theirs also was." 2 Timothy 3:8-9

"And when they had gone Pharaoh sent for Balaam the magician and to Jannes and Jambres his sons, and to all the magicians and conjurors and counsellors which belonged to the king, and they all came and sat before the king... And Aaron hastened and threw the rod out of his hand before Pharaoh and before his servants, and the rod turned into a serpent." Jasher 79:27,36

The Ancient Seder Olam is another Hebrew history book (not mentioned by Scripture) that dates from about AD 169. It records that Rabbi Eliezer was the most accurate when figuring dates and festivals because he used the Ancient *Book of Jasher* as the best source for his history. This tells us Jasher was in use and very well known in the first century AD. See chapter 4 of Ancient Seder Olam for details.

What is the history behind the *Book of Jasher*?

According to rabbinic legend, the *Book of Jasher* and several other ancient non-biblical Hebrew texts were brought from Jerusalem to Spain after the fall of Jerusalem in AD 70. One of the officers of Titus, Sidrus by name, was a believer in the God of the Hebrews. He made sure several sacred texts made it out of Jerusalem and into the Spanish city of Sevilia for safe keeping. The Sephardic rabbinate kept the texts safe. In the year AD 1613, the first official printed Hebrew copy of the *Book of Jasher* was published in Venice, Italy. The first translation from the Hebrew version of *Jasher* into English was completed in AD 1840.

Has the text been corrupted over the centuries?

The ancient scrolls of this book were in poor condition when the book was printed in Hebrew in 1613.

It is true that the Mormon publishing house, *J. H. Parry and Company,* first published the

> 1840 English translation of Jasher in 1887.
>
> Mormonism has long been fascinated with the *Book of Jasher*, but it is not officially recommended because some portions of *Jasher* contradict Mormon teaching. http://biblefacts.org/creation/Jasher_intro.pdf

The reviewer who stated that the "*Book of Jasher* is not authentic. What is being cited is an 18th century forgery..." provided the following link. http://www.gotquestions.org/book-of-Jasher.html

The first four paragraphs of this link are very helpful and filled with useful information. That is followed by dogmatic, unsupported, gratuitous assertions. It simply asserts without any evidence that "It is an eighteenth-century forgery that alleges to be a translation of the "lost" *Book of Jasher* by Alcuin, an eighteenth-century English scholar."

The *Jewish Encyclopedia* 1906 edition frequently quotes from the *Book of Jasher*. It is often quoted with the *Book of Enoch*.

> "In the compiling of the work the following sources were made use of, namely: the Babylonian Talmud; Bereshit Rabbah; Pirke R. Eliezer; the Yalkut; the Chronicle of Moses; Yosippon; Midrash Abkir; and various Arabic legends. As to the place and time of the work's origin various legendary accounts are given in the preface of the first edition (Naples, 1552).
>
> Modern Translations:
>
> In 1750 the London printer Thomas Ilive issued an English translation of the work, asserting that he had published the real "Book of Yashar" mentioned in the Bible; and in 1828 the London "Courier" (Nov. 8) reported that a man from Gazan in Persia, by name Alcurin (Noah has

"Alcuin"), had discovered the book named after Joshua, and brought it with him to London. Eleven days later (Nov. 19) a Jew of Liverpool named Samuel reported in the same paper that he was working on a translation of this work, which he had obtained in North Africa. Zunz thereupon found himself compelled to assert, in the "Berliner Nachrichten" of Nov. 29, 1828, that the work mentioned was the same as that published in Naples in 1552 or 1613; and in his "Gottesdienstliche Vorträge," 1832, the same author declared that the book originated in Spain in the twelfth century. That Italy, however, was the land of its origin seems evident from the author's knowledge of Italian names, as Tuscany, Lombardy, and the Tiber (x. 7-36), and also from the description of the rape of the Sabines (xvii. 1-14). The appearance of Arabic names, such as Sa'id, Allah, Abdallah, and Khalif, only tends to show that the book was written in southern Italy, where Arabic influence was strongly felt even in the eleventh century.

The "Yashar" has appeared in the following editions: Naples, 1552; Venice, 1625; Cracow, 1628; Prague, 1668; Frankfort-on-the-Main, 1706; Amsterdam, 1707; Constantinople, 1728; Fürth, 1768; Koretz, 1785; Frankfort-on-the-Oder, 1789; Grodno, 1795; Lemberg, 1816 and 1840; Warsaw, 1846; Wilna, 1848; Lemberg, 1850; Wilna, 1852; Warsaw, 1858. It was translated into Judæo-German by Jacob ha-Levi, and published with various annotations and Arabic glosses (Frankfort-on-the-Main, 1674; Sulzbach, 1783). A Latin version by Johann G. Abicht appeared in Leipsic in the middle of the eighteenth century under the title

"Dissertatio de Libro Recti." The work was first translated into English by Thomas Ilive, as mentioned above, and later by M. M. Noah under the title "The Book of Yashar" (New York, 1840). http://www.jewishencyclopedia.com/articles/15067-yashar-sefer-ha

2. Introduction

c Professor Romila Tharpar, *Frontline* magazine Volume 18, Issue 19, Sep. 15-28, 2001 India's National Magazine from the publishers of THE HINDU.)

c1 "Does God Play Dice ...?" https://www.hawking.org.uk/in-words/lectures/does-god-play-dice Also transcribed in *The Nature of Space and Time* (1996) by Stephen Hawking and Roger Penrose, p. 26

d *Scientific Naturalism as Science* by Larry Vardiman, Ph.D. *Larry Vardiman, Ph.D. 1997. Scientific Naturalism as Science. Acts & Facts. 26 (11).* http://www.icr.org/article/422/ (Dr. Vardiman is Chairman of the Astro/Geophysics Department at ICR.)

e *Demolishing Supposed Bible Contradictions Volumes 1, II, Ken Ham,* Bodie Hodge, and Tim Chaffey, *Master Books, 2010*

f *Rules For Interpretation,* Dr. David L. Cooper, *Biblical Research Monthly* 1947, 1949 http://www.biblicalresearch.info/page7.html This common quote might be older, but it is the oldest source we could find.

g *Rightly Dividing the Word of Truth,* Michael J. Findley, *August 6, 2012,* from our blog *https://findleyfamilyvideopublications.com/2012/09/2*

o/rightly-dividing-the-word-of-truth-interpreting-the-book-of-revelation/

h DUDE Acronym Joseph Felgenhauer, (Grand Canyon Park Ranger), "Inside Grand Canyon: How the Grand Canyon Was Shaped Over Time" (Podcast/oral talk). National Park Service, U.S. Department of the Interior. Grand Canyon National Park, Arizona. (No Date.) National Park Service Website

https://www.iheart.com/podcast/256-inside-grand-canyon-31110028/episode/how-grand-canyon-was-shaped-over-31910821/

i Bristlecone Pine Dendrochronology, more information:

https://ltrr.arizona.edu/content/dendrochronology-bristlecone-pine

j Fluctuating solar radiation

https://www.jpl.nasa.gov/news/solar-energy-fluctuations-detected

k Milkankovich Cycles (The full article is behind a paywall.)

https://www.science.org/doi/epdf/10.1126/science.1186256

l Factors in Cause of Ice Age Sandy Eldredge and Bob Biek, "Ice Ages: What are they and what causes them?" *Glad You Asked* article, Survey Notes, v. 42 no. 3, September 2010, Utah Geological Survey, Salt Lake City, UT.
http://geology.utah.gov/surveynotes/gladasked/gladice_ages.htm

m Scientists are not sure what causes an ice age Molly Edmonds, "How the Ice Age Worked" 13 May 2008. HowStuffWorks.com.

https://history.howstuffworks.com/historical-events/ice-age.htm

n BBC Ice age

https://www.bbc.co.uk/bitesize/guides/zy7cfrd/revision/1

o Missoula Ice Dam (No author), "Glacial Lake Missouri and the Ice Age Floods," (No date), Website for the Montana Natural History Center, Missoula, MT. www.glaciallakemissoula.org/

3. COA1 Main Text

1 "Stephen Hawking on Religion: 'Science Will Win,'" Interview with Diane Sawyer, as quoted on ABC World News (04 June 2010).

https://abcnews.go.com/WN/Technology/stephen-hawking-religion-science-win/story?id=10830164

2 "The Big Lie" quote comes from *Mein Kampf*, by Adolph Hitler, Eher Verlag, Munich, Germany, Vol. 1, Chap. 10, 1925.

3 (mendelsachs.wordpress.com) Dr. Mendel Sachs (born 13 April 1927, Portland, Oregon, is a US theoretical physicist who was Professor of Physics at the State University of New York at Buffalo (1966-1997) (Emeritus since 1997).https://mendelsachs.wordpress.com/

4 Stephen Jay Gould, "Nonoverlapping Magisteria," *Natural History* 106 (March 1997): 16-22.

http://blc.arizona.edu/courses/schaffer/449/Gould%20Nonoverlapping%20Magisteria.htm

5 Graham Hancock, *Fingerprints of the Gods*, Three Rivers Press New York, NY, 1996.

6 Erich Von Däniken, *Chariots of the Gods?* Penguin Group (USA) New York, NY January 1999.

7 Stephen Hawking . *The Illustrated A Brief History of Time.* New York, NY: Bantam Dell, a division of Random House, 1996. (Although the text refers to the better-known original *A Brief History of Time,* we cite from this illustrated version of the book because it is the one we own.)

8 Immanuel Velikovsky, *Ages in Chaos,* Harper, New York, NY, 1950.

9 _____. *Worlds in Collison* Harper, New York, NY, 1950.

(Reviews of these books are on our blog

https://findleyfamilyvideopublications.com/?s=ages+in+chaos+review

https://findleyfamilyvideopublications.com/2014/01/08/book-review-of-worlds-in-collision-by-michael-j-findley/

10 "Origin of Life: Critique of Early Stage Chemical Evolution Theories" by Duane Gish, Ph.D. *Impact,* Institute for Creation Research, Jan 1, 1976. footnote in Dr. Gish's article J. D. Bernal, in *The Origins of Prebiological Systems and of Their Molecular Matrices,* Ed. S. W. Fox, Academic Press, New York, 1965, p. 52.

11 The *Book of Jubilees* translated by R. H. Charles, published by the Society for Promoting Christian Knowledge, London, 1917.

12 Josh McDowell, *New Evidence That Demands a Verdict* Thomas Nelson; Nashville, TN, 1st edition, 1999.

13 "Leading anti-creationist philosopher admits that evolution is a religion" Ruse, M., How Evolution Became a Religion: Creationists Correct? *National Post*, pp. B1, B3, B7 May 13, 2000.
(The article quotes Michael Ruse, professor of philosophy and zoology at the University of Guelph,

Canada. The "sic" is because Duane Gish is a PhD in Biochemistry and properly referred to as "Dr.," not "Mr.") From *Answers in Genesis* website

https://answersingenesis.org/world-religions/leading-anti-creationist-philosopher-admits-evolution-religion/

14 Richard Dawkins, from *The Greatest Show on Earth, The Evidence for Evolution,* Ch. 1, Free Press, Simon and Schuster, New York, NY, 2009.

15 Augustine *City of God and Christian Doctrine,* Chapter 6, Book XI Translator, Schaff, Philip (1819-1893) Print Basis: New York: *The Christian Literature Publishing Co.*, 1890. From the Internet Sacred Text Archive, managed by John Bruno Hare.

16 Augustine *Confessions* Book 11 Chapter XXX paragraph 41. From the Internet Sacred Text Archive, managed by John Bruno Hare.

17 *Popol Vuh* ("Written Leaves") Book of the Mayas. The Book of the Community Book 1, English Version by Delia Goetz and Sylvanus G. Morley, copyright 1950 by the University of Oklahoma Press. Translation by Adrián Recinos. From the Internet Sacred Text Archive, managed by John Bruno Hare.

18 *The Book of the Cave of Treasures,* Part One, translation (Brit. Mus. MS. Add. 25875.) [The Title of the Work: *The Scribe's Prayer]* [Fol. 3b, col. 1.] "By the might of our Lord Jesus Christ we begin to write the "Book of the Succession of the Generations," that is to say, *ME'ÂRATH GAZZÊ*, which was composed by *SAINT MÂR APHRÊM* (i.e. Ephraim, commonly known as "Ephraim Syrus," or "Ephraim the Syrian," who died A.D. 373). "O our Lord, help Thou me in Thy Mercy. Amen." Translated from the Syriac by E. A. Wallis Budge [London, The Religious Tract Society] [1927] {scanned and edited by Christopher M. Weimer, June 2002} The text used from the *Book of the Cave of Treasures* comes from the *Internet Sacred Text Archive*, maintained by

John Bruno Hare, http://www.sacred-texts.com/index.htm A partial description of the work's history follows:

In the introduction it is attributed to Ephrem Syrus, or Ephraim the Syrian, born soon after A.D. 306 and died in 373. The present version is believed to date from the sixth century A.D.

This book presents a 'history' of the world from the creation to the death of Christ, partly from the Bible, partly other Jewish sources, partly Greek sources, and partly from Mesopotamian sources, according to the translator.

19 The *Book of Jubilees* .

20 *Oceanic Mythology* by Roland B. Dixon ©1916 Part I. "Polynesia Myths of Origins and the Deluge New Zealand," p. 6 Andersen, p. 127 (modified from Shortland, p. 12). From the Internet Sacred Text Archive, managed by John Bruno Hare.

21 *"THE SAMOAN STORY OF CREATION-A 'Tala.' " JOURNAL OF THE POLYNESIAN SOCIETY CONTAINING THE TRANSACTIONS AND PROCEEDINGS OF THE SOCIETY. VOL. I.* [WELLINGTON, 1892] {Reduced to HTML by Christopher M. Weimer, November 2002} Taken from the Internet Sacred Text Archive, www.sacred-texts.com, managed by John Bruno Hare.

22 *The Babylonian Legends of Creation,* by E.A. Wallis Budge, 1921. "The Legend of the Creation According to Berosus and Damascius, written in Greek by Berosus, a priest of Bel-Marduk about 250 BC at Babylon from Alexander Polyhistor." From the Internet Sacred Text Archive, managed by John Bruno Hare.

23 Garcia in his *Origin de los Indias* (Translation of Mixtec picture-manuscript) Quoted in *The Myths of*

Mexico and Peru by Lewis Spence 1913. From the Internet Sacred Text Archive, managed by John Bruno Hare.

24 Ovid's *Metamorphoses*, Book 1,Translator John Dryden et al, 1717. From the Internet Sacred Text Archive, managed by John Bruno Hare.

25 Flavius Josephus *Antiquities of the Jews* , *Book I,* Translated by William Whiston, 1737. From the Internet Sacred Text Archive, managed by John Bruno Hare.

26 Garcia in his *Origin*.

27 *The Theogony of Hesiod* (ll. 116-138) Translated by Hugh G. Evelyn-White. 1914.

28 *The Babylonian Legends of Creation.*

29 *Narration 28 Bundahis, E.W. West, translator. Narration 28 Bundahis,* Chapter I, "In the name of the creator Aûharmazd." (Persian*) Sacred Books of the East,* Volume 5, Oxford: the Clarendon Press, 1880. From the Internet Sacred Text Archive, managed by John Bruno Hare.

30 *Enuma Elish* ("When on High") (Babylonian/Assyrian/ Sumerian/ Chaldean/ Akkadian), Narration 1. London, 1902. From the Internet Sacred Text Archive, managed by John Bruno Hare.

31 "The History of Creation , A, The Book of knowing the Evolutions of Ra and of the overthrowing of Apep (Egyptian)", *Legends of the Gods The Egyptian Texts,* edited with Translations by E. A. Wallis Budge London: Kegan Paul, Trench and Trübner & Co. Ltd. [1912] Scanned at sacred-texts.com 1999 and 2003. J.B. Hare, redactor.

32 *Ancient Fragments* by I. P. Cory [1832 ed.] (reduced to HTML by Christopher M. Weimer, Dec. 2002) The Theology of the Phoenicians: From Sanchoniatho. From

the Internet Sacred Text Archive, managed by John Bruno Hare.

33 Oceanic Mythology.

34 Dr. Russell Humphreys, *Starlight and Time: Solving the Puzzle of Distant Starlight in a Young Universe*, Master Books, Green Forest, AR, 1996.

35 Oceanic Mythology.

36 Augustine *City of God and Christian Doctrine.*

37 *Ancient Fragments*.

38 Flavius Josephus.

39 *The Book of Chilam Balam of Chumayel* Ralph L. Roys, *The Book of Chilam Balam of Chumayel* (Mayan), XIII ("The Creation of the Uinal")Washington, D.C.: Carnagie Institution, 1933. From the Internet Sacred Text Archive, managed by John Bruno Hare.

40 Garcia in his *Origin de los Indias.*

41 Hurúing Wuhti and the Sun, from Field Columbian Museum Publication 96 Anthropological Series Volume VIII, The Traditions of the Hopi, by H.R. Voth The Stanley McCormick Hopi Expedition George A Dorsey, Curator, Department of Anthropology, Chicago, IL March, 1905 Scanned, proofed and formatted at sacred-texts.com, February 2001, by John Bruno Hare. Reformatted, August 2003

42 Garcia in his *Origin de los Indias* .

43 Ovid's *Metamorphoses.*

44 The Seven Tablets of Creation, by Leonard William King, [1902] V. Another Version of the Creation of the World by Marduk. From the Internet Sacred Text Archive, managed by John Bruno Hare.

45 Flavius Josephus.

46 The Annals of the World "The Origin of Time, and Continued to the Beginning of the Emperor Vespasian's Reign and the Total Destruction and Abolition of the Temple and Commonwealth of the Jews." by James Ussher 1650. From the Internet Sacred Text Archive, managed by John Bruno Hare.

47 Ovid's *Metamorphoses.*

48 Flavius Josephus.

49 The Annals of the World.

50 *The Poetic Edda* translated by Henry Adams Bellows Princeton University Press and American Scandinavian Foundation, Princeton, NJ: 1936. From the Internet Sacred Text Archive, managed by John Bruno Hare.

51 *Pahlavi Texts* Translated by E. W. West Part V Marvels of Zoroastrianism Sacred Books of the East, Volume 47 Oxford, the Clarendon Press 1897. From the Internet Sacred Text Archive, managed by John Bruno Hare.

52 *The Prose Edda of Snorri Sturlson* Translated by Arthur Gilchrist Brodeur *The Prose Edda of Snorri Sturlson* New York: Thc American-Scandinavian Foundation, 1916. From the Internet Sacred Text Archive, managed by John Bruno Hare.

53 *The Babylonian Legends of Creation.*

54 Time Dilation Russell Humphreys, PhD, "New time dilation helps creation cosmology", Journal of Creation 22(3):84–92 December 2008. http://creation.com/new-time-dilation-helps-creation-cosmology

55 *Clark's Foreign Theological Library* Keil and Delitszch (Multivolume Series) 1867ff Edinburgh T and T Clark, George Street Keil & Delitzsch Commentary on

the Old Testament Johann (C.F.) Keil (1807-1888) & Franz Delitzsch (1813-1890)

56 The Annals of the World.

57 Flavius Josephus.

58 Ovid's *Metamorphoses.*

59 *Clark's Foreign Theological Library* Keil and Delitszch (Multivolume Series) 1867ff Edinburgh T and T Clark, George Street Keil & Delitzsch Commentary on the Old Testament Johann (C.F.) Keil (1807-1888) & Franz Delitzsch (1813-1890)

60 Australian Aborigine "*Dreaming*" or "*Dreamtime*" Creation Story. http://www.fulbright.com.au/web-resources/docs/curriculum-projects/Bartels.pdf

61 Flavius Josephus.

62 Ovid's *Metamorphoses.*

63 Flavius Josephus.

64 Flavius Josephus.

65 Ovid's *Metamorphoses.*

66 Flavius Josephus

67 *The Orthodox Jewish Bible*, completed by Phillip Goble in 2002, is an English language version that applies Yiddish and Hasidic cultural expressions to the Messianic Bible. Copyright Information: The Orthodox Jewish Bible fourth edition, OJB. Copyright 2002,2003,2008,2010, 2011 by Artists for Israel International. All rights reserved. http://www.biblegateway.com/versions/Orthodox-Jewish-Bible-OJB/

68 Munro IR, Guyuron B (November 1981). "Split-Rib Cranioplasty." *Annals of Plastic Surgery* 7 (5): 341-346. http://www.ncbi.nlm.nih.gov/pubmed/7332200 (Skull

repair was successfully accomplished using rib graft. The rib portions removed completely regenerated.

B. Bibliography

For links to most of the sources we used, as well as why and how we use certain references, and background and further information on sources, please consult the appendix. This bibliography includes sources used in all the Conflict of the Ages modules 1-3.

Adam of Bremen. *Gesta Hammaburgensis Ecclesiae Pontificum*. Berlin. (translated and edited by G. Waitz, 1876).

Adams, Donald A. Pastor of Trinity Baptist Church, Weatherly PA. In the text of this work are emailed comments on the position that the Sons of God in Genesis 6 refers to descendants of Seth corrupting the godly line by intermarrying with female descendants of Cain. 11/18/2011.

Anonymous. "Antimony Poisoning" article from *Encyclopaedia Britannica* online.

______. Artificial coal made from wood substance. *Journal of Chemical Education* (J. Chem. Educ.), January 1929.

______. Australian Aborigine "Dreaming" or "Dreamtime" Creation Story. Fulbright Foundation. The Australian American Educational Foundation, T/A the Australian American Fulbright Commission

______. "Big Five Mass Extinction Events." Nature/Prehistoric Life. (No Date) *BBC.co.uk*

______. Bluecloud Dakota Creation Legend from the Black Hills of Western South Dakota. (No date.)

______. British Museum website. 'Adam and Eve' cylinder seal. Acquired from the John Robert Stewart Collection in 1846. T.C. Mitchell, *The Bible*

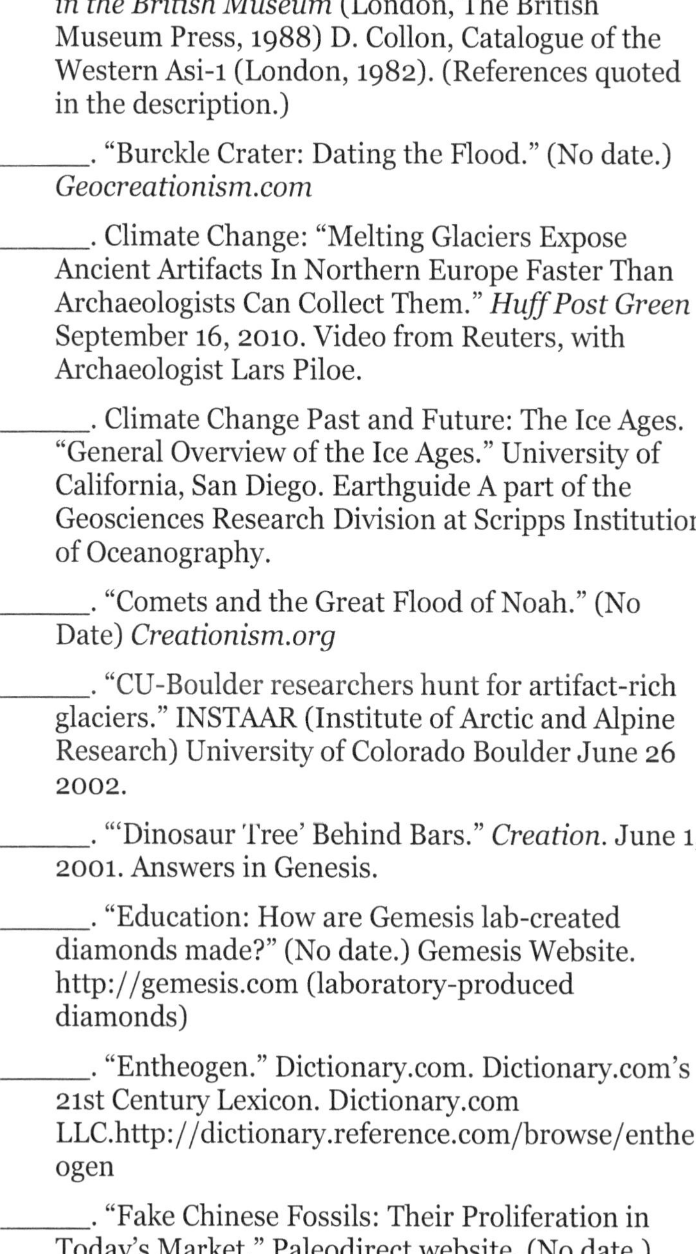

in the British Museum (London, The British Museum Press, 1988) D. Collon, Catalogue of the Western Asi-1 (London, 1982). (References quoted in the description.)

______. "Burckle Crater: Dating the Flood." (No date.) *Geocreationism.com*

______. Climate Change: "Melting Glaciers Expose Ancient Artifacts In Northern Europe Faster Than Archaeologists Can Collect Them." *Huff Post Green* September 16, 2010. Video from Reuters, with Archaeologist Lars Piloe.

______. Climate Change Past and Future: The Ice Ages. "General Overview of the Ice Ages." University of California, San Diego. Earthguide A part of the Geosciences Research Division at Scripps Institution of Oceanography.

______. "Comets and the Great Flood of Noah." (No Date) *Creationism.org*

______. "CU-Boulder researchers hunt for artifact-rich glaciers." INSTAAR (Institute of Arctic and Alpine Research) University of Colorado Boulder June 26 2002.

______. "'Dinosaur Tree' Behind Bars." *Creation*. June 1, 2001. Answers in Genesis.

______. "Education: How are Gemesis lab-created diamonds made?" (No date.) Gemesis Website. http://gemesis.com (laboratory-produced diamonds)

______. "Entheogen." Dictionary.com. Dictionary.com's 21st Century Lexicon. Dictionary.com LLC.http://dictionary.reference.com/browse/entheogen

______. "Fake Chinese Fossils: Their Proliferation in Today's Market." Paleodirect website. (No date.)

______. "Fallacies in Dating: Reason 8: Radioactivity," June 1, 2007, Answers in Genesis website.

______. "Fish that 'Fly'." December 1. 1997. *Creation* Answers in Genesis website.

______. "Folded Ferns: Simple, Logical Observation Shows How 'Slow and Gradual' Belief Systems Fail." September 1, 1996. Creation. Answers in Genesis.

______. "'Ghostly' Shrimp Update." September 1, 1994. *Creation*. Answers in Genesis.

______. "Glacial Lake Missouri and the Ice Age Floods." (No date.) Website for the Montana Natural History Center, Missoula, MT.

______. "Ice Ages." BBC Science/The Earth/Water&Ice (No Date.)

______. "Impressive Elephants." (No Date) SanDiegoZoo.org

______. "A majestic landscape reflecting a history of extremes. Ancient Bristlecone Pine Forest, Inyo National Forest." (No Date)The Sierra Web, Your complete guide to the eastern Sierra.

______. "Meteor Crater Sample Collection" US Geological Service Astrogeology Science Center. (No date.)

______. "Oilgae: Glossary. Synthetic petroleum Definition." Website promoting Algae-based biofuels. (no date) Oilgae.com

______. "Radiohalos." Wikipedia. Wikimedia Foundation Created by Jimmy Wales, Larry Sanger, Launched January 15, 2001.

______. "Rodent Resurrected." May 2, 2006. Answers in Genesis.

______. "Scientists Discover 356 Animal Inclusions Trapped In Opaque Amber 100 Million Years Old." European Synchrotron Radiation Facility. *ScienceDaily.* April 2008.

______. "Wonders of Geology: White Cliffs of Dover." August 21, 2008, Answers in Genesis.

Augustine. *City of God and Christian Doctrine,* Chapter 6, Book XI Translator, Schaff, Philip (1819-1893) Print Basis: New York: *The Christian Literature Publishing Co*., 1890. (Electronic version from the Internet Sacred Text Archive, managed by John Bruno Hare.)

______ *Confessions* Book 11 Chapter XXX paragraph 41 . (Electronic version from the Internet Sacred Text Archive, managed by John Bruno Hare.)

Austin, S.A. *Ten misconceptions about the geologic column.* ICR *Impact,* No. 137, 1984.

Banks, Norm, photographer. "Pyroclastic Flow." 1980 photograph. U.S. Geological Survey

Barnosky, Anthony, et. al. "Has the Earth's sixth mass extinction already arrived?" *Nature* (International Weekly Journal of Science), 471, 51-57 (03 March 2011)

Barry, Sharon, et. al. "The Dynamic Earth: Geogallery." Smithsonian Website. (No Date)

Beatty, Kelly. "Chelyabinsk Mega-meteor: Status Report" June 25, 2013. Sky & Telescope The Essential Guide to Astronomy website.

Bellows, Henry Adams, translator. *The Poetic Edda* Princeton University Press and American Scandinavian Foundation, Princeton, NJ: 1936. From the Internet Sacred Text Archive, managed by John Bruno Hare.

Bosch, F. et al., "Observation of bound-state b: decay of fully ionized 187Re," Physical Review Letters 77(26)5190-5193, 1996. For further discussion of this experiment, see: Kienle, P., Beta-decay experiments and astrophysical implications, in: Prantzos, N. and Harissopulus, S., Proceedings, Nuclei in the Cosmos, pp. 181-186, 1999.

Brazo, Mark W. and Steven A. Austin. The Tunguska Explosion of 1908. Institute for Creation Research, Origins 9(2):82-93 (1982).

Brodeur, Arthur Gilchrist, translator. *The Prose Edda of Snorri Sturlson* New York: The American-Scandinavian Foundation, 1916. From the Internet Sacred Text Archive, managed by John Bruno Hare.

James Brooke. "Lost Worlds Rediscovered as Canadian Glaciers Melt." *New York Times on the Web Learning Network,* October 5, 1999.

Brown, Walt, Dr. "24. Missing Trunk." *In the Beginning: Compelling Evidence for Creation and the Flood.* Center for Scientific Creation 2008

Budge, E.A. Wallis, translator. *The Babylonian Legends of Creation.* 1921. "The Legend of the Creation According to Berosus and Damascius, written in Greek by Berosus, a priest of Bel-Marduk about 250 BC at Babylon from Alexander Polyhistor." from the Internet Sacred Text Archive, managed by John Bruno Hare.

_____. *The Book of the Cave of Treasures,* Part One (Brit. Mus. MS. Add. 25875.) [The Title of the Work: *The Scribe's Prayer* Translated from the Syriac by [London, The Religious Tract Society] [1927] {scanned and edited by Christopher M. Weimer, June 2002}
from the *Internet Sacred Text Archive* managed by John Bruno Hare.

______. A History of Creation. "The Book of knowing the Evolutions of Ra and of the overthrowing of Apep (Egyptian)". *Legends of the Gods, The Egyptian Texts*. London: Kegan Paul, Trench and Trübner & Co. Ltd., 1912. Scanned at sacred-texts.com 1999 and 2003. J.B. Hare, redactor.

Carney, Scott. "Did A Comet Cause The Great Flood?" *Discover Magazine,* November 15, 2007 re-posted in Free Republic Website.

Catchpoole, David. "Lea, the spaghetti lioness." *Creation* 29(4):44–45, September, 2007.

______. "The Lion that wouldn't eat meat." *Creation* 22(2):22–23 March, 2000.

Catholic Catechism, English translation of the Catechism of the Catholic Church for the United States of America copyright © 1994, United States Catholic Conference, Inc.—Libreria Editrice Vaticana. English translation of the Catechism of the Catholic Church: Modifications from the Editio Typica copyright © 1997, United States Catholic Conference, Inc.—Libreria Editrice Vaticana.

Charles, R. H., translator. The *Book of Enoch* I. *The Apocrypha and Pseudepigrapha of the Old Testament*. Oxford: The Clarendon Press, 1913. From the Internet Sacred Text Archive, managed by John Bruno Hare.

______. *Book of Jubilees,* The. The Society for Promoting Christian Knowledge, London, 1917. (Electronic version from the Internet Sacred Text Archive, managed by John Bruno Hare.)

______. Zadokite or Damascus Document in *The Apocrypha and Pseudepigrapha of the Old Testament in English,* vol. 2: Pseudepigrapha (Oxford: Clarendon Press, 1913) http://famfaerch.dk/pseudigrapher/dsea/zadok01.html, (Webpage of Rolf Ivan Faerch)

Cooper, David L, Dr. *Rules for Interpretation*. Biblical Research Monthly, 1947, 1949.

Cory, I. P. *Ancient Fragments* [1832 ed.] The Theology of the Phoenicians: From Sanchoniatho (reduced to HTML by Christopher M. Weimer, Dec. 2002) From the Internet Sacred Text Archive, managed by John Bruno Hare.

Dalley, Stephanie, translator. *Epic of Atrahasis -- Myths from Mesopotamia: Creation, the Flood, Gilgamesh, and Others* Oxford World's Classics. Oxford University Press, 1998.

Von Däniken, Erich. *Chariots of the Gods?* Penguin Group (USA) New York, NY January 1999.

Dawkins, Richard. *The Greatest Show on Earth: The Evidence for Evolution*. Free Press, Simon and Schuster, New York, NY, 2009.

Dimichele, William A. and Howard J. Falcoln-Lang. "Pennsylvania: 'fossil forests' in growth position (T° assemblages): origin, taphonomic bias and palaeoecological insights." Journal of the Geological Society, London, Vol. 168, 2011, pp. 585-605.

Dixon, Roland B. *Oceanic Mythology* Part I. "Polynesia Myths of Origins and the Deluge New Zealand," 1916(Electronic version from the Internet Sacred Text Archive, managed by John Bruno Hare.)

Doyle, Shaun, "Noah's comet? Was Noah's Flood a tsunami caused by a comet impact?" 2 January 2008. Creation.com

Edmonds, Molly. "How the Ice Age Worked" 13 May 2008. HowStuffWorks.com.

http://geography.howstuffworks.com/terms-and-associations/ice-age.htm 12 April 2014.

Eldredge, Sandy and Bob Biek. "Ice Ages: What Are they and what causes them?" *Glad You Asked* article, Survey Notes, v. 42 no. 3, September 2010. Utah Geological Survey, Salt Lake City, UT.

Elias, Scott. Homepage. "Welcome to the World of Ice Age Paleoecology." University of Colorado at Boulder website.

Faulkner, Danny. "A biblically-based cratering theory." *Journal of Creation* 13(1):100-104 April 1999.

Felgenhauer, Joseph (Grand Canyon Park Ranger). "Inside Grand Canyon: How the Grand Canyon Was Shaped Over Time" (Transcript of oral presentation). National Park Service, U.S. Department of the Interior. Grand Canyon National Park, Arizona. (No Date.) National Park Service Website.

Ferdowsi, Hakim Abol-Ghasem (Toosi). *The Epic of Shahnameh Ferdowsi* (940-1020) Helen Zimmern translator. (*The Epic of Kings: Hero Tales of Ancient Persia* Chapter 1: The Shahs of Old (Zoroastrian). http://www.enel.ucalgary.ca/People/far/hobbies/iran/shahnameh.html

Findley, Michael J. *Rightly Dividing the Word of Truth. Elk Jerky for the Soul blog, August 6, 2012.* (from findley family video publications website)

Froede, Carl R. Jr. "Precambrian Plant Fossils and the Hakatai Shale Controversy." Volume 36(3):106-113 December 1999. Creation Research Society Quarterly Journal.

Gao, Ke-Qin & Neil H. Shubin. "Earliest known crown-group salamanders." *Nature* 422:428, March 27, 2003.

Gentry, Robert, Dr. "Creation's Tiny Mystery." Earth Science Associates 3rd edition (May 1992).

______, et. al. "Fingerprints of Creation" video. Earth Science Associates Knoxville, TN, 1996.

Gish, Duane, Ph.D. "Origin of Life: Critique of Early Stage Chemical Evolution Theories." *Impact*. Institute for Creation Research, Jan 1, 1976

Goble, Phillip. *The Orthodox Jewish Bible*. English language version that applies Yiddish and Hasidic cultural expressions to the Messianic Bible. fourth edition. Copyright 2002,2003,2008,2010, 2011 by Artists for Israel International. All rights reserved.

Goetz, Delia and Sylvanus G. Morley, English translators. (Spanish translation by Adrián Recinos.) *Popol Vuh* ("Written Leaves") Book of the Mayas. The Book of the Community Book 1, copyright 1950 by the University of Oklahoma Press. (Electronic version from the Internet Sacred Text Archive, managed by John Bruno Hare.)

Gornitz, Vivien. "Sea Level Rise, After the Ice Melted and Today." *Science Briefs*. National Aeronautics and Space Administration Goddard Institute for Space Studies, January 2007.

Gould, Stephen Jay. "Nonoverlapping Magisteria," *Natural History* 106 (March 1997): 16-22. http://www.stephenjaygould.org/library/gould_noma.html

Halafta, Yose ben, rabi. *Seder Olam* or *Seder Olam Rabbah* (The Hebrew words mean "The Great Order of the World"). approximately 160 AD. English Translation of the *Seder Olam* http://www.betemunah.org/sederolam.html

Ham, Ken, Bodie Hodge, and Tim Chaffey. *Demolishing Supposed Bible Contradictions. Volumes 1, II. Master Books, Green Forest, AR, 2010.*

Hancock, Graham. *Fingerprints of the Gods*. Three Rivers Press. New York, NY, 1996.

______. *Supernatural: Meetings with the Ancient Teachers of Mankind*. Disinformation Books. New York, NY, Revised edition 2006.

Hardy, Julia. "Afterlife and Salvation." Religion Library: Buddhism. *Patheos Library: Hosting the Conversation on Faith*. (No Date.)

Hawking, Stephen. *The Illustrated A Brief History of Time*. New York, NY: Bantam Dell, a division of Random House, 1996.

Heinlein, Robert A. *Time for the Stars*. Tor Books, New York, NY, 1956.

Herzenhorn, David M. "Lifted From a Russian Lake, a Big, if Fragile, Space Rock." October 16, 2013. New York Times website.

Hesiod. *The Theogony*. (ll. 116-138) Hugh G. Evelyn-White, translator. 1914. From the Internet Sacred Text Archive, managed by John Bruno Hare.

Hinduism http://marbaniang.wordpress.com/2010/08/22/hinduism-4-stages-of-life-and-3-ways-of-salvation-parallels-with-christianity/

Hitler, Adolph. *Mein Kampf*. Franz Eher Verlag (Publisher), Munich, Germany, 1925.

Hodge, Bodie. "Biblical Overview of the Flood Timeline." August 23, 2010 Answers in Genesis.

Hong, S.W. et al. Safety investigation of Noah's Ark in a seaway, *Journal of Creation* 8(1):26-36, 1994. (English version of a 1992 Korean study by on the seaworthiness of the ark supported by the Korea Association of Creation Research.) Proceedings of the International Conference on Creation Research, Korea Association of Creation Research, Taejon, 1993

Houdmann, S. Michael. Question: "How to get to heaven - what are the ideas from the different religions?" Answer concerning Confucianism. From the website *Got Questions.org? The Bible has answers! We'll help you find them!*

Humphreys, D. Russell. *Earth's Magnetic Field is Decaying Steadily –with a Little Rhythm,* CRSQ (Creation Research Society Quarterly) July 1, 2010.

______. *Helium Diffusion Rates Support Accelerated Nuclear Decay* 2003 Abstract [in part] The entire paper is available for download as a .pdf file. http://logosresearchassociates.org/Documents/Baumgardner/Helium-Diffusion-Rates-Support-Accelerated-Nuclear-Decay.pdf

______. "Helium Evidence For A Young World Remains Crystal-Clear." Institute for Creation Research. April 27, 2005. The True Origin Archive.

______. "New time dilation helps creation cosmology." *Journal of Creation* 22(3):84–92 December 2008.

______. *Starlight and Time: Solving the Puzzle of Distant Starlight in a Young Universe.* Master Books, Green Forest, AR, 1996.

Ilive, Thomas and M. M. Noah, translators (based on the Jewish Encyclopedia article). *Book of Jasher*, The. Also called *Sepher HaYasher*. Copyright Ken Johnson, 2013. Biblefacts Edition.
also; Salt Lake City, J.H. Parry and Company, 1887.

Inman, Mason. “New Asian Rodent Found as Food Is ‘Living Fossil,’ Gene Study Confirms.” *National Geographic News*. April 24, 2007.

Jewish Encyclopedia http://www.jewishencyclopedia.com/ The unedited full-text of the 1906 Jewish Encyclopedia

Josephus, Flavius. *Antiquities of the Jews , Book I.* William Whiston, translator. 1737. From the Internet Sacred Text Archive managed by John Bruno Hare.

Kelsen, Hans. *The Flood Myth*. Alan Dundes, editor. University of California Press: Berkeley and Los Angeles, California, University of California Press, Ltd., London, England, The Regents of the University of California, 1988.

Al-Khatib, Talal. “Dino do-overs: Fixes to paleontology” Published August 14, 2013, *Discovery News*. *Foxnews.com/*Science

Kurtén, B. Pleistocene Mammals of Europe (Chicago: Aldine, 1968).

King, Leonard William. *The Seven Tablets of Creation.* Another Version of the Creation of the World by Marduk. Luzac’s Semitic text and translation series. vol. xii-xiii Luzac and Co. London, 1902. From the Internet Sacred Text Archive, managed by John Bruno Hare.

______. *Enuma Elish* (“When on High”) (Babylonian/Assyrian/Sumerian/ Chaldean/ Akkadian), Narration 1. London, 1902. From the Internet Sacred Text Archive, managed by John Bruno Hare.

Knapp, Alex. “Radioactive Decay Rates May Not Be Constant After All.” *Forbes* Tech. May 3, 2011.

Larson, Kirsten. "Neutrinos!" IceCube South Pole Neutrino Observatory. National Science Foundation. University of Wisconsin-Madison. (No date.)

Livingston, David, Jr., PhD. *Correlating the Texts of Ancient Literature with the Old Testament* © 2003 David Livingston http://davelivingston.com/corancienttexts.htm From the site "Ancient Days"

López, Raúl Erlando. "The Antediluvian Patriarch and the Sumerian King List." *Journal of Creation* 12(3):347-357, 1998.

McDonald, Charlotte. "Who, What, Why: Is the Earth getting lighter?" BBC News Magazine, 31 January, 2012.

McDowell, Josh. *New Evidence That Demands a Verdict*. Thomas Nelson; Nashville, TN. 1st edition, 1999.

Meyer, T. and J. Martin. *Clark's Foreign Theological Library* 1854-1858. Keil and Delitszch (Multivolume Series) 1867ff Edinburgh T and T Clark, George Street Keil & Delitzsch Commentary on the Old Testament Johann (C.F.) Keil (1807-1888) & Franz Delitzsch (1813-1890).

Miller, Brandon. "Presto! Instant Petrified Wood Created in Lab." Tech. January 27, 2005. LiveScience website.

Morris, J. 2010. "The Real Nature of the Fossil Record." *Acts & Facts*. 39 (2): 12-14. Institute for Creation Research.

Mortenson, Terry, Dr. "Fossil Turtles Confound Evolutionists." April 18, 2005. Answers in Genesis.

Munro IR, Guyuron B "Split-Rib Cranioplasty". *Annals of Plastic Surgery* 7 (5): 341-346, November 1981.

Murray, Richard. "Missouri Watershed Profile." 14 November 2013. Prezi.com (A site for creating and sharing presentations.)

Naso, Publius Ovidius. (Ovid) The *Metamorphoses,* Book 1. John Dryden, et al, translators, 1717. From the Internet Sacred Text Archive, managed by John Bruno Hare.

Oard, Michael J. "Chapter 8: The Snowblitz, October 1, 2004." From the book *Frozen in Time,* Masterbooks, a division of New Leaf Press (Green Forest, Arkansas) 2004.

______. "The Geological Column Is a General Flood Order with Many Exceptions." *The Geologic Column: Perspectives Within Diluvial Geology*. Reed, J.K and M.J. Oard (editors). Creation Research Society.

______. "How did 90% of large Australian Ice Age animals go extinct?" *Journal of Creation* 22(1):17–19, April 2008.

______. *The New Answers Book Where Does The Ice Age Fit?* Master Books, Green Forest, AR, 2007.

O'Neil, Dennis, Dr. "Interpreting the Fossil Record." RECORD OF TIME: An Introduction to the Nature of Fossils and Paleoanthropological Dating Methods. Website created and maintained by , Behavioral Sciences Department, Palomar College, San Marcos, California Copyright © 1998-2012 by Dennis O'Neil. All rights reserved.

Orr, James, editor. *ISBE* (*International Standard Bible Encyclopedia*) originally published in 1939 by Wm. B. Eerdmans Publishing Co. Website HTML copyright 2011.

Parker, Gary. Dr. "Fossil Plants." *Creation Facts of Life, Answers in Genesis website,* January 1, 1994.

______. "How Fast?" *Creation Facts of Life, Answers in Genesis website,* January 1, 1994.

Plato. *Cratylus.* 360 B.C.E Benjamin Jowett, translator.

Post, Vincent, Dr. et al. News and Media. Media release: "Scientists find vast new freshwater sources under the sea." 05 Dec 2013 The National Centre for Groundwater Research and Training is an Australian Government initiative, supported by the Australian Research Council and the National Water Commission.

______ "Offshore fresh groundwater reserves as global phenomenon." *Nature* 504, 71-78 (05 Dec 2013). International weekly journal of science. Nature.com

Quran and Islam http://www.truthnet.org/islam/Quran/Rodwell/50/

Reedy, Anaru, *Ngā Kōrero a Mohi Ruatapu, tohunga rongonui o Ngāti Porou: The Writings of Mohi Ruatapu.* Canterbury University Press: Christchurch, 1993.

Remy, Melina. ("Our Amazing Planet" staff writer.) "The World's Longest Rivers." June 23, 2010. Livescience.com

Riddle, Mike, "Does Radiometric Dating Prove the Earth Is Old?" October 4, 2007 Excerpted from *The New Answers Book,* Answers in Genesis. Master Books/New Leaf Press: Green Forest, AR, 2006.

Roys, Ralph L. *The Book of Chilam Balam of Chumayel* (Mayan), XIII ("The Creation of the Uinal")Washington, D.C.: Carnagie Institution, 1933. From the Internet Sacred Text Archive, managed by John Bruno Hare.

Ruse, M. "Leading anti-creationist philosopher admits that evolution is a religion. How Evolution Became a Religion: Creationists Correct?" *National Post*, pp. B1, B3, B7 May 13, 2000.

Russell, Eric. "The Biology Classics: Paramecium Reproduction." Biomedia Associates: Learning Programs for Biology Education. (No Date.) Beaufort, SC.

Sachs, Mendel, Dr. from his website.

St. John, James. "Replacement." (Fossil preservation involving change in crystal structure and mineralogy of an organism's hard parts.) (No date) Ohio State University at Newark Website.

Sarfati, Jonathan. "Flood models and biblical realism." Journal of Creation 24(3):46–53 December 2010.

______. "How did dinosaurs grow so big?" Creation 28(1):44–47 December 2005

______. *'Millions of years' are missing.* (Interview with biologist and geologist Ariel Roth.) Creation.com

Sawyer, Diane. "Stephen Hawking on Religion: 'Science Will Win,'" Interview with Diane Sawyer, as quoted on ABC World News (07 June 2010).

Scheven, Joachim. "Living Fossils." Creation. September 1, 1993. Answers in Genesis.

Shakespeare, William. *Romeo and Juliet*. Act 3, Scene 1.

Sherwin, F. 2006. Amber: A Window to the Recent Past. *Acts & Facts*. 35 (7). Institute for Creation Research.

Shoemaker, Eugene M. "Impact Mechanics at Meteor Crater, Arizona." Prepared on behalf of the U.S. Atomic Energy Commission. US Geological service Publications.

Smith, George. *The Chaldean Account of Genesis*. London: Thomas Scott, 1876. From the Internet Sacred Text Archive, managed by John Bruno Hare.

Snelling, Andrew A., PhD. The Cause of Anomalous Potassium-Argon "Ages" for Recent Andesite Flows at Mt. Ngauruhoe, New Zealand, and the Implications for Potassium-Argon "Dating" Answers in Genesis Presented at the Fourth International Conference on Creationism, Pittsburgh, Pennsylvania, August 3–8, 1998. Published in: Proceedings of the Fourth International Conference on Creationism, R. E. Walsh (editor), pp. 503–525.

______. "Coal Beds and Noah's Flood." June 1, 1986. Creation Ex Nihilo; Answers in Genesis.

______. "Did Meteors Trigger Noah's Flood?" December 6, 2011, Answers in Genesis website.

______. "The Earth's magnetic field and the age of the Earth," first published: *Creation (Creation Ministries International)*, 13(4):44-48 September 1991.

______. "The Fallacies of Radioactive Dating of Rocks: Basalt Lava Flows in Grand Canyon. *Answers*. Sept. 5, 2006.

______. "Order in the Fossil Record." November 23, 2009. *Answers*. Answers in Genesis.

______. "Polonium Radiohalos: Still 'A Very Tiny Mystery'." *Acts & Facts*. 29 (8). 2000.

______. Radioactive "Dating" Failure: Recent New Zealand Lava Flows Yield "Ages" of Millions of Years. December 1, 1999. Creation Answers in Genesis website.

______. "Radiocarbons in Diamonds Confirmed." November 7, 2007. AiG-U.S. (Answers in Genesis website).

______. Radiohalos: The Flood's Smoking Gun. (Three-Part series) Answers in Genesis Website.
1. Mysterious Bullet Holes in Rocks March 5, 2012
2. Radiohalos: The Mysterious Vanishing Bullets June 6, 2012
3. Solving the Mystery of the Missing Bullets. Sept. 11, 2012

______. "Radioisotope Dating of Rocks in the Grand Canyon." June 1, 2005. Creation Answers in Genesis website.

______. "Snelling's Reply to Gentry." Nov 17, 2002. Earth Science Associates website.

______. "The World's a Graveyard: Flood Evidence Number Two." Answers in Genesis. February 12, 2008

Solomon, S., et. al., (eds.). "Changes Before the Industrial Era?" IPCC, 2007: Climate Change 2007: The Physical Science Basis. Contribution of Working Group I to the Fourth Assessment Report of the Intergovernmental Panel on Climate Change. Cambridge University Press, Cambridge, United Kingdom and New York, NY, USA.

Spence, Lewis. *The Myths of Mexico and Peru,* 1913. Garcia's *Origin de los Indias* (Translation of Mixtec picture-manuscript) quoted in this work.

Swanson, D.A., (photographer). Phreatic Eruption, Mount St. Helens 18 May 1980.

Swenson, Keith. "Radio-Dating in Rubble: The Lava Dome at Mount St Helens Debunks Dating Methods." Creation Magazine June 1, 2001 Answers in Genesis Website.

al-Tabari, Ibn Jarir. (Muslim historian 838-923.) *The History of al-Tabari*. English translation of *The History of the Prophets and Kings*.

Than, Ker. "Huge Ocean Discovered Inside Earth." February 28, 2007. Livescience.com.

Tharpar, Romila. *Frontline* magazine Volume 18, Issue 19, Sep. 15-28, 2001.

Theoi Classical E-Texts Library, New Zealand.

Thom, Harrie. "How could Noah care for the animals?" Creation 30(1):50–51, December 2007.

Thomas, Brian, M.S. "Canadian 'Mega' Dinosaur Bonebed Formed by Watery Catastrophe." July 13, 2010. Institute for Creation Research.

______. "Chinese Dinosaurs Were Fossilized by Flood." April 8. 2011. Institute for Creation Research.

______. Dinosaur Fossil "Wasn't Supposed to Be There." April 14, 2011. Institute for Creation Research. icr.org

Ussher, James. The Annals of the World "The Origin of Time, and Continued to the Beginning of the Emperor Vespasian's Reign and the Total Destruction and Abolition of the Temple and Commonwealth of the Jews." London: Printed by E. Tyler for F. Crook and B. Bedell, 1658. From the Internet Sacred Text Archive, managed by John Bruno Hare.

U.S. Geological Survey. Geologic Names Committee, 2010, Divisions of geologic time—major chronostratigraphic and geochronologic units: U.S. Geological Survey Fact Sheet 2010–3059, 2 p.

______. Graphic of Index Fossils. http://pubs.usgs.gov/gip/geotime/fossils.html

Valentine, J. W. "How Good Was the Fossil Record? Clues from the California Pleistocene," *Paleobiology* 15 no. 2 (1989): 83 -94.

Vardiman, Larry, Ph.D. Scientific Naturalism as Science. *Acts & Facts* (Institute for Creation Research), 26 (11). 1997.

_____. and D. R. Humphreys. 2010. *A New Creationist Cosmology: In No Time at All* Part 1. Acts & Facts. 39 (11): 12-15, 40 (1): 12-14, 40(2): 12-14.

Velikovsky, Immanuel. *Ages in Chaos*. Harper, New York, NY, 1950.

_____. *Worlds in Collison*. Harper, New York, NY, 1950.

Voth. H.R. Hurúing Wuhti and the Sun. From Field Columbian Museum Publication 96 Anthropological Series Volume VIII, The Traditions of the Hopi. The Stanley McCormick Hopi Expedition George A Dorsey, Curator, Department of Anthropology, Chicago, IL March, 1905 Scanned, proofed and formatted at sacred-texts.com, February 2001, by John Bruno Hare. Reformatted, August 2003. From the Internet Sacred Text Archive, managed by John Bruno Hare.

Walker, Tas. Walker/Klevberg chart. "Time/Rock Transformation" Chart based on the Walker system modified by Klevberg. Tas Walker's Biblical Geology website.

WELLINGTON. *"THE SAMOAN STORY OF CREATION-A 'Tala.' " JOURNAL OF THE POLYNESIAN SOCIETY CONTAINING THE TRANSACTIONS AND PROCEEDINGS OF THE SOCIETY. VOL. I.* [Wellington, 1892] {Reduced to HTML by Christopher M. Weimer, November 2002

West, E.W., translator. Narration 28 Bundahis, Chapter I, "In the name of the creator Aûharmazd." (Persian)

Sacred Books of the East, Volume 5, Oxford: the Clarendon Press, 1880. From the Internet Sacred Text Archive, managed by John Bruno Hare.

______. *Pahlavi Texts.* Part V "Marvels of Zoroastrianism." *Sacred Books of the East,* Volume 47 Oxford: the Clarendon Press, 1897. From the Internet Sacred Text Archive, managed by John Bruno Hare.

Whitten, D.G.A. and J.R.V. Brooks. The Penguin Dictionary of Geology. Middlesex, England: Penguin Books, 1972.

Wilkins, W. J. *Hindu Mythology, Vedic and Puranic.* Calcutta: Thacker, Spink & Co.; London: W. Thacker & Co. 1900. Kamadeva/Madana. From the Internet Sacred Text Archive, managed by John Bruno Hare.

Wise, K. "The Fossil Record: The Ultimate Test Case for Young-Earth Creationism," Opus: A Journal for Interdisciplinary Studies (1991-92): 17-29. Answers in Genesis.

Woodmorappe, John. "Billion-Fold Acceleration of Radioactivity Demonstrated in Laboratory." Journal of Creation. Answers in Genesis. August 1, 2001.

______. "Caring for the Animals on the Ark." March 29, 2007. *Answers.* Answers in Genesis. (This may be a valuable source, given that the author's *Feasibility Study* book is out of print. See entry below.)

______. "*National Geographic* Plays the Dating Game." April 1, 2002. Answers in Genesis website.

______. *Noah's Ark: A Feasibility Study.* Institute for Creation Research, Dallas, TX, July 1996.

Woody, Todd. "Gulf oil spill methane bloom disappears." *Grist: A Beacon in the Smog.* January 7, 2011.

Woolley, Joanna F. "The Origin of the Carboniferous Coal Measures Part 1: Lessons from History" Journal of Creation 24(3):76–81.

Xocipilli information: http://www.biroz.net/visions2012/xochipilli.htm

Zenkova, Olga. "Libra did not survive the severity of Chelyabinsk meteorite." (Translation provided on the site page. It is in Russian). Novosti website, 10/16/2013.

C. Articles from Elk Jerky for the Soul

1. The Problem with Dates in History: Hammurabi's Law Code https://findleyfamilyvideopublications.com/2012/10/17/the-problem-with-dates-in-history-hammurabais-law-code/

In 1901-1902 AD a French team excavating in Susa, one of the ancient Capitals of Elam, then Persia, now modern Iran, discovered pieces of a basalt stele. It was completely reconstructed and now sits in the Louvre, in Paris. The head of the French team, M. de Morgan used the surroundings where it was found to date the stele, the now famous Law Code of Hammurabi around 1100-1200 BC.

An American/German team headed by the German born American Hermann Hilprecht was excavating in Nippur at the same time. Nippur is in ancient Mesopotamian, an area ruled over by the Assyrians, Babylonians, Persians, Greeks, Ottoman Turks and is now modern Iraq. They found a kings list with the name Hammurabi on it. This list made Hammurabi a ruler in the 24th century, BC. Hermann Hilprecht immediately (January 1903) proclaimed the Hammurabi stele as the oldest law code ever found in a lecture at the University of Pennsylvania.

A book entitled *The Oldest Code of Laws in the World, by Hammurabi, King of Babylon* was immediately published in early 1903 and is available as an ebook through Project Gutenberg. It proclaims that Hammurabi ruled from 2285-2242 B.C. The forward is by C.H.W. Johns, M.A. of Cambridge. The book was printed in Edinburgh.

Since 1903, several other Sumerian kings lists were discovered. A rather brief but thorough article in the Roman Catholic online encyclopedia New Advent describes the major positions mainstream archaeologists take on the time Hammurabi actually ruled. Most 21st century archaeologists hold to some type of a "middle" position, that Hammurabi ruled around 1700 B.C.

It is very important to Liberals and Secular Humanists that the law code of Hammurabi be older than the Law Code of Moses. They insist that the Mosaic Code "evolved" from the lower Hammurabi Code, and that our laws today have "evolved" beyond the Mosaic Code. Since the Law was divinely given by God, it makes no difference if Hammurabi wrote his Law Code before God gave Moses the Law on Sinai. Since God revealed His Law to Noah, Hammurabi's Law code is still a corruption of God's revealed Law. God saw that man had corrupted His Law and needed to reveal it once more in writing to Moses.

If the 1700 date for Hammurabi is correct, then Hammurabi ruled while the Children of Israel were slaves in Egypt. They would remain slaves for another 250+ years before Moses would lead them out.

However, if the original date of M. de Morgan is correct, then Hammurabi's Law Code was written about 250 years after God revealed His Law to Moses on Sinai. While this seems to make very little difference, it is anathema to Evolutionists.

The important point is how can the uncertain date of Hammurabi's Law Code be a "backbone" on which to base history? "Human history has become too much a matter of dogma taught by professionals in ivory towers as though it's all fact. Actually, much of human history is up for grabs. The further back you go, the more that the history that is taught in the schools and universities begins to look like some kind of faerie story." (Graham Hancock *Fingerprints of the Gods*

2. A Very Simple Overview Of Relativity

https://findleyfamilyvideopublications.com/2012/09/19/the-big-bang-or-the-big-crunch-pick-your-religion/

"The Big Bang or the Big Crunch? Pick Your Religion."

Certain types of relativity can be traced to the ancient Greeks, but an adequate study really begins with the classical or mechanical relativity of Sir Isaac Newton. He used the concept of inertia (an object at rest remains at rest or an object in motion remains in motion until an outside force acts upon it) to explain the universe as we find it.

To visualize Newton's mechanical relativity, imagine you are standing on a platform. A vehicle with a window is traveling past. You can see a ball bouncing up and down on a table inside the vehicle. To a person inside the vehicle the bouncing ball appears to bounce straight up and down. To those standing on the platform and looking in the window, the ball is taking a zigzag path as it both bounces up and down and moves past you. The path the ball takes is *relative* to your point of view. Except for the path of the ball, everything else is the same to both those in the vehicle and those on the platform. Most important, time is the same to those on the platform and those in the vehicle. Albert Einstein called this *absolute time*, time which is same for everyone.

Albert Einstein first developed what we call *special relativity*. To use Einstein's own illustration, imagine that you are in an idealized elevator that is forever falling to the earth. You are in perpetual free fall. You release a steel ball and a handkerchief at the same time. Because you, the ball, the handkerchief and the elevator are all falling at the same rate, you, the ball and the handkerchief seem to "float." You are all part of what Albert Einstein calls "the same co-ordinate system (CS)."

At this point you realize that you are falling and every part of your CS is in fact moving. Inertia is only apparent within your CS and time is another dimension which is also moving with your CS and is also relative. Today we would understand this illustration better if we replaced the elevator image with a space station orbiting the earth.

The last stage is the well-known theory of *general relativity*. You are now an observer outside of the elevator, watching someone inside it. You have a different CS. Time is different to you and to the man in the elevator. While he sees stationary objects, you see that everything is falling. There is no true inertia. Everything is always moving and this movement is *relative* to your CS, to your point of view.

Einstein found flaws in Newton's mechanical theory. Newton taught that time was absolute. Einstein's theory of Special Relativity, based on his discovery of the space-time continuum, taught that time is a dimension, like length width and height. Einstein thought at first that the universe was static. In 1917, fifteen years after developing his theory of Special Relativity, Einstein included what he called a Universal Constant to make formulas work in General Relativity. This was based on an assumption that the universe was static. Stars would move within the universe but the universe itself was a static force.

The theory that developed as a result of this conclusion taught that the universe will simply run out of energy and will cease expanding. Gravitational forces are not strong enough to cause contraction or collapse, but the universe will die a "heat death." Everything will arrive at a uniform temperature, near absolute zero. There will be a uniformity of elemental composition. Everything will be dead and motionless.

Years later Einstein retracted his universal constant statement as the greatest mistake of his career, when the astronomer Hubble pointed out to him that stars have a Doppler Red Shift, proving that the universe is in motion. We know the universe is in motion because of the Doppler effect, the shift to the infrared spectrum, visible in stars, indicating they are moving away from us. That may indicate that the universe is either expanding or contracting.

A common illustration of the Doppler effect uses trains and a train station. When a train is approaching, passing, and going away, the changes in the sound of the whistle and the engine noises are an example of the Doppler effect. In the case of light and more distant objects such as stars, the Doppler effect will appear as a shift in the light spectrums. A star approaching us will have a shift toward the ultraviolet spectrum. For stars receding or going away, the shift will be toward the infrared spectrum.

The second theory is that the big bang is true and the universe is infinite. Gravitational forces are too weak to hold it together and it will expand for eternity. This is the current position of mainstream Physics and Astronomy today, and the one you must hold to if you expect to be published in academic circles. This is Stephen Hawking's position.

The third possibility is that the universe will run out of the expansion force from the big bang. Gravitational force will pull it back together in what is sometimes called the Big Crunch, collapsing it back into a Black Hole. Some "mainstream" physicists hold this view, but believe that it does not matter since we are still in the expansion stage and the Big Crunch is billions of years into the future. But the appearance of the Doppler effect, that of distance increasing between Earth and other bodies, might actually be the universe collapsing. The Doppler red shift might mean we are pulling away from all other stars because we are in the lead, rushing toward a Black Hole and we are the closest to the event horizon.

The same Doppler effect is achieved whether you are at the station listening to a passing train's whistle, or riding past in a train, listening to a whistle on a train sitting at the station. This is a minority position among physicists and implies that we are rapidly approaching the "Big Crunch," the end of the universe as we know it, where we return to the original singularity.

These are the major positions postulated by Physics. Though there are many, many other positions and many, many variations on these positions, the important fact is that they are all religious beliefs which can never be proved. Physics uses mathematical formulas to arrive at their conclusions, but mathematics is a language. Like all languages, we must start with certain assumptions. We can observe and measure the universe and some observations fit some models better than others. There is no scientific data on origins

Albert Einstein, *The Evolution of Physics,* Touchstone (an Imprint of Simon and Schuster) New York, NY, 1967.

Stephen Hawking, *A Brief History of Time and The Universe In a Nutshell.* Bantam Books for Young Readers, New York, NY, 1996.

3. A Not So Simple Look at Relativity

https://findleyfamilyvideopublications.com/2014/01/23/a-not-so-simple-look-at-relativity-post-by-michael-j-findley/

The importance of the theory of relativity is the religious conclusions rammed down our throats by religious bigots. This strong language is necessary to understand the unyielding priesthood these men have erected. These people have convinced themselves and many others that they are open minded, kind and gentle. In their world, however, disagreements are only tolerated within their general framework of their view of the universe.

The first tenet of their religion is that the current universe and the way it operates can be examined to discover all truths. The second tenet of their religion is that the universe is at least billions of years old, if not eternal. The third tenet is the necessary and important conclusion of the first two. The entire human race is an infinitesimally small and insignificant part of an eternal, or nearly eternal cosmos. The only significance anyone can ever have is the decisions we choose to call significant. At one time the concept of God creating the universe was permitted, but even that kind of a God is now intolerable. Everything is relative and the guardians (as they were to do in Plato's *Republic*) tell us what is good and how to live in order to best serve society.

Though it took longer than predicted, *1984* has arrived. The uniforms are blue jeans. Newspeak is a combination of psychobabble and pseudoscience jargon. All their conclusions claim a basis in relativity. In reality, Einstein's theory of general relativity has no relationship with moral relativism. The principles of general relativity are only observable on the cosmic level. Personal relationships, physical as well as personal, do not use relativity. We are all in the same co-ordinate system.

The concept of a space/time continuum is essential to understand general relativity. Time is just as much a dimension as space. The universal constant is the speed of light. Time can be altered in two ways. The first is the well-known Twins Paradox. If you are not familiar with the Twins Paradox, the 1956 juvenile story *Time for the Stars* by Robert Heinlein is an interesting introduction. A pair of twins have telepathic abilities which are not limited by distance. Because of this ability, one twin is placed on a spacecraft with near light speed and heads for the stars while the other twin remains on earth to receive and relay messages As the mass of the starship approaches the speed of light, the relative time on the starship slows down. Both twins experience a "normal" life with what they perceive to be a normal timeframe. As the twin on the spaceship travels and the twin on earth ages and the telepathic responsibilities are transferred first to his twin's daughter on earth, then his granddaughter and finally his great granddaughter. By the end of the book, the traveling twin has aged only a few years while time on earth has gone through decades. If you are not familiar with the book, there is a somewhat cute ending. This Twins Paradox concept is a frequent topic in space travel discussions, because people and spaceships have mass.

According to the theory of general relativity, an object with mass will have its perception of time altered as it approaches the speed of light. Since the amount of energy needed to propel a spacecraft at the actual speed of light is infinite, actual light speed is impossible. But as mass approaches the speed of light, time will seem to slow down those in other co-ordinate systems. A spacecraft near the speed of light will have normal time to those on board the spacecraft. Those on the spacecraft would view those on earth as racing around furiously as time raced by. Those on earth will view those on the spacecraft as moving in extreme slow motion.

Since we are unaware of any actual starships, our real, daily experience is actually reversed. On page 43 of Stephen Hawking's book *A Brief History of Time* there is a picture of a tower with two clocks, one in the base and one in the top. The clock at the top runs faster than the one in the base. "Another prediction of general relativity is that time should appear to run slower near a massive body like the earth." He takes several pages to explain this, but the important point is that satellite navigation systems which fail to account for this time difference caused by general relativity can be off by miles. Massless particles, such as light photons, traveling completely outside of gravitational fields, such as between galaxies, could easily travel at the speed of light yet travel for millions or even billions of years while only brief periods of time, perhaps only seconds, transpire on earth. The same principles apply to any electromagnetic energy. This important aspect of general relativity is rarely, if ever mentioned.

The reason for this sin of omission is explained by Dr. Russell Humphries in his work, *Starlight and Time.* The idea that the universe is billions of light years across and therefore the earth is millions or billions of years old is the single greatest deception in the secular humanist's arsenal. They frequently say that a look at distant galaxies is a look at the beginning of the universe because the light we see left those galaxies just after the big bang. Relativity is ignored when it is convenient.

Robert A. Heinlein, *Time for the Stars,* Tor Books, New York, NY, 1956.

Dr. Russell Humphreys, *Starlight and Time: Solving the Puzzle of Distant Starlight in a Young Universe*, Master Books, Green Forest, AR, 1996.

4. *The Training Place of Mankind; God's Creation Explained For Normal Folk* by David Bergsland

A Book Review by Michael J. Findley

https://findleyfamilyvideopublications.com/2013/05/27/the-training-place-of-mankind-gods-creation-explained-for-normal-folk-by-david-bergsland-a-book-review-by-michael-j-findley/

I have read several books by this author and enjoy both his writing style and the content of his works. But I must admit that I am not part of the target audience; Normal Folk. No one has ever accused me of being "normal."

On my Android 7" ebook reader, type set to 100%, this is an eighty page book. According the author and the title, our brief life on earth is a training place. The table of contents and all links work. While a table of contents and working links is something you might just expect, sadly many ebooks fail in these simple basics. Our daughter, an elementary school teacher, believes this is one of the best book covers she has ever seen.

This is an overview of mankind on earth, from the original creation to the New Heavens and the New Earth. It does not cover every topic I would like, but in such a brief work that is simply not possible.

If you have never looked at an overview of God's Word, or you know someone like this, this book is a must read. If you know someone who is curious about the Bible but has never read it, then this book is a must read for them.

It is both an easy, enjoyable read and introduces most major topics of the Word of God in a single book. Not to mislead anyone; this is neither a theology book nor a Bible Doctrines overview. More than half of this brief book is devoted to the book of Genesis, creation, the flood, the birth of civilization and the beginning of the Jewish nation.

The three-plus pages titled, *So what happened to science?* and *My point is this: Creationism is basic to Christianity* are very important points that are both brief and thorough. *The Creation Week: 4000 B.C.* might just be the best nine-page overview of the Creation Week available.

This book looks at the Bible from a very Gentile perspective. The central chapter, *The pivot of history: Jesus* assumes that the reader is not even familiar with the most basic information about the Messiah. Sadly, that is probably a valid assumption and makes it so necessary. Many pastors I talk to would likely find the basic information in this book a real eye opener. That is so sad.

The book concludes with *Israel is Transformed* and *The End of Creation*. He explains prophecy with science to examine what the earth's future will be like.

Once again, it does not answer everything. But it is a great eye opener for anyone not familiar with the Word of God.

C. Excerpts from *Antidisestablishmentarianism*

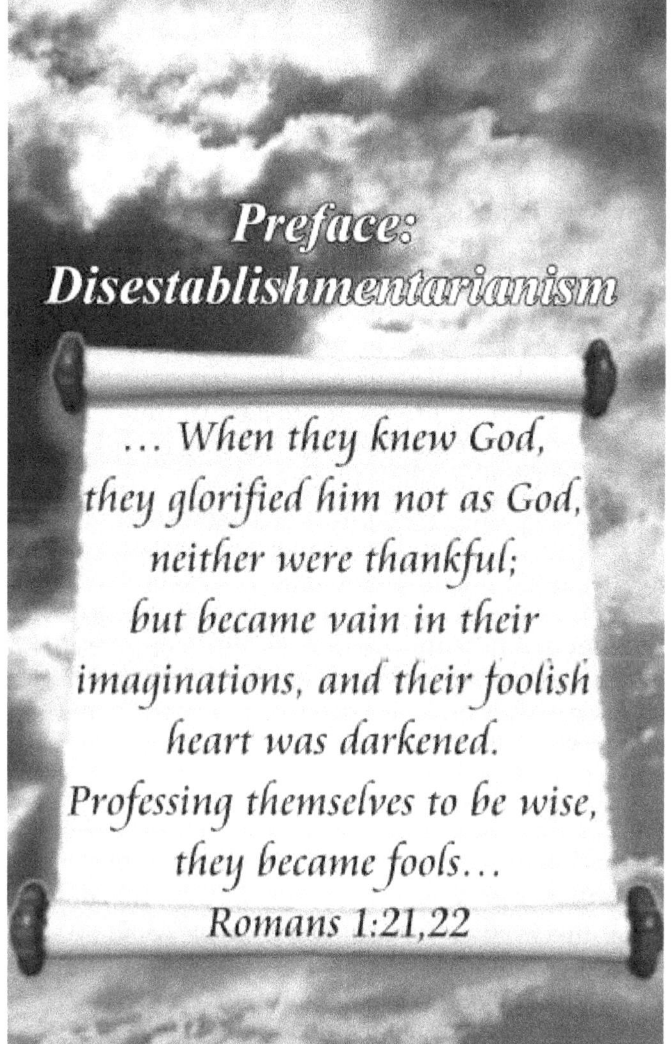

Graphic from the Preface of Illustrated Antidisestablishmentarianism and includes Romans

1:21-22 which is given in text form in the chapter header below.

1. Preface: Disestablishmentarianism

... When they knew God, they glorified him not as God, neither were thankful; but became vain in their imaginations, and their foolish heart was darkened. Professing themselves to be wise, they became fools...
Romans 1:21,22

The most religious people on earth are those who claim not to have any religion. Dogmatic, intolerant, and bigoted, they refuse to allow anyone to so much as speak their opposition. Yet these same people demand political power and tax support. The mildest opposition, such as the mere mention of Intelligent Design (not God), has blacklisted tenured professors. Just two parents in a middle school in Texas made the national news by objecting to Gideon Bibles placed, without comment, on a table outside the school office.[1] Such people dishonestly claim that they are not religious and "religion" is a group of mythologies. The truth is that they are the ones promoting mythology. In every aspect of life they promote this mythology with unproven dogmatic assertions under the guise of "Science" vocabulary. After hijacking the word "Science," they use the courts to elevate their misuse of the term to an established religion.

Science is the study of the world around us, the use of the experimental method and the improvement of our lives through the application of technology. It is divided into various academic disciplines such as Chemistry, Physics, Mathematics and Biology. However, what the federal courts, the Academic community and the mainstream Western media mean by science is uniformitarianism. It is the cosmological foundation of the religion of Secular Humanism. "Since the fathers fell asleep, all things continue as they were from the beginning of the creation" (II Peter 3:4). This concise description of Uniformitarianism clearly shows that it is completely and entirely a religious belief in antiscientific myths.

Secular Humanists use words which have been in the English language for hundreds of years but give them "new" meanings. However, "there is no new thing under the sun" (Ecclesiastes 1:9, KJV). The words believe, faith and trust are all historic judicial terms and they also form the foundation of the true scientific method. What Secular Humanists promote as their version of the scientific method consists of preconceptions, presuppositions and assumptions. It is the opposite of an open mind.

A true open mind is founded in belief, faith and trust. The historic meaning of believe is to perceive or understand with the mind and then make an informed decision.[2] The most basic use of the word believe which the average American would understand is that of a juror in court. Which witness do you believe? Which piece of evidence is believable? A synonym would be the word credible. When we believe something or someone and then act on that belief, that is faith. The active part of belief is faith. The passive part of belief is trust. Suppose your brother says that he will drive you to the doctor. If you believe him, then you understand what he says and you make a decision to get ready. If you get in the vehicle with him, that is faith. You act on your belief. When you sit in the vehicle as he drives, that is trust, a passive reliance on what you have proven true. You trust in his driving skills. You trust in the vehicle. You trust the roads, etc. Everything we do is a combination of belief, faith or trust. By restoring their historic definitions, belief, faith and trust re-emerge as the clear language of true experimental science. These terms were deliberately segregated from science to deceive people into believing Secular Humanism.

Liberals, Secular Humanists and materialists, however, use the word "belief" as a synonym for a philosophical position, just an opinion. Faith and trust to them are metaphysical words which mean different things to different people. And this is just the tip of an enormous iceberg. Secular Humanists have redefined hundreds of words to support their religion, such as sin, judgment and anthropology. A conversation with them can be very difficult since they use historical English words but mean something entirely different.

The traditional role of religion is to place priesthood as intermediary between God and man. The traditional role of an establishment of religion places the government in that intermediary role between God and man. In the Middle Ages the Roman Catholic Church put itself between man and God, as other religions have in the past. Johann Tetzel, a "professional pardoner," sold indulgences representing forgiveness for sins in Germany. Indulgences were based on the "storehouse" of good works believed to exist because of the sacrifice of Christ and the good deeds and prayers of past saints. Tetzel was said to promise that, "As soon as a coin in the coffer rings, a soul from purgatory springs."[3]

Selling indulgences was the final act of many which brought on the Reformation. People wouldn't have bought them if they hadn't believed the Catholic Church alone could placate God on their behalf. Martin Luther convinced the princes of Germany that they did not need to send their money to Rome because they could go to God directly. Rome sent armies to collect the money. Even Modern Roman Catholics who do not believe that their church today claims to stand between them and God have to admit that the medieval Roman Catholic Church did.

The combined power of Church and State restricted personal worship, scientific study and access to historical truth. Today Secular Humanism has done the same by removing foundational truths from education. It excludes study and discovery that contradicts uniformitarianism. It rewrites history to undermine morality and freedom of expression.

The union between the medieval Romanist church and the state came to an end in two ways. In Southern Europe during the Renaissance, art, architecture, literature, and learning opened up to all men, not just those who were part of the church and state system. The Renaissance left the power intact, however. In Northern Europe, the Reformation abolished the need for a church like Rome through the great affirmations of the Reformation: The Scriptures are the absolute authority; Justification is by faith alone apart from works; and every believer is his own priest with direct access to God. The Reformation made a special priesthood class unnecessary because men could pray directly to God and read His Word on their own.

The medieval Roman Catholic Church kept the Scriptures almost exclusively in Latin to prevent ordinary people from studying them, forcing people to come to the priest. The priest would not only tell them what the Scriptures said, but he also mingled that with the church's interpretation. In order for ordinary people who did not know Latin to read the Bible for themselves, the Scriptures had to be translated into the language of the ordinary people. Translation work by Reformers was essential to enable ordinary men to read the Scriptures for themselves, even though it was punishable by death under the Church-State system. The Renaissance and the Reformation worked together in the development of moveable type to make printing and distribution of translations of the Scriptures easier. Renaissance scholars revived interest in studying forgotten manuscripts and making translations into the vernacular. Erasmus's Greek New Testament provided a basis for more accurate translations of the Scriptures.

The Medieval Romanist Church-State system took away freedom by forcing man to rely on and accept its teachings. The Renaissance and the Reformation restored freedom by returning art, science, and all forms of learning to ordinary people. In particular the people were able to worship God as the Scriptures taught, without Church-State control. Modern western culture, and American culture in particular, was founded on this religious freedom. American culture is more Christian than European cultures, but neither of these cultures can survive if the foundation of religious freedom is destroyed.

It is this Christian foundation of religious freedom which is the real target of Secular Humanists. These Secular Humanists have taken outrageous liberties in their unrelenting quest to replace religious freedom with their established religion of Secular Humanism, which they incorrectly call science or Natural Law. Their major tool is the US court system. Sympathetic US courts have consistently supported Secular Humanism by using every possible opportunity to replace the word religion with the ancient concept of Natural Law. However, since Natural Law has been used so many different ways, the courts had to standardize the term Natural Law. Their version of Natural Law goes back to Plato's *Republic*. Though Plato never used the phrase "natural law" in his *Republic,* translator Benjamin Jowett's notes state that, "Plato among the Greeks, like Bacon among the moderns, was the first who conceived a method of knowledge... "[4] Plato's *Republic* is at least the foundation of modern Natural Law, if not the detailed finished product. Together with Aristotle, Plato is supposed by secularists to have laid the foundation for learning and development of the Sciences. This really is the essence of Natural Law.

Jowett goes on to say that Plato provided for a means to spread his method of acquiring knowledge. "In the ideal

State which is constructed by Socrates, the first care of the rulers is to be education."[4] Jowett makes it clear that Socrates meant to impart much more than mere academic knowledge, just as Natural Law means to teach more than mere Science. Socrates promoted "the conception of a higher State, in which 'no man calls anything his own,' and in which there is neither 'marrying nor giving in marriage,' and 'kings are philosophers' and 'philosophers are kings;' and there is another and higher education, intellectual as well as moral and religious, of science as well as of art, and not of youth only but of the whole of life."[4]

Many know that Plato in his *Republic* based his state on a philosopher/king. Few, however, are aware that he believed in communism and free love and that these two "natural" principles were to be foundational principles of the state.

Though the preceding condensation by Benjamin Jowett is an excellent job, as you can read for yourself, the actual words of Socrates, as quoted by Plato, are much longer and more difficult to understand. "None of them will have anything specially his or her own." "... Their legislator, having selected the men, will now select the women and give them to them [the legislator gives selected women to selected men]... they must live in common houses and meet at common meals ... they will be together ... And so they will be drawn by a necessity of their natures to have intercourse with each other... " "... Until philosophers are kings, or the kings and princes ... have the spirit and power of philosophy, and political greatness and wisdom meet in one ... cities will never have rest from their evils."[5]

The philosopher/king, according to Socrates, was to lay these foundational ideas through education. Though he did not use the phrase "establishment of religion," Plato clearly advocated an established religion. It was to be put in place by a philosopher/king through education based on a state where "no man calls anything his own" and where there is neither "marrying nor giving in marriage." Though this education would begin with children, it would continue throughout a person's entire life. This is the Natural Law which the US Court system has imposed.

The US needs to disestablish its Establishment of Religion and reestablish religious freedom. In the 1800's churches which tried to break away from the Church of England were called disestablishmentarians. The people who fought against the disestablishment of those churches within the Church of England in the 1800s were called Antidisestablishmentarians. Today, the mainstream media, liberal politicians, the academic community, the liberal courts and all others who file lawsuits, blacklist, fire, refuse to hire, tax, legislate against, libel, slander and do whatever is necessary to maintain their positions of privilege and power are modern Antidisestablishmentarians.

---

1 (No author) "Parents Fuming as Texas Schools Let Gideons Provide Bibles to Students," Tuesday, May 19, 2009, *Fox News.com*. "A spokeswoman for the school district said that a number of materials are made available to students this way, including newspapers, camp brochures and tutoring pamphlets. College and military recruitment information is available all year long. The Gideon Bibles were made available for just one day. 'We have to handle this request in the same manner as other requests to distribute non-school literature: in a view-point neutral manner,' Shana Wortham, director of communications for the district, wrote in an e-mail to *FoxNews.com*.

2 Alexander Hamilton, in an 1802 letter to James Bayard. "I have carefully examined the evidences of the Christian religion, and if I was sitting as a juror upon its

authenticity I would un-hesitatingly give my verdict in its favor. I can prove its truth as clearly as any proposition ever submitted to the mind of man."

3 Philip Schaff, *History of the Christian Church,* Volume 7, "The Reformation," Charles Scribner's Sons, 1910.

4 Plato, *The Republic* (c. 360 B.C.), translated by Benjamin Jowett over a period of 30 years until his death in 1893, completed posthumously by Lewis Campbell. (Introductory material (in double quotes) and paraphrases of Plato's ideas (in single quotes) were written by Jowett.)

5 Plato, *The Republic*, Book Five Dialogue excerpts among Socrates, Adeimantus, Glaucon and Thrasymachus have been placed in parentheses within Jowett's introductory material.

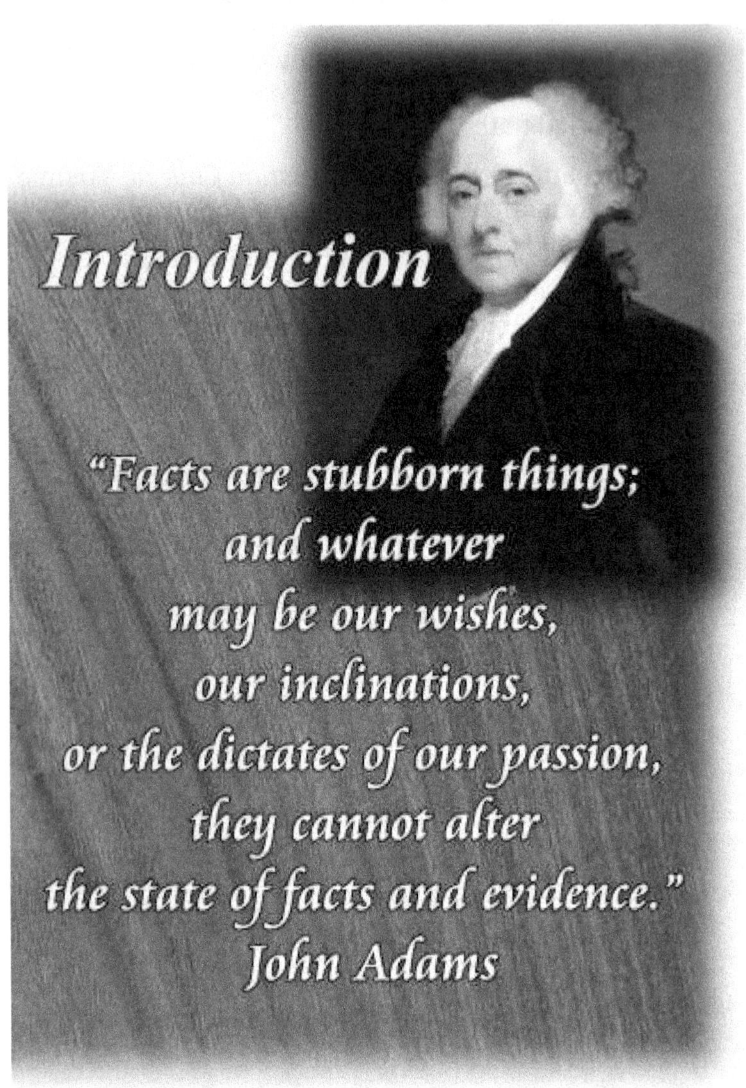

Graphic from the Introduction of Illustrated Antidisestablishmentarianism and includes the John Adams quote given in text form in the chapter header below.

2. Introduction

Facts are stubborn things; and whatever may be our wishes, our inclinations, or the dictates of our passion, they cannot alter the state of facts and evidence.[1]
John Adams

Sometime in the early twentieth century, Secular Humanist indoctrination convinced almost everyone in the United States that "an establishment of religion" in the first phrase of the first amendment of the United States Constitution is vague and can mean just about anything. "The state of the facts and evidence," as John Adams so eloquently put it, is the exact opposite.

Section One of this work documents what the founders meant by the phrase "an establishment of religion. " The Founding Fathers made as clear a statement as the English language permitted. The Constitution of the United States is founded on English law and to a lesser extent, various European laws, especially German and Dutch. In each of these countries, an Establishment of Religion was the collection of taxes to support education, welfare and public worship. The various governments appointed the teachers, welfare workers and pastors and expected these people to support the government in turn.

The original state constitutions not only permitted, but openly encouraged establishments of religion, especially in the areas of welfare and education. The foundation of the US Constitution is the fact that federal government was to have no control whatsoever in these areas. Their concept of a separation of Church and State was the exact opposite of what the courts have rammed down our throats for the past hundred years. The church should have the right to pray and teach without any federal intervention whatsoever. Judges should have the right to post any Scriptures they want. The courts should have no authority whatsoever to comment. Removing a state judge from office for posting the Ten Commandments is not merely an Establishment of Religion. It is the Inquisition.

Section Two documents the foundations of Secular Humanism and how it grew to become America's Establishment of Religion. The words "Secular Humanism "come from various groups in the 1950's. The phrase "Secular Humanist " is found in court documents to describe this set of beliefs. Secular Humanism is as old as civilization, but the primary foundation of twenty first century Secular Humanism is Plato's *Republic*. In America, Secular Humanism can be said to have originated with Thomas Paine. Secular Humanism has specific beliefs which are written down in various manifestos. Like Christianity, Islam and Judaism, Secular Humanism has many variations. Though Secular Humanists do not like the term, the most accurate words to describe these variants are "sects " or "denominations. " Like Christians, Muslims and Jews, many Secular Humanist denominations do not get along with one another. Therefore, we have attempted to point out the beliefs which have the greatest agreement.

Section Three defines science, since Secular Humanists claim that science separates them from all other religions. Since true science is founded in the belief, faith and trust of the Bible, all of these words are defined carefully and in detail. In the Bible, belief, faith and trust are legal terms. Believe means to examine the evidence and come to a reasoned conclusion. Action taken on that belief is faith. Trust is the passive version of faith.

The Scientific Method is the biblical version of belief, faith and trust applied to the material world which God created for us. In the Bible, the Scientific Method recognizes that God is the creator, that we are required to be responsible managers of the material world God has given us and that there is a final judgment after death which will include how well we managed the gifts God allowed us to use.

Our book concludes with Section Four, the results of having Secular Humanism as an Establishment of Religion. With the exception of America's founding documents and the ancient documents such as Plato, Plutarch and Genesis, hundreds of other quotes could easily be substituted for the quotes that appear here. There is nothing new or unique in this book. It is a combination of what used to be common knowledge in America before Secular Humanism took over and destroyed the education system and current events. If we were to start over today, we would pull different stories from the daily news. Though the individual stories would be different, the points would be the same. "There is nothing new under the sun " (Ecclesiastes 1:9). Or to state the same thing another way, the more things change, the more they stay the same.

America's Established Religion is Secular Humanism. This work is dedicated to exposing, defining and disestablishing it.

---

1 John Adams, "Argument in defence of the [English] soldiers in the Boston Massacre trial," December 1770.

2 "Alabama's Judicial Ethics Panel removed Chief Justice Roy Moore from office Thursday for defying a Federal judge's order to move a ten commandments monument from the State Supreme Court building. " Friday, November 14, 2003. Posted 6:56 AM Eastern time. *CNN.com*

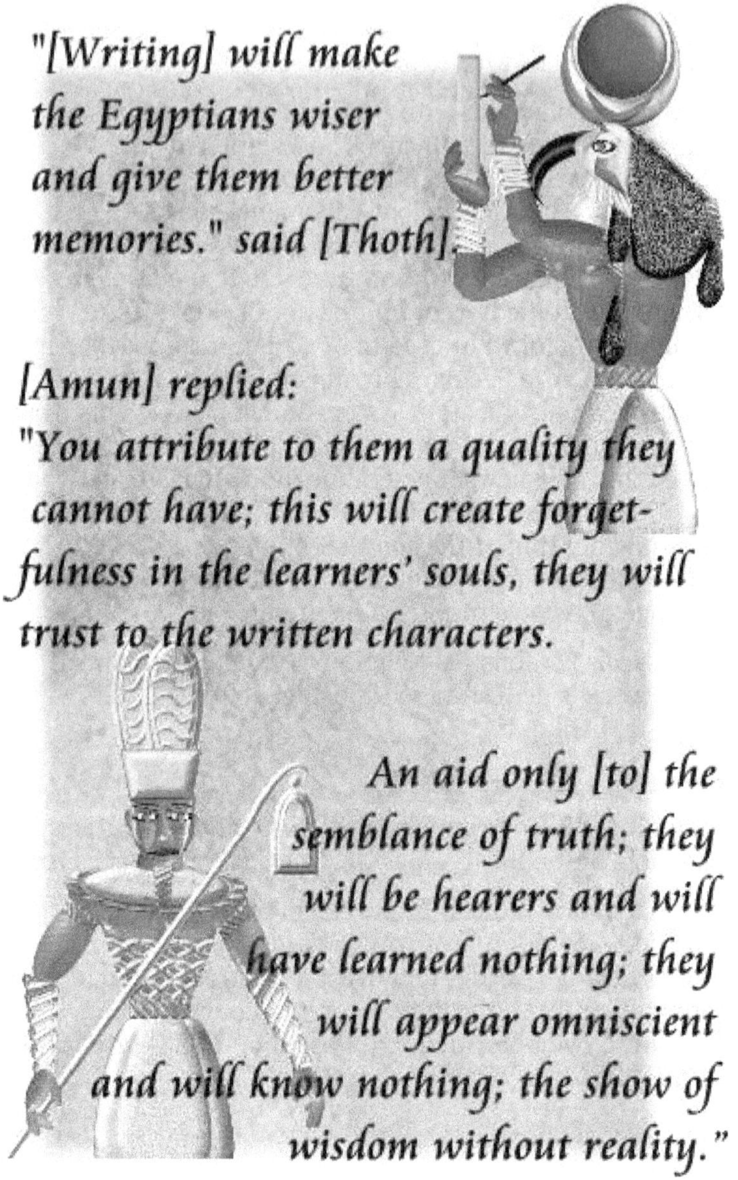

"[Writing] will make the Egyptians wiser and give them better memories." said [Thoth].

[Amun] replied:
"You attribute to them a quality they cannot have; this will create forgetfulness in the learners' souls, they will trust to the written characters.

An aid only [to] the semblance of truth; they will be hearers and will have learned nothing; they will appear omniscient and will know nothing; the show of wisdom without reality."

Graphic shows images of Egyptian gods Thoth and Ammun and a portion of their conversation included in the text on the next page.

Excerpt from Chapter Six: "What Is Secular Humanism?" This excerpt discusses the oral versus written tradition in literature.

Since the opposite is drilled into everyone through western culture and western education, we need to think the following example through slowly and carefully. The Exodus of the children of Israel from Egypt is told in the Bible as a straightforward, factual, historic event. Charlton Heston, in his narration of the picturesque Bible video series, presents the Bible as part of the "oral tradition in storytelling " as if teachings passed on orally were understood to be less accurate or reliable and therefore merely legends and myths. Socrates, in Plato's Dialogue *Phaedrus,* addresses the subject of oral versus written history.

> *Theuth [Thoth] ... was the inventor of many arts, ... but his great discovery was the use of letters. ... Thammus [the god Ammun] was the king of ... Egypt; ...To him came Theuth ... desiring that the other Egyptians might be allowed to have the benefit of [his inventions]; ... when they came to letters, "This," said Theuth, "will make the Egyptians wiser and give them better memories; " ... Thammus replied: ... "You ... attribute to them a quality which they cannot have; for this ... will create forgetfulness in the learners' souls, ... they will trust to the external written characters ... This is an aid not to memory, but to reminiscence, ... not truth, but only the semblance of truth; they will be hearers of many things and will have learned nothing; they will appear to be omniscient and will generally know nothing; they will be tiresome company, having the show of wisdom without the reality. "*[4]

Plutarch, in his discourse on the life of Lycurgus and his rule in ancient Greece, expresses the belief that oral tradition is a way of making the law more firmly fixed in the mind.

> *None of his laws were put into writing by Lycurgus, indeed, one of the so-called "rhetras "forbids it. For he thought that if the most important and binding principles which conduce to the prosperity and virtue of a city were implanted in the habits and training of its citizens, they would remain unchanged and secure, having a stronger bond than compulsion in the fixed purposes imparted to the young by education, which performs the office of a law-giver for every one of them.*[5]

There is considerable disagreement about whether the Scriptures were in some part orally communicated before being written down. The point is that even if they were it does not make them less authoritative or reliable. Socrates may not be entirely justified in discounting the value of written records but he reinforces the point that oral communication of history does not make it unreliable or inaccurate. Memorizing and passing on history demands great discipline and does not result in a form of the child's game "gossip. "

Gossip, sometimes called Telephone or other names, consists of a group made to stand in a line. The first person in line is given a piece of paper on which is written a phrase to whisper into the ear of the second person. Frequently there is only one opportunity to whisper the message. The second person whispers what he heard to the third, and so on down the line. The last person is to write down or speak aloud what he heard the person before him say. When the final form of the "gossip " message is made public, frequently it bears little resemblance to the original phrase. The distortion of the oral message in the game gossip is simply due to the indifference of the people playing the game. In fact, one simple change in the rules of the game of gossip produces correct transmission of the message even by children. Simply offer everyone who is playing a large enough reward, or punishment, if the final message is correct.

Modern prisoners of war, inmates in prison, gang members, spies and others today pass on important information without writing it down and without changing the message. Most American Indian tribes had no written language and saw no need for one, until Europeans demonstrated the ability to talk to people far away. In the popular TV series *Mission: Impossible*, the leader of the team received his orders on a recording that self-destructed after he had heard it one time. He was forced to memorize the mission immediately or he would be unable to complete it.

*****

But the predominant form of unbelief in the world today is Secular Humanism. We use the term "Secular Humanist" or "Secular Humanism" because that is what they called themselves. *The Humanist Manifesto I* is a religious document, written by a Unitarian Minister, Raymond B. Bragg, in 1933. Thirty men who believed themselves to be representative of a vast multitude "forging a new philosophy " signed it. "... There is no new thing under the sun. " (Ecclesiastes 1:9, KJV)

The Humanist Manifestos I, II and *III* can be viewed on the website *americanhumanist.org*. They cannot be reprinted here because of the following notice on the site:

> *Copyright renewed 1973 by the American Humanist Association. Permission to reproduce this material, complete and unmodified, in electronic or printout form is hereby granted free of charge by the copyright holder to nonprofit humanist and freethought*

> *publications. All other uses, and uses by all others, require that requests for permission be made through the American Humanist Association.*[15]

These men quickly learned that using the word “religion” actually hampered their cause. If they could deceive people into believing that secular humanism was not a religion and that religion was bad, then they could get state funding (follow the money trail) and political power while putting ungodly restrictions on those who actually dared to call themselves religious. Humanist Manifestos II and III call traditional religions “traditional theism “ and describe them as “obstacles to human progress. “ Many have also dropped the word “secular “ and simply call themselves “humanists.”

This is an effective propaganda technique, since they are now denying that they are a religion. The 1973 *Humanist Manifesto II* is lengthy and filled with doublespeak. It is exactly what George Orwell in 1984 and Aldous Huxley in *Brave New World* warned us about. It is important because it was signed by more than one hundred influential people, including doctors, university professors, and others like Isaac Asimov, scientist and writer, B. F. Skinner, Prof. of Psychology, Harvard University, Betty Friedan, Founder of *N.O.W*, and Sir Julian Huxley, former head, *UNESCO,* Great Britain. All the manifesto texts can be viewed online. *Humanist Manifesto III* is the most seductive. True intentions are cleverly obscured and it sounds very good. As commentator Bill O’Reilly points out, the term Secular Humanist is not very accurate. It is, however, the oldest and most accurate of the labels they have chosen for themselves.

It is also the term used in court documents, including the US Supreme Court, so we will continue to use it. “Among religions in this country which do not teach what would generally be considered a belief in the existence of God are Buddhism, Taoism, Ethical Culture, Secular Humanism, and others."[16] Justice Black based his comments on the 1957 case of *Fellowship of Humanity v. County of Alameda.* In this case an organization of humanists sought a tax exemption on the ground that they used their property "solely and exclusively for religious worship. " The court ruled that the activities of *Fellowship of Humanity* entitled it to an exemption. These activities included weekly Sunday meetings. The *Fellowship of Humanity* case used the word humanism, not secular humanism.[16]

Secular Humanism also made a separate manifesto, first published in 1980 as *A Secular Humanist Declaration* by *CODESH (Council for Democratic Secular Humanism)* co-authored by Paul Kurtz and Edwin H. Wilson, both editors of *The Humanist* magazine. Its principle purpose was to declare its compatibility with democracy and how enlightened man should view traditional religions as inferior to secular humanism.

Still," ...There is nothing new under the sun. " (Ecclesiastes 1:9, NIV). Plato praised many of these same follies in his dialogue *The Republic.* Since Plato is so verbose, few study him in detail today, which is good. Where Aldous Huxley in *Brave New World* and George Orwell in 1984 viewed the following principles as deplorable, Plato praised them as necessary. His philosopher king would use thugs he called guardians to enforce the will of the legislators on a hapless society divided into classes. Plato's philosopher/king together with legislators and guardians would determine what the classes would be and who would belong to which class. The class you belonged to would determine every aspect of your life.

But Secular Humanism is older than Plato. It is older than anything written which is still in existence. "What has been will be again, what has been done will be done again; there is nothing new under the sun. " (Ecclesiastes 1:9, NIV). Contrary to scientific facts, the modern version of the religion of Secular Humanism believes that a simple, chaotic universe evolved into a complex, ordered universe. To oversimplify, everything came from nothing. Secular Humanists deny that they are a religion for the express purpose of attacking all other religions, collecting tax money and obtaining political power. They also deny that same political power to anyone who disagrees with them. As no two Christians, Jews, Taoists, etc. believe exactly the same way, so no two Secular Humanists believe the same thing. Despite their differences, Secular Humanists hold many beliefs in common.

People who hold beliefs in common can be labeled by those common beliefs. For example, the *Niagara Bible Conference* is where the term Fundamentalism first began to be used. The term was also used to describe "The Fundamentals," a collection of twelve books funded by Milton and Lyman Stewart. These men collected as many addresses of Christian teachers, preachers and other leaders as they could find. They published the books and sent them to these addresses over a period of time ending around 1910. This group of beliefs became known as Fundamentalism.

Fundamentalists defined their beliefs so clearly that anyone willing to be called a Fundamentalist told others something about what they believe.[17] The term Fundamentalist, however, applies to every aspect of life. A football coach who emphasizes the basics of blocking and tackling as opposed to trick plays or a wide open offence like the West Coast offence is known as a Fundamentalist. An architect who designs simple, inexpensive buildings using the basics of engineering is a Fundamentalist. And a believer in the following list of fundamentals for Secular Humanism makes a person a Fundamentalist in Secular Humanism.

The Fundamentals of Secular Humanism

1. Secular Humanism is a religion based on feelings and emotion, not reason.

2. Secular Humanism denies anything non-material. Anything spiritual is redefined as "energy." Various humanists use terms such as "Life Energy," "Life-Force," "Interdimensional Energy," etc. The source of the energy is always material or natural, not supernatural.

3. Secular Humanism denies the existence of a supreme being including Intelligent Design.

4. While acknowledging the existence of evil it denies the concept of original sin. It believes in the perfectibility of man.

5. Though Secular Humanism is open to things not yet discovered, at this time there is no scientific evidence for life after death.

6. Man's existence on the Earth, like everything else in the universe, is a result of chance and not a plan. The most likely explanation for this chance is evolution, which is based on uniformitarianism.

7. Secular Humanism demands that science include only what is within the scope of "natural law " but does not allow for any explanation for the origin of natural law, and therefore the origins of matter or energy; nor is there any reliable information on a possible end to the universe.

8. Only secular humanist beliefs are reasonable; all other religions raise false hopes, restrict personal fulfillment, or both.

9. The purpose of life is to make you a better person. This is accomplished by service to others and seeking fulfillment in this life. Though each person might have a different concept of fulfillment, no one has the right to tell another person that what he is doing is wrong, unless

it harms someone else. This is especially true with sexual gratification.

10. The accumulated improvements of many individuals will drive the evolution of the human race.

11. The best way for society to survive and thrive is to allow enlightened leaders complete freedom to guide all institutions and organizations that serve all people from the beginning to the end of life.

12. Man exists only as a member of the world community. The world community is responsible to provide for the protection and guidance of the enlightened society from the earliest age. Children must not be separated from the world community. Any persons of majority age who oppose the ideals of the world community must be forced into conformity through employment sanctions or reeducation. Opposition must be suppressed by any necessary means.

13. Improvement of society is the essential duty of the enlightened guardians and includes guidance to prevent nonproductive, undesirable or inferior types.

14. Enlightened leaders guide others to fulfillment in this life. The community chooses the values of these enlightened leaders. The enlightened leaders help to guide the community in developing their values system.

15. Compulsory education indoctrinates the citizen of the world community. It is the catechism of the new society.

16. Personal property is evil. This includes any type of marriage since marriage is a property arrangement. Since Secular Humanists recognize evil, it is the responsibility of the guardians to supervise the distribution of material possessions, including social contracts. Individuals corrupt material possessions by unnecessarily hoarding them.

17. National sovereignty is the cause of war, poverty, overpopulation, and waste or destruction of resources. A unified world government is essential to stable economics and freedom in the areas of communication, travel, arts, sciences and education.

18. Unity means eradication of opposition. Secular Humanists characterize anyone who differs from them on these fundamentals as opponents. Opponents are characterized as being oppressive, divisive, fearful of change, bigoted or guilty of hatred.

Some of these items may seem extreme, even to those who claim to be humanists. Some will protest, "I don't believe that!" As was said before, not all humanists believe all these points exactly in these words. The position of the Secular Humanists has been evolving over millennia, not just centuries, and in the next chapters some surprising adherents will come to light. Prepare to hear from people who lived in times when they could see and touch the gods the state demanded they worship, yet their words produced the echoes secularists proclaim today as "new ideas for new times. " Look for parallels of these "modern " beliefs in the words of ancient writers who were required by law to believe in the gods of Sumeria, Babylonia, Egypt, India, Meso-America, Greece and Rome. They still spoke clearly about how they had already forged their own beliefs with man as his own prophet, priest and object of worship. Moving closer to modern times, hundreds of well-known humanists will make it clear that those who are influencing every aspect of our culture have believed these concepts for centuries and do, in fact, believe them and work for their realization today.

4. Comments on *Segraves vs. State of California,* 1981

from *Antidisestablishmentarianism,* Chapter 9, How Was Secular Humanism Established?

Segraves vs. State of California, 1981, took up the case of a man who sued because he said his children's free exercise rights were being violated by the teaching of evolution in the schools. California had a provision of accommodation that included the following:

> *The anti-dogmatism policy provided that class discussions of origins should emphasize that scientific explanations focus on "how," not "ultimate cause," and that any speculative statements concerning origins, both in texts and in classes, should be presented conditionally, not dogmatically.*
>
> *Now, when you begin to think of textbooks that talk about belief, now to me belief is not a scientific word. One knows, one accumulates data, one has a comprehension of, one understands, one does a lot of things, but to me belief always, in my situation, has been something I associate with my theology. I would not like to see my theology and my science get mixed. I have never dealt with a scientific process where somebody says, 'I believe.' I have dealt with theological processes where one believes. In short, I think at that point you begin to mix epistemologies, and that's confusing.*

The judge seems to have forgotten his historic jurisprudence, because belief is a legal term. It's like a jury examining evidence on a case and reaching a verdict. It's not even primarily a religious term, and it applies to Science as well as law when properly defined. There's no question that Evolution is a belief by the judge's definition, dealing in more presuppositions and theories than facts. And it certainly can become confusing when it gets mixed up with Science.

Court case source: *Segraves v. California* (1981) Sacramento Superior Court #278978) excerpts from the personal website built by Frank Fire.

5. Evidences of a Young Earth

14. What Does The Scientific Evidence Prove?

Integrity without knowledge is weak and useless, and knowledge without integrity is dangerous and dreadful.
Samuel Johnson

Image shows Samuel Johnson, a space background, and a microscope. The Johnson quote included is in the text that follows.

14. What Does The Scientific Evidence Prove?

"I am quite conscious that my speculations run quite beyond the bounds of true science."
Charles Darwin[1]

"Facts are stubborn things; and whatever may be our wishes, our inclinations, or the dictates of our passion, they cannot alter the state of facts and evidence."
John Adams[2]

"In the space of one hundred and seventy-six years the Mississippi has shortened itself two hundred and forty-two miles. Therefore ... in the Old Silurian Period the Mississippi River was upward of one million three hundred thousand miles long ... seven hundred and forty-two years from now the Mississippi will be only a mile and three-quarters long. ... There is something fascinating about science. One gets such wholesale returns of conjecture out of such a trifling investment of fact."
Mark Twain[3]

Samuel Johnson said, "Integrity without knowledge is weak and useless, and knowledge without integrity is dangerous and dreadful."[4] Christians often believe that science is an enemy. They think this way because most who use the word "science" have completely abandoned Johnson's demand that integrity go hand-in-hand with knowledge. Uniformitarians replace truth with selective evidence which supports preconceived conclusions. Christians should neither develop an antagonism toward true science, nor should they ignore the very real contributions of true science. True scientists should not ignore the very real foundation of science in Christianity. Dennis Prager, author, columnist, radio show host and historian, laments the unthinking reliance on pseudo-science in today's society.

"In much of the West, the well-educated have been taught to believe they can know nothing and they can draw no independent conclusions about truth, unless

they cite a study and 'experts' have affirmed it. 'Studies show' is to the modern secular college graduate what 'Scripture says' is to the religious fundamentalist."[5]

"I am quite conscious that my speculations run beyond the bounds of true science."
Charles Darwin

"Facts are stubborn things; and whatever may be our wishes, our inclinations, or the dictates of our passion, they cannot alter the state of facts and evidence."
John Adams

"In the space of one hundred and seventy-six years the Mississippi has shortened two hundred and forty-two miles. In the Old Silurian Period [it] was one million three hundred thousand miles long. [In]Seven hundred and forty- two years [it] will be only 1 and 3/4 miles long. There is something fascinating about science. One gets such wholesale returns of conjecture out of such a trifling investment of fact.
Mark Twain

illustration includes images of Charles Darwin, John Adams, and Mark Twain with quotes included in the text on the previous page.

In everyday life, probably the greatest area of conflict between Christianity and those who misuse the word science is moral relativism. This came about because of the dishonest use of the word relativity. The theories of relativity (special and general) neither support nor have any reference to moral relativism. The similarity in the sound of the words is simply a propaganda technique. Neither do the moral absolutes of the Word of God belittle true science. However, since the established religion of Secular Humanism teaches just the opposite, the following list of scientific facts can help us understand that true science can only be explained by the world as described in the Bible. None of these scientific facts prove the Bible. Each does prove the religious belief in deep time to be a scientific impossibility.

Sun Energy Source

Until shortly after WWII, the majority of scientists believed the sun shrank by an average of .01 percent per year. They concluded, based on 400 years' worth of scientific observations, that this was proof that the sun was powered by gravitational collapse. In the late 1800s the Kelvin-Helmholtz Contraction Theory was developed to explain both the observed contraction and how the sun was powered.[6]

In the 1930s religious Secular Humanists, understanding the consequences of this theory, proposed nuclear fusion as the energy source for the sun. In 1928 George Gamow published a paper proposing a theory. The Gamow theory included what came to be known as the Gamow factor.[7] This was the first serious step toward the idea that stars are powered by nuclear fusion. General acceptance was slow. Gamow's ideas were further explored in the 1930s. This exploration grew into Hans Bethe's theory of Stellar Nucleosynthesis.[8] Bethe won a Nobel Prize for this work in 1967. The detonation of the atomic bombs actually did more to convince people than the theoretical papers. According to the Kelvin-Helmoltz

Contraction Theory, with gravitational collapse powering the sun, the sun would have been so large and hot around 50,000 years ago that it would have boiled all the water out of all the oceans on the earth. A mere million years ago the orbit of the earth would have been inside the sun.[9]

These are not just creationist rantings. While we might disagree about the exact numbers, there is no questioning the basic principle. Here are the words of very committed uniformitarians.

"But Kelvin-Helmholtz contraction cannot be the major source of the Sun's energy today. If it were, the Sun would have had to be much larger in the relatively recent past. Helmholtz's own calculations showed that the Sun could have started its initial collapse from the solar nebula no more than about 2.5 million years ago. But the geological and fossil record shows that the earth is far older than that, and so the Sun must be as well. Hence, this model of a Sun that shines because it shrinks cannot be correct."[10]

Why is the Kelvin-Helmholtz contraction incorrect? Because they *believe* "that the earth is far older than that."

Secularists' religious belief that life on earth has existed for billions of years required the sun to be billions of years old. So they eagerly accepted that the sun was powered by nuclear fusion. It is also true that the sun's surface is not static, as is the case with water, rock, or ice on a planet's surface, so a consistent measurement of the sun's diameter is not possible. Two different measurements on the same day might yield different diameters because of massive fluctuations on the sun.

The sun's life cycle in this theory would be 9.2 billion years. At 4.6 billion years the sun would be roughly half way through its life cycle. The problem with this theory is that the sun would have been too cool; forty percent of its present brightness, 4.6 billion years ago, and the earth would have been a frozen wasteland. This is also known as the early faint sun paradox.

"While the early faint Sun paradox does not tell us that the Solar System is only thousands of years old, it does seem to rule out the age being billions of years."
Dr. Danny R. Faulkner

Image of sun with flares and quote by Dr. Danny R. Faulkner "While the early faint Sun paradox does not tell us that the Solar System is only thousands of years old, it does seem to rule out the age being billions of years." from "The Young Faint Sun Paradox and the Age of the Solar System." Acts & Facts. 27 (6).

Project *SOHO*, launched in 1995, has provided us with more information about the sun. Unwilling to change their belief about the age of the sun and life on earth, some Secular Humanists now believe that the sun is powered by a perfect balance of different types of nuclear fusion combined with gravitational collapse, which has produced a uniform temperature for life on earth for the last 4.6 billion years. The best way to describe this kind of balance is "miraculous."[11]

NASA's Solar Dynamics Observatory Satellite, or SDO, was launched in February 2010 and chief scientist Dean Pesnell said it has already reshaped our theories of how the star works.[12]

ScienceBlogs.com contributor Ethan Siegal, PhD in theoretical astrophysics at the University of Florida, writes a blog called "Starts with a Bang." In a post titled, "How the Sun works, from the inside out", originally written August 12, 2011 he has included crossed out and updated information, indicating how rapidly information changes. Theories about the sun must be changed, updated, and corrected to match the most up-to-date information.[13]

Many who insist on billions of years agree that 4.6 billion years is just a rough estimate. They explain that the 9.2 billion year figure is correct, but that they simply are not certain how far our sun is into its 9.2 billion year lifecycle. With such rapid changes in information, how is it possible to state dogmatically that the sun has a lifespan of 9.2 billion years?

Radiohalos and Radiometric Dating

The 4.6 billion year figure comes from radiometric dating. The most common radiohalos are found in zircons. Zircons are found all over the earth and range in size from microscopic to the size of rocks. Zircons are crystals of zirconium silicate. Zircons can be of gemstone quality and large zircons are often used as substitutes for diamonds (cubic zirconia is a close man-made synthetic). Most zircons, however, are around the size of very small grains of sand. Though the wide range of impurities creates an enormous variety of zircons, the most important geological use for zircons is radiometric dating. Zircons contain trace amounts of uranium and thorium. Tiny zircons are sliced open to examine fission tracks produced by decaying uranium. These fission tracks and the U→Pb (Uranium to lead) methods of radiometric dating have dated zircons as old as 4.404 billion years.[14] This means, according to uniformitarian assumptions, that the original crystal formation of these tested zircon samples occurred 4.404 billion years ago. As with all radiometric samples, there is no scientific way of knowing the original condition of the sample tested.

The same zircons also contain helium, which provides another dating method. Helium retention rates in these zircons have a date range beginning as young as 4000 years.[14] While there are a tremendous number of articles attacking this datc as too young, most of thcsc articlcs read like tabloids reporting on British royalty, not honest science. A true scientist would look for an explanation that accounted for both the uranium radiohalos and helium retention. It is far easier to come up with an explanation for the radiohalos' presence if the rocks have a young age. It is nearly impossible to explain the retained helium if the rocks are ancient. One possible explanation for young radiohalos is that they were created at the same time the earth was created.

Another possible answer is that a massive thermonuclear event such as the sun exploding and losing an outer layer sent thermonuclear radiation through the entire planet. Since such an event would have destroyed all nonaquatic life on earth, this would have happened around 2350 BC, at the time of the flood.

Whatever the trigger, the most likely scenario is accelerated nuclear decay during the flood. The accelerated nuclear decay during the flood is the only explanation we are aware of which properly balances all the existing evidence.

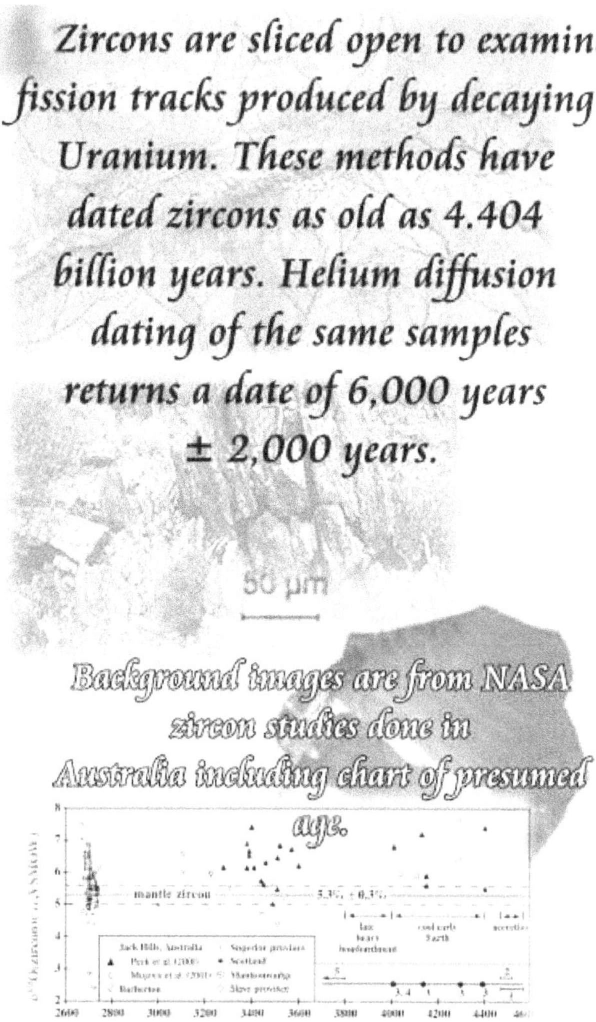

Zircons are sliced open to examine fission tracks produced by decaying Uranium. These methods have dated zircons as old as 4.404 billion years. Helium diffusion dating of the same samples returns a date of 6,000 years ± 2,000 years.

50 μm

Background images are from NASA zircon studies done in Australia including chart of presumed age.

mantle zircon

*The graphic shows NASA zircon study images done in Australia including chart of presumed age. Tiny zircons are sliced open to examine fission tracks produced by decaying uranium. These fission tracks and the U*Pb (Uranium to lead) methods of radiometric dating have dated zircons as old as 4.404 billion years.*

Dating Rock Formations

Travel anywhere and you will see signs proclaiming various rocks or layers of rocks to be millions or even billions of years old. "The Little Willow Formation consists primarily of contorted quartz schist and gneiss; at 1.7 billion years old, it is the oldest rock in the Salt Lake City area."[15] This religious belief in the myth of great ages is proclaimed in textbooks, school classrooms, museums, and, most importantly, by employers, who will either refuse to hire or actually fire anyone who refuses to openly support this religious myth. Though many supposed scientific facts are used to support these dates, radiometric dating is the foundation for all dating methods.[16]

Since fossils have no direct methods of dating, such as radiometric dating, how is the age of a particular fossil determined? It is compared to other fossils of a "known" age or it is dated according to strata where it was found. How is the age of the other fossils or the strata determined? The usual answer is more fossils of a "known" age or strata of a "known" age. This circular reasoning is standard textbook content. Radiometric dating is the only dating method that does not rely on a comparison with something else already dated. Radiometric dating is not valid on fossils. Radiometric dating must be used on the rocks in the surrounding strata.

Every form of radiometric dating always depends on an unstable radioactive isotope deteriorating (decaying) to a stable isotope at a known, stable rate. K*Ar (Potassium to Argon) and U*Pb (235U to Lead) are just two examples of isotopes used as radiometric clocks. All radioactive isotopes used as radiometric clocks work the same way. A sample is taken and analyzed. The result is always a ratio of radioactive isotope to the stable final element. The ratio can be found on a chart because the rate of decay is stable, that is, unaffected by any known outside influence.

The graphic says, "Wherever modern man travels on planet earth, people have erected signs proclaiming various rocks or

layers of rocks to be millions or even billions of years old." It includes photos by the authors of rock layers and roadside educational sites depiction formation age suppositions.

Everyone who uses radioactive isotopes as clocks must, however, rely on three invalid religious assumptions. The first is the unscientific religious leap of faith that the sample being tested had no daughter material when it was formed. For radiometric clocks to work, it is an absolutely essential scientific necessity to know the original condition of the sample. If the original condition of the sample is less than one hundred percent radioactive, then the date is less than the published date. These widely publicized dates, however, assume that the tested sample began its existence (at the time it was formed) one hundred per cent radioactive with no daughter element present. In reality, the only scientific information we learn from these radiometric tests is the current ratio of radioactive material to nonradioactive material. The published dates are always the upper possible date of a range of possible dates.

The second assumption is that nothing contaminated the sample during its existence. It is impossible to know the conditions of the sample during its existence. Simply to assume that contamination never occurred is not science. It is especially bad science when the very people claiming the accuracy of radiometric dating also claim that the earth underwent a series of what they call extinction events which catastrophically changed the surface of the earth.

The third assumption is that nothing changed the decay rate. While the second assumption is something changed the individual sample or the immediate environment of the sample, this assumption is worldwide or throughout the universe. In other words, is the present really the key to the past? How can we know that?

If there was a sample with a known date, other samples could be calibrated against it. Not only do such calibration samples not exist, without a time machine to go back in time and obtain a calibration sample, it is not possible to have a calibration sample. With very few exceptions, the published dates of tens of thousands to billions of years are based purely on mythological religious assumptions.

There are a few exceptions, however. Thermoluminescence is used to date pottery. Thermoluminescence is based on the time the pottery was fired, a known event. ^{14}C is another one of these exceptions. The radioactive isotope ^{14}C is integrated into the tissue of living organisms throughout the lifetime of that organism. At the time of death that amount of ^{14}C becomes a fixed amount and begins to radioactively decay into ^{14}N. That amount of ^{14}C at the time of death is equal to the amount of ^{14}C in the atmosphere at the time of death. The ratio of ^{14}C in the sample tested at the time of death compared to the assumed amount of ^{14}C in the atmosphere at the time of death should be an almost perfect radiometric clock. However, certain conditions can alter that ratio. If the ratio is in some way tampered with, that tampering is normally leaching. That particular sample will then test to be older than it really is. ^{14}C dates older than 1000 B.C. also assume atmospheric amounts of ^{14}C and absorption rates of ^{14}C similar to current absorption rates. That is almost certainly an invalid assumption, making many, if not all ^{14}C dates for items dated older than 1000 B.C. older than they actually are.

Finally, radiometric dating never gives an absolute date. It only tells us the upper limit of a range of possible dates. One of the most important but rarely published conclusions by secularists about ^{14}C dating is that even they admit that after approximately 60,000 years, the remaining ^{14}C is such a small amount that it is difficult to test for it. They have also concluded that ^{14}C disappears entirely after a little more than 100,000 years. Though fossils which are pronounced older than 100,000 years are rarely tested for ^{14}C, those few which have been tested usually have some trace of ^{14}C.

"Carbon-14 (^{14}C) dating of multiple samples of bone from 8 dinosaurs from Texas, Alaska, Colorado, and Montana revealed that they are only 22,000 to 39,000 years old."

"After the AOGS-AGU conference in Singapore, the abstract was removed from the conference website by two chairmen because they could not accept the findings. Unwilling to challenge the data openly, they erased the report from public view without a word to the authors or even to the AOGS officers, until after an investigation. It won't be restored.

The researchers presented their findings at the 2012 Western Pacific Geophysics Meeting in Singapore, August 13-17, a conference of the American Geophysical Union (AGU) and the Asia Oceania Geosciences Society (AOGS)."[17]

Lunar Recession

"Scotty, I need power now!" pleads a desperate Captain Kirk, on *Star Trek* the original series, only to hear his Chief Engineer reply, "He's turned the engines off. Completely cold. Thirty minutes to startup. I canna change the laws of physics, Captain!" The only hope of pulling out of a decaying orbit and saving the *Enterprise* is a restart of her engines.

Why? The Earth is surrounded by nonpowered satellites. Why does the *Enterprise* need power? The *Enterprise* needs to remain in a slow orbit as near the planet as possible while maintaining a fixed point over it. The only way to accomplish that is to keep the engines powered up to constantly change the orbit and counter the pull of gravity. The closer a satellite is to the object it is orbiting, the faster it has to travel to maintain a stable orbit without engine power. Mercury is the fastest-traveling planet orbiting the sun. Venus, Earth and Mars are all progressively slower at their greater distances.

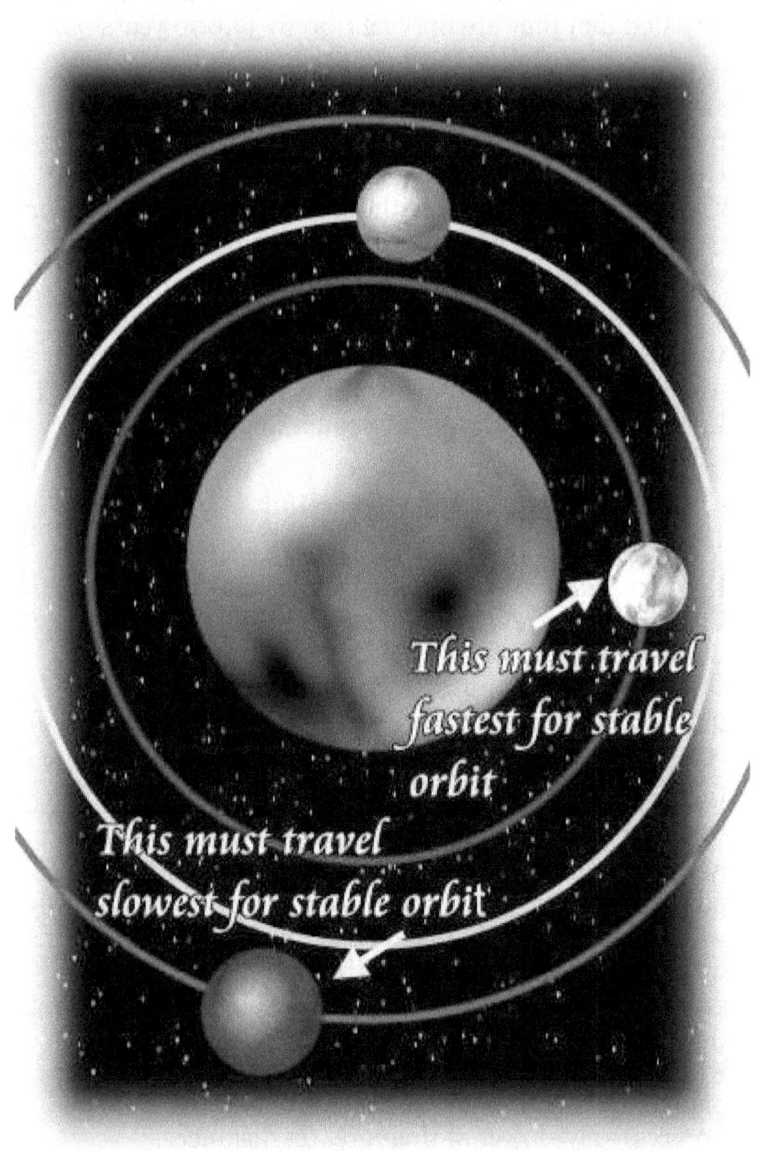
This must travel
fastest for stable
orbit
This must travel
slowest for stable orbit

Graphic shows relative orbits and speeds of satellites around a larger body in space.

For a given velocity there is only one stable orbit around (distance from) a planet (or sun). The closer the satellite (or starship) is to the object it is orbiting, the faster it needs to travel (without power or thrust). Otherwise it needs power (thrust) to maintain the orbit.

All orbiting objects have one of three types of orbits.

1) The orbit is a decaying orbit (being pulled into the planet),

2) A stable orbit (no change in orbit over time) or

3) A receding orbit (moving away from the planet).

The closer the satellite (or starship) is to the object it is orbiting, the faster it must travel or the more power (thrust) it must use to counteract the attraction of gravity.

The laser reflectors left by the Apollo missions on the lunar surface have been hit with lasers from earth many times. It proves the moon is moving away from the earth at a rate of about 1.5 inches per year.[18] Assuming the Moon has not changed mass, velocity or direction of orbit, sometime in the past it would have possessed a stable orbit closer to the Earth. Even closer to the earth, inside that stable orbit, the moon's orbit with no change in mass, velocity, or orbital direction, would have decayed.

The important point is the stable or equilibrium orbit.

At the current rate of recession, the moon is receding from the earth at a rate of approximately one mile every 42,240 years. If the Moon were to remain unchanged in mass, velocity and rate of recession, just over 42 million years ago, the moon would be more than one thousand miles closer to the earth. With no change in its mass and velocity, in far less than 42 million years the moon's orbit would be a decaying orbit, not a receding orbit. The moon would be drawing closer to the Earth and not moving away from the earth as it is now. Just like the *Enterprise,* the moon would have a decaying orbit.

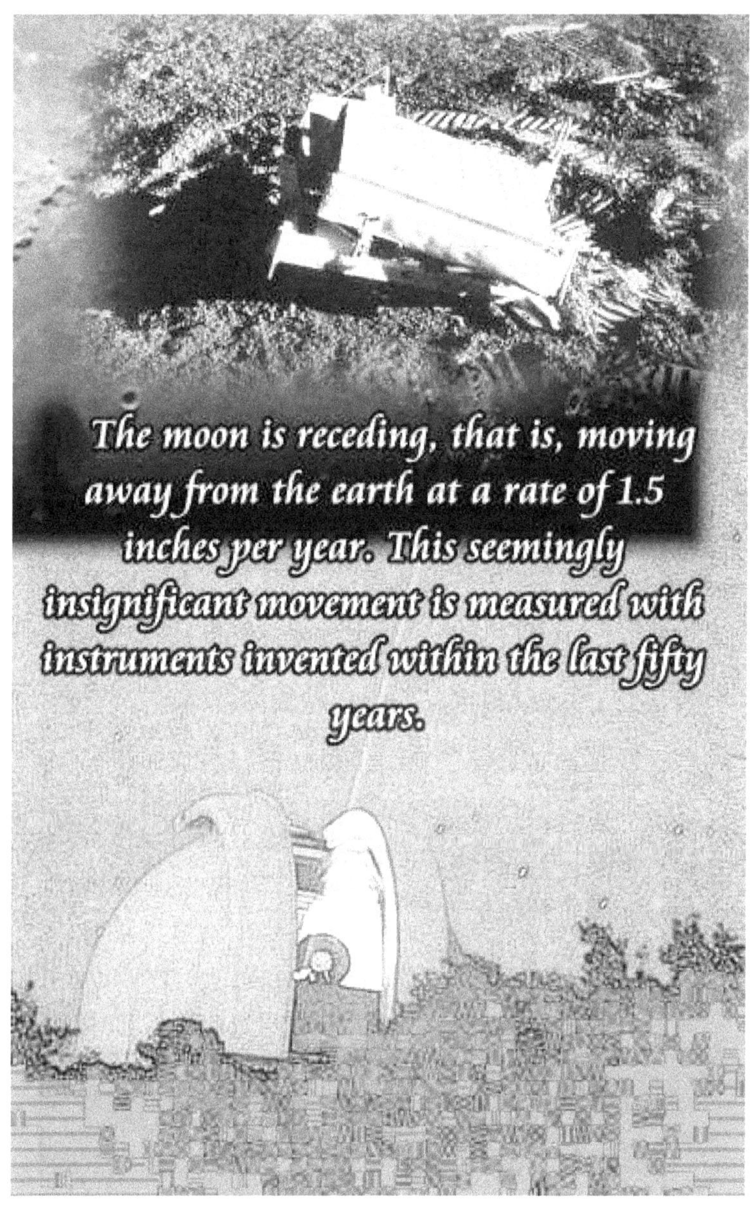

Image shows equipment for measuring the moon's recession. "The moon is receding, that is, moving away from the earth at a rate of 1.5 inches per year. This seemingly insignificant

movement is measured with instruments invented within the last fifty years.

Since the lunar orbit is receding, not decaying, it means that the existing lunar orbit is, geologically speaking, very young. If you reject the conclusion that this indicates a recent creation, you are left with only two choices:

1) The Moon is a very recent addition to the Earth or

2) Some sort of catastrophe has relatively recently altered the Moon's orbit. This catastrophe would have required far more energy than what could be produced by the simultaneous detonation of all the nuclear weapons on Earth.

That catastrophic event would have occurred quite recently, even according to uniformitarians. Any catastrophe powerful enough to alter the moon's orbit would also have catastrophically affected the Earth as well.

Geomagnetic Field Decay

The earth's magnetic field seems to have a half-life of around 1400 years. Assuming that to be correct, just 11,200 years ago the earth's magnetic field would have been 256 times stronger than it is now. 14,000 years ago the earth's magnetic field would have been 1024 times stronger than it is now. That would make animal life impossible.[19]

Dr. Russell Humphreys has continued to work in this field. He believes that a strict linear half-life is unlikely and concludes his article with the following: "These ideas weigh heavily against the idea that there is currently a "dynamo" process at work in the core that would ultimately restore the lost energy back to the field. Without such a restoration mechanism, the field can only have a limited lifetime, in the thousands of years. So the clarity of this new fit, especially the exponential part, is further evidence that the earth's magnetic field is young."[20]

The *dynamo process* Dr. Humphreys references is the theory that instead of continually decaying, earth's magnetic field is continually rebuilding or restoring itself. Its existence would make the entire life cycle of the earth's magnetic field much more stable and therefore much, much older.

Many articles purport to "debunk" these observations. They usually begin with personal attacks on the original authors. Even if the "debunkers" are correct that the half-life of the earth's magnetic field is longer than 1,400 years, for life to exist hundreds of millions years ago, the half-life must be hundreds of times larger. Instead of making personal attacks, detractors should present data supporting a much longer half-life. Instead, they use data based on the presupposition that the earth is millions of years old to insist that the earth's magnetic field must have a large half-life.

An excellent response to these uniformitarian proposals is Jonathan Sarfati's article, *The Earth's Magnetic Field: Evidence That the Earth Is Young*. After including many detailed examples, it concludes, "The clear decay pattern shows the earth could not be older than about 10,000 years."[21]

A key element of the decay of the earth's magnetic field is the evidence of magnetic field reversals found in cooled lava flows. "Lava flows in Nevada's Sheep Creek Range may have preserved evidence that the planet's magnetic field rapidly changed direction." Other evidence in the paleomagnetic lava flow at Steens Mountain in Oregon shows that the earth's magnetic field reversed its polarity in just over two weeks. This is in line with a magnetic field half-life of 1,400 years, but entirely unexplainable with a magnetic field hundreds of millions or billions of years old. Also, the sun reverses the polarity of its magnetic field every eleven years. [22]

The earth's magnetic field has a half-life of 1,400 years. Just 14,000 years ago the earth's magnetic field would have been ten times stronger than it is now. 1.4 million years ago the earth's magnetic field would have been 1,000 times stronger than it is now. That would make animal life impossible.

"The earth's magnetic field has a half-life of 1,400 years. 14,000 years ago the earth's magnetic field would have been 1,000 times stronger than it is now. That would make animal

life impossible." Image also shows Paleomagnetic lava flow at Steens Mountain in Oregon.

Mount Saint Helens Canyon Formation

Though the eruption of this volcano was observed by millions via television, internet and print media, few are aware of the significance. It carved another "Little Grand Canyon" similar to the Grand Canyon in Arizona in days or perhaps only hours. Millions witnessed this event. We saw it happening live or on video in real time. To those who understand, the evidence is so overwhelming that even some evolutionists are admitting it, though quite grudgingly. They still believe, without any evidence, that the catastrophe creating most other prominent geologic sites happened millions of years ago. But the evidence has forced them to admit that the Grand Canyon's formation was rapid, created with massive amounts of water.[23]

"The Eruption of Mt. Saint Helens also carved another 'Little Grand Canyon' similar to the Grand Canyon in days or perhaps only hours." Image shows Mt. St. Helens' canyon formation.

Varves

Image shows an example of Varves with a Paint brush placed to show scale. Photo Information/Credit[24]

Mount Saint Helens produced more scientifically observable evidence, in the form of something remarkably like varves. According to most dictionaries, a varve is a layer of alternating fine and course (light and dark) silt at the bottom of a pond or lake. Counting varves used to be considered a very important method of dating. Each layer has two parts, one lighter and the other darker. One part is the time of year when water moves quickly and brings many deposits. The other part is the time of year when water is stationary, perhaps even stagnant, such as the winter when the lake is covered in ice. All honest scientists admit that there might be more than one varve per year. A core sample, which counts varves to determine the age of a lake, might give a date older than the actual date. The assumption that conditions in the past were similar to the present is an assumption that the difference in dates is slight. Though the varve count might be slightly older than the actual date, it is yon in Arizona in days or perhaps only hours still assumed to be reliable.

The eruption of Mt. St. Helens discredited the use of varves as a dating method (based on the assumption that one mud/silt layer equals one year). Ash and mud sandwiched together in thin light and dark layers, just like varves, accumulated up to twenty-five feet thick with thousands of layers and within hours, perhaps only minutes.

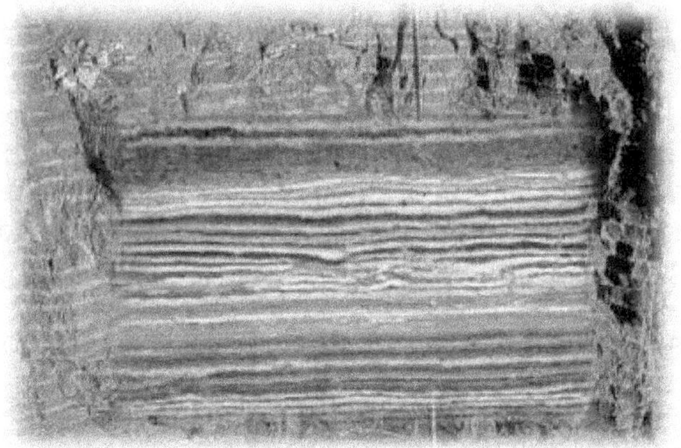

The eruption of Mt. St. Helens discredited the use of varves as a dating method (based on the assumption that one mud/silt layer equals one year). Ash and mud sandwiched together in thin light and dark layers, just like varves, accumulated up to 25 feet thick with thousands of layers and within hours, perhaps only minutes. Image shows examples of these layers.

The eruption of Mount St. Helens on May 18, 1980 scientifically proved that assumption to be in error. Ash and mud up to twenty-five feet thick with thousands of layers filled the region. Though these layers are never called varves, they display the same characteristics as varves, a thin light and dark layer sandwiched together. These thousands of layers, put down in a matter of hours, perhaps minutes, completely discredit the concept of using layers for dating. People who use varves for dating never acknowledge or even mention this.[25]

Lake Titicaca

Catastrophes change the shape of the land where they occur forever. Few places have been changed more dramatically than Lake Titicaca. It rises 12,500 feet (3,800 meters) above sea level in South America between Bolivia and Peru. Fresh water rivers and streams feed the lake now, but the salt content is about five-and-a-half parts per thousand, classifying the lake as brackish. No current conditions explain the salt content of the lake. The most likely explanation is that Lake Titicaca was once at or below sea level and that a catastrophic uplift moved a lake full of seawater almost two and a half miles above sea level. Marine fossils are preserved around the lake. The current salt level of Lake Titicaca is about fifteen percent of the Pacific Ocean off Peru, where the Pacific Ocean varies from 34 to 37 parts per thousand.

"In the heart of the Andes ... is Lake Titicaca." [Its saltiness and the present fauna (It contains sea horses)] strongly suggested that the present fauna of Lake Titicaca has survived from a time when the lake communicated directly with [was connected to] the ocean."[26]

Theories other than uplift have been postulated. These theories, however, require completely speculative processes that have never been observed. That is not a scientific process. Some evolutionists believe the uplift theory because the scientific evidence is so overwhelming, but say that the catastrophe occurred millions of years ago. A past waterline is slanted in relation to the current waterline.

A catastrophic upthrust during the time of civilized habitation is the only explanation for the presence of a former seaport city and corn terraces up to 17,000 feet surrounding Lake Titicaca, which is situated 12,500 feet above sea level.

"A catastrophic upthrust during the time of civilized habitation is the only explanation for the presence of a former seaport city and corn terraces up to 17,000 feet *surrounding Lake Titicaca, which is situated 12,500 feet above sea level." Image shows the lake and corn terraces.*

At one time Lake Titicaca had more water than it does now, and this waterline is much higher at one end of the lake, proving that a catastrophe tipped the lake in the past.

"The strandline [near Lake Titicaca] was carefully surveyed for a length of about 375 miles [603 km]. And then it was established that it is not 'straight.' ... Its level showed a slant of a most peculiar character in relation to the present ocean-level, or, which amounts to the same, relative to the present level of Lake Titicaca."[27]

Past irrigation and buildings in and around the lake prove an ancient civilization built the port city of Tiahuanaco. It is approximately 800 feet higher than the current lake surface. Tiahuanaco was a harbor, but is now twelve miles south of the lake, and the ship berths are of a size most likely built for ocean-going vessels. The lake "is large, 3,261 square miles. It contains sea horses, suggesting that this region or its water were once below sea level. On the mountain sides ... are terraces of ancient corn fields going up to 17,000 feet. Yet corn will not germinate [sprout] above 11,500 feet!"[20] There is also a building beneath the lake, about 660 feet long, with a road running to it and roads and steps leading down into deeper water. It is twice the size of a modern soccer field and modern archaeologists believe it to be a temple.[28]

Himalayan Yellow Band Ammonites

Geological features suddenly and catastrophically created by water can be found all over the world. Near the top of the Himalayan Mountains, reaching up to 29,029 feet (8,848 m) above sea level, is a layer of rock known as the yellow band. This yellow band is filled with marine fossils called ammonites. "Marine fossils are also found high in the Himalayas, the world's tallest mountain range, reaching up to 29,029 feet (8,848 m) above sea level. For example, fossil ammonites (coiled marine cephalopods) are found in limestone beds in the Himalayas of Nepal. All geologists agree that ocean waters must have buried these marine fossils in these limestone beds. "[29] Ammonites are common fossils found all over the earth and are similar to a modern marine creature known as the Nautilus. These fossilized marine creatures lived in oceans, not a freshwater lake. All of the Himalayan mountain chain had to have been under seawater. This many fossilized ammonites were not transported somehow after the mountains were formed. Sometime in the past either the entire Himalayan Mountain chain was five miles lower than it is now or the entire planet had more than twice the water volume than it has now.

"Near the top of many Himalayan mountains, including Everest, is a layer of rock known as the Yellow Band. This yellow band is filled with marine fossils called Ammonites." The image shows fossil ammonites, a modern nautilus,

similar to the extinct sea creatures, and the yellow band on the mountains.

Also, these ammonite fossils are not crushed. They were moved by a catastrophic (sudden) event while the entire layer was plastic (mud). The ammonites had to be protected to keep them from being crushed. The only scientific answer is that the surrounding mud protected them. A slow uplift over a long period of time would have dried out the surrounding mud. Instead of protecting the ammonites, the hardened rock would have ground the ammonites to powder. Since water weighs approximately eight pounds per gallon, the energy necessary to create the Himalayan Mountains was thousands of times greater than all the nuclear weapons in all the nuclear arsenals in every country on earth detonating at the same time.

On a much smaller scale, highway engineers have carved into mountains all over the earth. Thousands of mountains at every possible elevation all over the earth show bent, folded and twisted layers intact without cracks. These layers had to be plastic [mud] when they were put in place. This is the only way these mountains could have formed.

"Thousands of mountains at every possible elevation all over

the earth show bent, folded, and twisted layers intact without cracks." Images by the authors show examples.

Catastrophic Fossil Formation

Fossils like the ammonites of the yellow band were formed in a catastrophic event. Even evolutionists have to admit that. Insects, microbes and weathering combine to destroy everything except bones in less than one hundred years, often in less than a week. Tissue deteriorates too rapidly for fossilization without a catastrophe. The question is: When did this catastrophe occur? Once again, the only available scientific evidence indicates a more recent event. Since fossils were bones, they once contained ^{14}C. If a standard test for ^{14}C discovered any ^{14}C, the tested sample would scientifically prove a date less than 60,000 years old.

Since the religion of Secular Humanism demands that these fossils are millions of years old, and they control both the fossils to be tested and the testing procedures, ^{14}C testing is never done on fossils. There is only the dogmatic assertion that fossils are now stone and there is no carbon to test.

There have been carbon tests on mollusks that indicate a much younger date on certain samples. Without ^{14}C testing, however, there is no scientific dating of fossils, only religious pronouncements.[30]

"Secular Humanists must admit that fossils were formed in a catastrophic event." Examples of fossil beds.

Warm Antarctica

Piri Reis Map

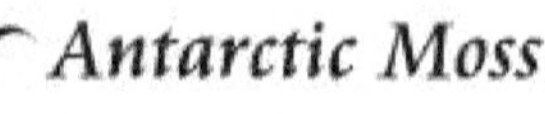

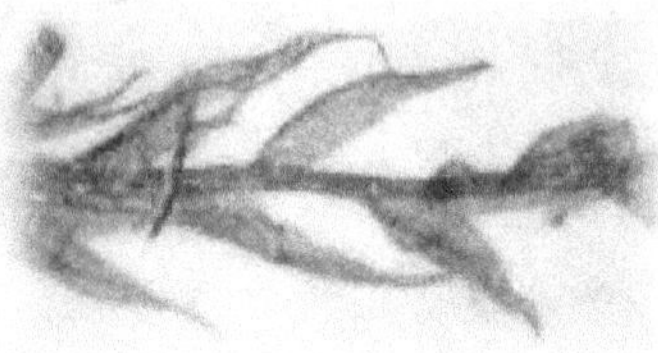

Giant Salamander Fossil

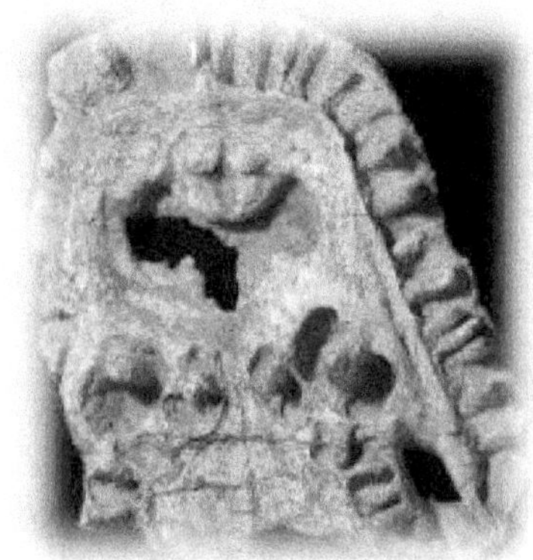

There is abundant evidence that Antarctica was once warm. Warm climate animal and plant fossils abound.

Ice core samples have revealed that many of these fossils are below sea level.

Images are a giant salamander fossil, the Piri Reis Map, and Antarctic moss. Caption says: "There is abundant evidence that Antarctica was once warm. Warm climate animal and plant fossils abound. Ice core samples have revealed that many of these fossils are below sea level."

Antarctica also has a coal bed. Formation of a coal bed requires a massive number of warm climate plants. [31] The question is, why? Possible explanations include that Antarctica was once in a warmer latitude and moved, or that the magnetic poles have shifted (as mentioned earlier), or that the oceans have changed dramatically. The facts are clear. A once warm-climate land mass now lies beneath ice three miles thick in spots. The common thread through all of these explanations is the scientific fact of a catastrophic change. Sadly, instead of completely scientific explanations, supposed scientific and academic articles lead off with dogmatic mythological assertions: “around 40 million years ago,” “millions of years ago,” “40,000 year cycles.”

A catastrophe could turn Antarctica from a warm climate into a frozen wasteland very quickly. The articles describing Antarctica’s past might have much correct scientific data, but these dogmatic mythological foundational assertions make the entire article read like something from a tabloid.

Ice Core Samples and *Glacier Girl*

Researchers annually take core samples of glaciers and massive ice caps such as those covering Antarctica. They count each layer as a single year and publish a date. As with radiometric dating, it is not possible to know the original condition of the ice cap or glacier. However, unlike radiometric dating, starting with a zero condition (no ice, bare ground) is reasonable. Assuming that the earth is older than the glacier or ice cap is also reasonable. So the speed with which a glacier or ice cap forms is critical to an accurate date.

The layers (of annual ice core samples) are counted as if each layer was a single year and a date is published. The speed with which a glacier forms is critical to an accurate date.

A squadron of P-38s made an emergency landing on a glacier in Greenland on July 15, 1942. For 50 years the squadron of planes had flowed with the glacier, being covered with more ice. One plane was buried in 268 feet of ice. The recovered plane was restored and renamed Glacier Girl.

Captions: "The layers (of annual ice core samples) are counted as if each layer was a single year and a date is published. The speed with which a glacier or ice cap forms is critical to an accurate date.

(The second caption on the image is an abbreviated version of the paragraph that follows.)

A squadron of P-38s made an emergency landing on a glacier in Greenland on July 15, 1942. The pilots were rescued and the planes abandoned. On July 15, 1992, the final piece of one P-38 was dug out of the glacier. For 50 years the squadron of planes had flowed with the glacier while being covered with more ice. One plane was pulled out of the glacier more than two miles from the landing point, buried in 268 feet of ice. The recovered plane was restored and renamed *Glacier Girl.*[32]

If the same techniques which boldly pronounce with absolute certainty that core samples are tens of thousands of years old were applied to the ice which covered *Glacier Girl*, then that ice would have to be thousands of years old. Yet the scientific fact is that *Glacier Girl* was covered by 268 feet of ice. It is also a scientific fact that this ice was fifty years old. This particular glacier grew at a rate of almost 5.5 feet per year. At this rate, the thickest ice sheet in the world, Terre Adelie in Antarctica, could be formed in just over 2,500 years. Secular Humanists would insist that different conditions in the past required a much longer formation time. Any change in the conditions could just as easily have resulted in a shorter time for formation.

Besides counting the layers in core samples, methods of dating a glacier include testing the oxygen content of the water, studying the presence of CO_2, finding evidence of radioactive decay, and examining pieces of volcanic material. Fred Hall wrote a brief article, “Ice Cores Not All That Simple,”[33] showing how complicated glaciers really are. None of these methods are entirely reliable. While there have been hundreds, perhaps thousands, of computer and theoretical models developed to explain glacier formation, the only scientific observations are in line with the glacier which covered *Glacier Girl.*

Water Scale

Formations like the Grand Canyon were carved by water action. No one disputes this, but water action is a topic on which scientists can still find points of disagreement.

Bridges built in powerful rivers, especially rivers prone to flood, are often washed away. Engineers building a new bridge over the Mississippi River at Alton, IL, between 1990 and 1994, built a scale model to help prevent that from happening. The scale model they built used real water to examine the direction and amount of force the Mississippi River would exert on the new bridge.

Image of the bridge in Alton, IL described in the article. "Bridges built in powerful rivers, especially rivers prone to flooding, are often washed away. Engineers building a new bridge over the Mississippi River at Alton, IL, between 1990 and 1994, built a scale model to help prevent that from happening. The scale model they built used real water to examine the direction and amount of force the Mississippi River would exert on the new bridge."

Anyone who has watched a movie from the 1950s or earlier has seen the common, at that time, technique of filming a scale model ship in a tank of water. Even with rather large ships, such as the ones used in Ben Hur, the water never looks quite real. The explanation is that water does not scale, that is, large amounts of water look and behave differently than smaller amounts of water. For realistic water, producers and directors had to either build full sized models or wait decades for 3-D animation.

Since water does not scale visually, scale models using water were believed to be inaccurate also. For example, water can cut channels through layers of mud. The resulting canyons look something like a scale model of the Grand Canyon. These models have been dismissed as unrealistic simply because water does not scale. This idea that water does not scale, however, is not always true. Bridges built in powerful rivers, especially rivers prone to flooding, are often washed away. Engineers building a new bridge over the Mississippi River at Alton, IL, between 1990 and 1994, built a scale model to help prevent that from happening. The scale model they built used real water to examine the direction and amount of force the Mississippi River would exert on the new bridge.[34]

Though the water did not "look" to scale, the water flow and pressure information was accurate enough to allow the engineers to see what forces they had to contend with. Because of the model, modifications were made in the bridge's design. These modifications are likely the reason the bridge is still standing today.

Water Salinity

The study of water and its properties gives scientists many ways to learn about the earth. It is also a very much-abused study when it comes to dating the earth. One of the most unusual methods of dating is measuring the salt content of the sea. This method assumes a constant and steady addition of salt to the sea by freshwater rivers and a constant and steady evaporation rate.[35]

One of the most unusual methods of dating is measuring the salt content of the sea. This method assumes a constant and steady addition of salt to the sea by freshwater rivers and a constant and steady evaporation rate.

(Pictured are Computer models of ocean salinity)

Images are computer models of ocean salinity. Caption: "One of the most unusual methods of dating is measuring the salt content of the sea. This method assumes a constant and steady addition of salt to the sea by freshwater rivers and a constant and steady evaporation rate."

While this method is often cited in textbooks as one of many dating methods "proving" an ancient earth, it is fraught with so many difficulties that it has few educated defenders. It is usually referred to as an "additional" or "support" method of dating.

The first major scientific problem with using the salt content of the sea as a dating method is the wide disparity in salt content among the world's bodies of water. The Mediterranean Sea has a much higher salt content than the Atlantic, which has a higher salt content than the Antarctic. Is the Mediterranean older than the rest of the oceans of the world? Are the rivers that flow into the Mediterranean saltier than the rest of the rivers of the world? The scientific answer to both of these questions is either "no" or "we do not know."

People have attempted to date the seas using salt content since at least Sir Isaac Newton's time. Simply measuring the contact of salt requires a date no more than 100 million years old. Drs. "Austin and Humphreys calculated that the ocean must be less than 62 million years old. It's important to stress that this is not the actual age, but a maximum age. That is, this evidence is consistent with any age up to 62 million years, including the biblical age of about 6000 years."[36]

Providence Canyon

Water's power to shape the landscape provides us with another amazing creation in southwest Georgia. Providence Canyon, sometimes called "Georgia's Little Grand Canyon" is 1100 acres of canyons carved out by erosion since the early 1800s.[37] Though much smaller than the Grand Canyon, it is still one of the largest canyons in America. As the model of the Alton, Illinois bridge helped engineers understand the Mississippi River; Providence Canyon helps us understand the Grand Canyon in Arizona. While neither the Alton Bridge nor the Providence Canyon are perfect models, on a small scale they both accurately model the effects of far greater amounts of water.

Providence Canyon in southwest Georgia, sometimes called "Georgia's Little Grand Canyon" is 1100 acres of canyons carved out by erosion since the early 1800s.

Image of Providence Canyon. Caption: "Providence Canyon,

sometimes called 'Georgia's Little Grand Canyon' is 1100 acres of canyons carved out by erosion since the early 1800s.

Though Providence Canyon is smaller than the Grand Canyon, it has many similar features. The formation of Providence is a scientific fact. Since Providence Canyon is less than two hundred years old, there is no scientific reason to believe the Grand Canyon, or any other canyon, must be millions of years old. All that is needed to make a canyon larger than Providence Canyon is more water, not more time.

Arches National Park

Just a few hundred miles north of the Grand Canyon is Arches National Park in Southeast Utah. When the National Park Service took over management of the park in 1971 there were over 2000 natural sandstone arches. Since then many arches have collapsed, the most famous being the collapse of Wall Arch on August 4-5, 2008. Though the exact number of collapsed arches is not documented, if only one arch were to collapse every three years, in less than 675 years there would not be any arches left. There is no evidence that there were ever hundreds of thousands or millions of arches. The evidence indicates that there were never many more arches than we see now. And there is evidence that many arches have fallen since 1971.

The scientific conclusion, based on the scientifically observed collapse of arches, is that either conditions in the recent past were drastically different to preserve the arches or that the arches are much younger than Secular Humanism proclaims them to be. If conditions were similar to the conditions we know now, the arches could be not older than about 4000 years old. They could easily be younger.[38]

Images are Landscape Arch, collapsed in 1991 and Wall Arch, collapsed in 2008. Caption: When the National Park Service

took over management of the park in 1971 there were over 2000 natural sandstone arches.

Stalactites and Stalagmites

The picture was taken in late 1987 at level 5 workings in the lead-zinc mine at Mt Isa, in north-western Queensland, Australia.

Photo taken beneath the Lincoln Memorial in the 1960s

Images of fast-growing modern-formed stalactites in Australia and Washington D.C. Captions: "The picture was taken in late 1987 at level 5 workings in the lead-zinc mine at Mount Isa, in north-western Queensland." "Photo taken beneath the Lincoln Memorial in the 1960s." Photo Credits[40]

Stalactites and stalagmites are another geologic feature formed by water. The Lincoln Memorial was built between 1914 and 1922 over land formerly at the bottom of the Potomac River. Stalactites and stalagmites have formed beneath the stairs in the period since the construction was completed (less than 100 years at the time of this writing) as described below.

"... Supports were driven down almost 100 feet to bedrock. This cavernous foundation provides an ideal location for cave-like formations to actively grow. Water on the surface slowly makes its way down through cement stairs into the empty space below. Cement is 'glued' together by calcium carbonate. As the water passes through the cement, it dissolves some calcium carbonate and carries it downward. When the water reaches the open space, it leaves behind the calcium carbonate, creating stalactites and stalagmites. This is the same way cave stalactites and stalagmites form, only instead of passing through cement stairs, natural cave features usually form when ground water passes through limestone. Since the cave formations at the Lincoln Memorial aren't in an actual cave, maybe we should call them 'under-the-stair-ites'."[40]

Dave E. Matson attempts to claim that all the stalactites and stalagmites in existence could not have formed in less than 5000 years.

"The Bulletin of the National Speleological Society (37: p.21, 1975) gives a stalactite/stalagmite growth rate of ... 0.1 to 10 centimeters per thousand years. An exceptional spurt of growth might exceed ... 10 centimeters or 2.5 inches per thousand years. ...Thus, a 60 foot giant, as might be found in Carlsbad Caverns, would have a minimum estimated age of about 180,000 years."[41]

Timpanogos Cave National Monument, in American Fork, Utah, is described in park literature as being roughly 65 million years old. Although the claim that the stalactites and stalagmites are millions of years old is no longer being made, secularists still demand thousands of years for the formation of these cave features, usually tens or hundreds of thousands, not the less than a hundred necessary in the Lincoln Memorial.

"Water trickling through the limestone overlying the caves dissolved calcite and other minerals from the rock. ...The water deposited its mineral load as tiny crystals on a cave ceiling, wall, or floor. Over thousands of years, as countless crystals were deposited, a variety of cave formations took shape--stalactites, stalagmites, flowstone, helictites, and others." [42]

Julia E. Cole, University of Tucson professor of Geosciences, studied a limestone cave in southern AZ. The article described the cave formations as "natural climate archives" and said, "The stalagmite yielded an almost continuous century-by-century climate record spanning 55,000 to 11,000 years ago. ... Each climate regime lasted from a few hundred years to more than one thousand years."[43] The article's photo shows Sarah Truebe, a geosciences doctoral student, with a cave formation less than 2 feet tall. The cave itself appears to be less than ten feet in height. The use of these cave features as "natural climate archives" is based on utter conjecture and uniformitarian presupposition.

Each of these claims is nothing more than a gratuitous assertion. The evidence shows the formation of these features, especially of stalactites, take only decades.[44]

Diamonds

Diamonds are reported by Secular Humanists to be at least 45 million years old, formed 75 miles or deeper beneath the earth. Yet laboratory-produced diamonds are made commercially. In 1953 the first industrial grade laboratory-produced diamonds were made. These tiny laboratory-produced diamonds were and still are manufactured for industrial applications such as cutting tools and electrical coatings. More advanced processes coat lenses with laboratory-produced diamond. The laboratory produced diamond industry gradually increased the size and quality of laboratory-produced diamonds. In early 2010 a 2-carat laboratory-produced gemstone-quality diamond was produced in about three days.

Russian Diamond Mine

Laboratory-produced diamonds were commercially made in 1953.

The first laboratory-produced diamonds were industrial grade.

Caption: "Laboratory-produced diamonds were commercially made in 1953. The first laboratory-produced diamonds were industrial grade." Images are of diamonds, a Russian diamond mine, and H. Tracy Hall.

The FTC (Federal Trade Commission) requires the label of laboratory-produced, laboratory-manufactured, or for the product to be identified by the name of the manufacturer along with the specific type of gem rather than using the term synthetic when referring to the type of gem. A laboratory-produced diamond is identical to a geologically-produced diamond is every way; chemically, structurally, and appearance, even on the microscopic level.

A synthetic diamond is still a technically correct term when applied to a laboratory-produced diamond, but some vendors use the term "synthetic" diamond to refer to cubic zirconia, cut glass or any other manmade substitute for a diamond. So the FTC wants to distinguish between real diamonds, both geologic and laboratory-produced, and other crystals which are not diamonds. These other crystals which are not diamonds are often marketed as synthetic diamonds, which they are not.

The existence of laboratory-produced diamonds is a scientific fact. They are produced and reproduced under controlled conditions. Depending on color desired, other chemicals can be added to the crystal-growing process and the resulting gemstone can be pink, green, blue, yellow, and colorless (white). The diamond mining industry is concerned about the number of laboratory-produced diamonds being manufactured. Proclaiming the youngest naturally-occurring diamond to be 45 million years old is a dogmatic religious pronouncement contrary to science. The most reasonable scientific theory is that diamonds were formed suddenly under the correct conditions.[45]

The RATE (Radioisotopes and the Age of The Earth) research project at the Institute for Creation Research found Carbon 14 in both natural diamonds and ten US coal beds. The upper range of the possible dates for the diamonds was 55,000 years.[46]

"R.E. Taylor of the Department of Anthropology at the University of California-Riverside and of the Cotsen Institute of Archaeology at the University of California-Los Angeles teamed with J. Southon at the Keck Accelerator Mass Spectrometry Laboratory of the Department of Earth System Science at the University of California-Irvine to analyze nine natural diamonds from Brazil. All nine diamonds are conventionally regarded as being at least of early Paleozoic age, that is, at least several hundred million years old. So if they really are that old they should not have any intrinsic ^{14}C in them. Eight of the diamonds yielded radiocarbon 'ages' of 64,900 years to 80,000 years."[46]

Coal and Oil

Carbon can be turned into diamonds, coal and oil. Most of the world uses coal and oil to heat homes and run electric generators. Coal and oil are abundant. Coal was made from plant material that was covered with water and neither coal nor oil is being formed geologically today. There is, however, one possible exception.

When Mount St. Helens erupted in 1980, the explosion filled Spirit Lake with logs. The bottom of the lake was filled with plant material covered in mud from the eruption. This was under the lake water. Examination of this material showed the early stages of the formation of coal. This, however, is a very tiny deposit compared to the massive coal deposits worldwide.[47]

Crude petroleum is also produced on a small scale in laboratories from garbage. Like diamonds and petrified wood, the processes that formed coal beds and oil deposits are not going on today. Something is dramatically different about conditions today. Like diamond formation and petrified wood formation, the only possible scientific example of oil and coal formation shows coal and oil being formed rapidly in a catastrophic event.[48]

Spirit Lake Log Mat

Coal was made from plant material which was covered with water and is not being made today. There is, however, one possible exception. When Mount St. Helens erupted in 1980, the explosion filled Spirit Lake with plant material covered in mud from the eruption. Examination of this material showed the early stages of the formation of coal.

Mount Saint Helens Eruption

Synthetic Petroleum Resin

Images are of Spirit Lake log mat, Mt St Helens eruption, and synthetic petroleum resin. Caption: "Coal was made from plant material that was covered with water and neither coal nor oil is being formed geologically today. There is, however, one possible exception. When Mount St. Helens erupted in 1980, the explosion filled Spirit Lake with logs. The bottom of the lake was filled with plant material covered in mud from the eruption. This was under the lake water. Examination of this material showed the early stages of the formation of coal.”

Petrified Wood

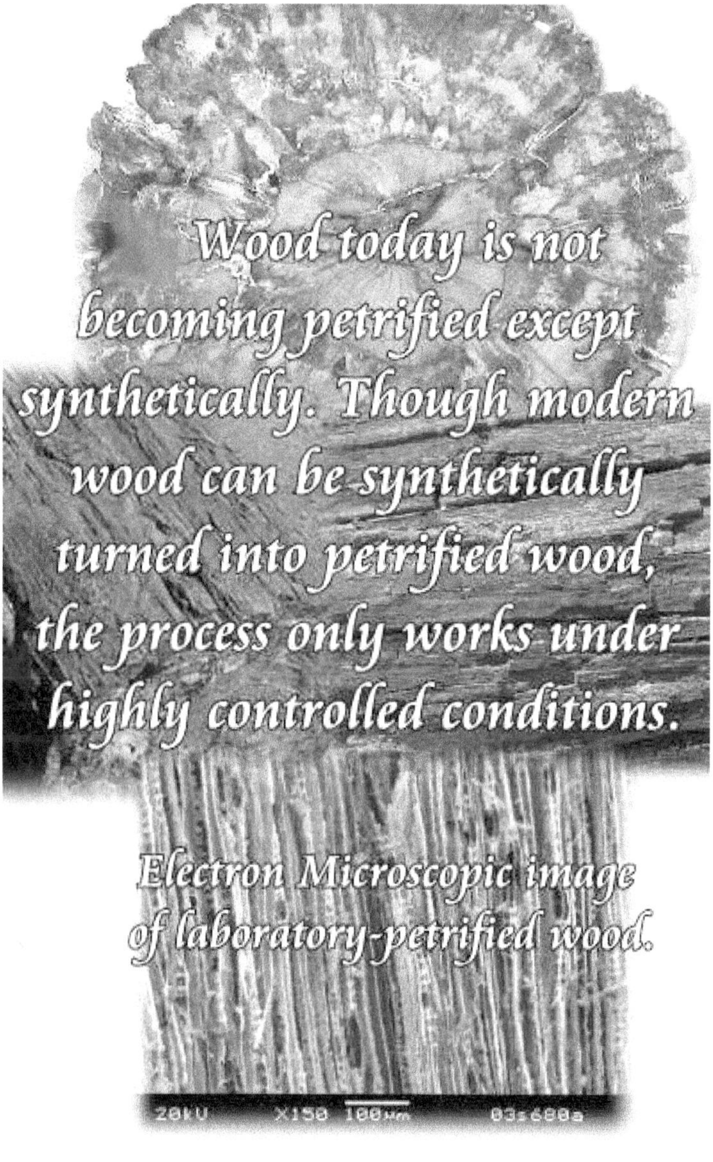

Wood today is not becoming petrified except synthetically. Though modern wood can be synthetically turned into petrified wood, the process only works under highly controlled conditions.

Electron Microscopic image of laboratory-petrified wood.

20kV X150 100µm 03 680a

Images: Electron microscope image of laboratory-petrified wood and naturally petrified wood. "Wood today is not becoming petrified except synthetically. Though modern wood can be synthetically turned into petrified wood, the process only works under highly-controlled conditions."

Just off of Interstate 40 in the Navajo Indian reservation in northeast Arizona is the Petrified Forest. While the Petrified Forest in Arizona is the most well-known of the Petrified Forests, petrified wood can be found all over the world, though it is abundant in dry regions of the western United States. Petrified wood is wood that has turned to stone. The authors have seen petrified tree stumps in South Dakota more than twenty feet in diameter. Perhaps there is a rare exception somewhere, but wood today is not becoming petrified except synthetically. Though modern wood can be synthetically turned into petrified wood, the process only works under highly-controlled conditions.

The existence of synthetic diamonds and manmade petrified wood both scientifically prove that these substances require not immense periods of time but proper conditions to form them. They can be made in days, weeks or months. The religious belief that wood petrified over a great period of time and that the process took place thousands or millions of years ago is without scientific evidence. Even people who insist that wood petrified thousands or millions of years ago must admit wood is not naturally petrifying today. Therefore, something has dramatically changed. Though the most reasonable scientific explanation is a catastrophe, religious dogmas refuse to allow for these scientific explanations.[49]

Japanese scientists fastened pieces of wood in a hot acid lake. They observed that “after only 7 years the wood had turned into stone, petrified with silica.”[50]

Preservation in Ice, Tar, and Peat

Images: Tar entombed remains. Caption: "There is an entire class of creatures entombed in tar, peat bogs, muck and sand; organic remains clearly younger than fossils."

Some of the more well-known of these creatures are woolly mammoths, mastodons, saber-toothed tigers, woolly rhinos, and giant ground sloths. These creatures are not fossilized, that is, turned to stone, but frozen. Though some were preserved in warmer areas by tar, most specimens are frozen and decay quickly when thawed.

Undigested plant remains in their stomachs prove that the animals were frozen quickly. Though pop culture places these animals in the Ice Age, the types of undigested plants found in their stomachs suggest that at the time the animals were frozen they and the plants lived in a warm climate. This indicates that tropical, subtropical or at least temperate conditions existed even in Siberia, Alaska, and northern Canada. Though these creatures obviously died in a catastrophe, this catastrophe was far more recent than the catastrophe which fossilized billions of other creatures worldwide.[51]

Soft Tissue in Dinosaur Bones

Creatures found in tar and ice are said by evolutionists to have come from a later time period than those fossilized, thus minimizing the troublesome issues of their real age. It is harder to dismiss one discovery, soft tissue from the bone of a dinosaur. There is no question that soft tissue deteriorates very rapidly. There is no question as to what such a discovery must mean. Dinosaurs, at least the ones leaving remains with soft tissue, had to have been living at the same time humans lived. The question is, has such a discovery actually been made? Paleontologist Mary Higby Schweitzer of North Carolina University has published her discovery of the remains of blood cells in dinosaur fossils and soft tissue remains in a T. Rex. John Asara of Harvard Medical School and researchers at Palo Alto have verified it.

Blood for transfusions can only be stored for about six weeks. Cryopreservation is only good for about ten years. These facts should help put this discovery into perspective. Not only did Dr. Schweitzer's team find bone cells, blood cells, and proteins, they also found dinosaur DNA.[52]

We should also compare this to the soft tissue discovered in a female wooly mammoth carcass. Even uniformitarians only date this to be 10,000 years old. We know that this is more than twice the actual age of the wooly mammoth. The conditions for preservation of the tissue were much better. It was preserved in permafrost at -10° C. Physiologist Kevin Campbell of the University of Manitoba wrote in an email to Kate Wong in a May 30, 2013 article that, “ancient DNA is highly fragmented and by no means “ready to go” into the next mammoth embryo.” He also said “how were these samples preserved in this state for so long?”[53]

So the soft tissue of Ice Age woolly mammoths preserved in very favorable conditions is puzzling. The preservation of dinosaur soft tissue for millions of years is, by comparison, impossible.[54]

The evidence is overwhelming. The conclusions, however, are even more astounding. Rather than admit the obvious, that the bones with the remains of soft tissue were young, the published reports maintain that the bones are millions of years old, but some process not now understood preserved the soft tissue. There is no evidence of such an unknown process. This is a classic attempt to make the evidence fit the preconception.[54] It is also a glaring example of professional bigotry. This kind of article can never be published without a claim that the bones are millions of years old.

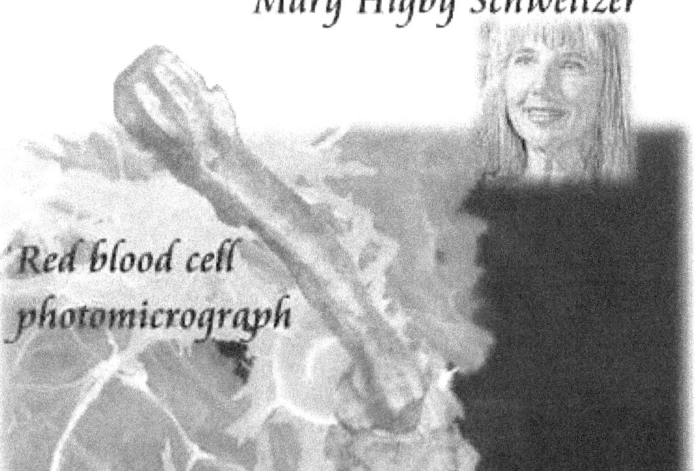

One highly controversial discovery is soft tissue from the bone of a dinosaur. There is no question that soft tissue deteriorates very rapidly and can be at most a few thousand years old.

Images: T-Rex leg bone and picture of Mary Higby Schweitzer. Caption: "One highly controversial discovery is soft tissue from the bone of a dinosaur. There is no question that soft tissue deteriorates very rapidly and can be at most a few thousand years old."

Mary Schweitzer is firmly committed to ignoring the implications of her work, that these bones are very, very young. That secures her professional position. If she were to acknowledge this implication, that would be the end of her professional career. Eventually well-orchestrated condemnation would cost the author her job, as documented repeatedly in Ben Stein's movie *Expelled*.[55]

No Great Ape Fossils

"No fossils of any of the great apes: gorillas, chimpanzees or orangutans; have ever been found. As far as the fossil record is concerned, they never existed; and yet we know from the evidence of our own eyes that they did, and do."[56]

Though hundreds, perhaps thousands, of news releases, newspaper articles, magazine articles, radio, video, and internet announcements have proclaimed the discovery of a fossil of a great ape, none has ever been verified. Such discoveries have either proven to not be fossilized, and therefore much younger, or not to be a great ape. Some who carefully examine the evidence come to the reasoned conclusion that evolution is not scientifically valid. They do not find reproductive links in the evolutionary chain. Creationists are frequently charged with ignoring the evidence. Richard Dawkins claims to refute the fossil gap arguments in his numerous books, although he doesn't really refute them at all. He just dismisses the arguments with a bald, unsupported statement that large numbers of intermediates exist.

"Creationists are deeply enamored of the fossil record ...[They] repeat, over and over, the mantra that it is full of 'gaps': 'Show me your "intermediates!"' ...We [have]...massive numbers ... to document evolutionary history ... beautiful 'intermediates.' ... The fossil evidence for evolution in many major animal groups is wonderfully strong. Nevertheless there are, of course, gaps, and creationists love them obsessively."[57]

The truth is that there is nothing for mankind to link to. Neanderthals interbred with modern man. A skull found in *Pestera cu Oase,* "The Cave of Bones" in Romania, has characteristics of both so-called "species."

"The skull bearing both older and modern characteristics is discussed in a paper by Erik Trinkaus of Washington University in St. Louis. The report appears in today's [January 15, 2007] issue of *Proceedings of the National Academy of Sciences.*

"...The researchers said the skull had the same proportions as a modern human head and lacked the large brow ridge commonly associated with Neanderthals. However, there were also features that are unusual in modern humans, such as frontal flattening, a fairly large bone behind the ear and exceptionally large upper molars, which are seen among Neanderthals and other early hominids.

"Such differences raise important questions about the evolutionary history of modern humans," said co-author João Zilhão of the University of Bristol, England.[58]

Therefore, Neanderthals are men. Without any fossil evidence of creatures for man to evolve from, evolution of humans is a religious leap of faith. There is no evidence of any link and no fossil evidence of anything to link to.

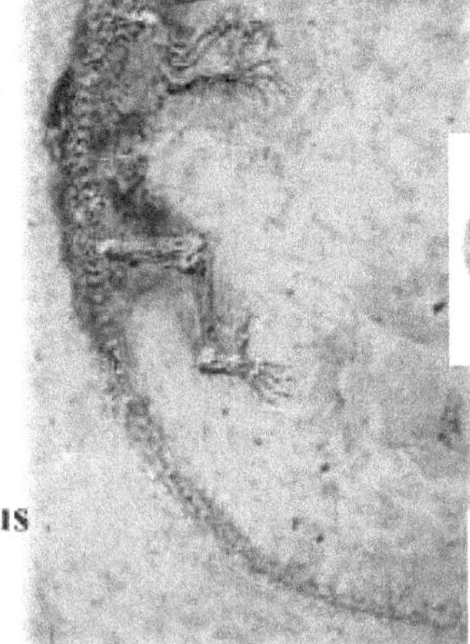

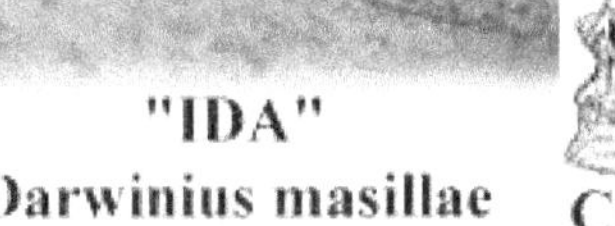

"No fossils of any of the great apes - gorillas, chimpanzees or orangutans - have ever been found. As far as the fossil record is concerned, they never existed; and yet we know from the evidence of our own eyes that they did, and do."

Images of fossils speculated to be human evolutionary ancestors, including "Ida," Darwinius masillae. *"No fossils of any of the great apes: gorillas, chimpanzees or orangutans; have ever been found. As far as the fossil record is concerned, they never existed; and yet we know from the evidence of our own eyes that they did, and do."*

Mitochondrial DNA

Any link would be controlled by DNA. The most important aspect of the soft tissue discovery in the dinosaur is the DNA. DNA is in all cells of all living organisms. The tiniest cell in the human body contains the same DNA in the nucleus as the largest cell. This genetic coding determines hair color, shape of our nostrils, and every other detail of our body. As every student of high school biology knows, this DNA inside the nucleus contains genetic material from both our mother and our father. But many people are unaware of another type of DNA known as mitochondrial DNA. Mitochondrial DNA exists within the cell's mitochondria outside of the nucleus and contains only genetic material from our mothers. Since there is no mixing of genetic material, a child's mitochondrial DNA should be an exact duplicate of the mother's mitochondrial DNA.

Mitochondrial DNA controls individual cell functions, not genetically encoded information. Infinite generations with genetically different fathers can have identical mitochondrial DNA but radically different physical characteristics. This should allow for a trace of mitochondrial DNA back to the beginning the human race. We could perform this trace, except for the problem of genetic mutations. Since a child's normal mitochondrial DNA is identical to his mother's, any mutation starts a new line. Minor mutations are difficult to detect and major mutations, such as those caused by massive radiation exposure, produce children who are unable to survive. But a few extremely rare mutations have produced traceable lines.

In 1997, *Nature Genetics* published an article with the innocuous title "A high observed substitution rate in the human mitochondrial DNA control rate." An abstract is available online for free. Though the technical language is absolutely necessary for accuracy, it distracts the average reader. Even with nothing but the abstract, the force of this study is overwhelming.

> *"...We report a direct measurement of the intergenerational substitution rate in the human CR [Control Region – a section of the DNA that controls other sections of DNA]. We compared DNA sequences of two CR hypervariable segments from close maternal relatives, from 134 independent mtDNA lineages spanning 327 generational events. Ten substitutions were observed, resulting in an empirical rate of 1/33 generations, or 2.5/site/Myr. This is roughly twenty-fold higher than estimates derived from phylogenetic analyses. This disparity cannot be accounted for simply by substitutions at mutational hot spots, suggesting additional factors that produce the discrepancy between very near-term and long-term apparent rates of sequence divergence. The data also indicate that extremely rapid segregation of CR sequence variants between generations is common in humans, with a very small mtDNA bottleneck."*[59]
>
> What this study did was take mitochondrial DNA samples from living volunteers and compared it to mitochondrial DNA from their ancestors. The test subjects had to have accurate records of their ancestors for hundreds of years, so all test subjects had to be European. Corpses had to be available with accurate records and preserved well enough that mitochondrial DNA could be obtained. The study went back approximately 550 years.

The test results proved that mutations happen at a significantly higher rate than geneticists thought possible. The resulting statistical analysis came to two stunning conclusions.

First, applying this data to other studies gives an approximate date of 6000-6,500 BP (Before Present) for Mitochondrial Eve.[60]

The most important aspect of the soft tissue discovery in this dinosaur is the DNA. Many people are unaware of another type of DNA known as mitochondrial DNA. Mitochondrial DNA exists within the cell's mitochondria outside of the nucleus and contains only genetic material from our mothers.

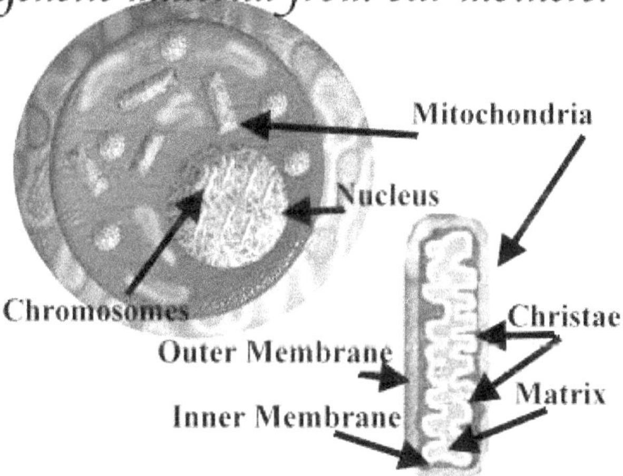

Mitochondrial DNA is not contained in the Nucleus but is in the cytoplasm of the Cell.

Image: illustrations of cell contents including mitochondrial DNA. Caption: "The most important aspect of the soft tissue discovery in the dinosaur is the DNA. many people are unaware of another type of DNA known as mitochondrial DNA. Mitochondrial DNA exists within the cell's mitochondria outside of the nucleus and contains only genetic material from our mothers."

Catastrophes powerful enough to move marine ammonites to the top of Mount Everest, and tilt Lake Titicaca, could easily, temporarily and dramatically, increase the mutation rate, making even the 6000-year-old date too old.

Second is the "very small mtDNA bottleneck." This means that at some point in the history of the human race there were very few women. Bryan Sykes, author of *The Seven Daughters of Eve* believes that all Europeans currently alive can be traced back to one of seven women. Though Sykes is a well-respected English geneticist, as a committed Secular Humanist he makes two common though critical errors. These two errors have become the "standard" which any geneticist who expects to be published must adhere to. These errors are required by the religious dogma of Secular Humanism. Because his religious dogma demands that the human race is much older than the scientific evidence shows, he makes the leap of faith that the 2.5/site/Myr was lower in the past. His second error is assuming by a leap of faith, without any scientific evidence, that these seven women represent the smallest point of the bottleneck.

The Bible says that the sons of Noah brought their wives on the ark. These three women are the smallest point of the bottleneck. Their daughters or granddaughters might be the seven women of Bryan Sykes. Since conditions at that time could easily cause increased genetic mutations, their daughters, granddaughters or great granddaughters could easily be the seven women isolated by Bryan Sykes. When you read *The Seven Daughters of Eve,* understand that the last part of the book is devoted to fictional indoctrination. He novelizes each of these women and places each of them in a "cavewoman" setting. This is as antiscientific an approach as possible. Nevertheless the book was published. The scientific evidence of Mitochondrial DNA concludes that the human race is much younger than the published dates, less than 10,000 years, and that at one time in the very recent past the entire human race had no more than seven women. Bryan Sykes added the cavewoman fictions to assure publication. Such fabrications are the essence of the academic requirements for upholding the secularist dogma.[56]

He also claims that this genetic bottleneck of seven women is only for women of European descent, not the entire human race.

A much better study, without the approval of the academic community, therefore without the publicity, is Dr. Robert W. Carter's *Adam, Eve and Noah vs Modern Genetics.* This article also explores why the Y chromosome supports a recent genetic bottleneck. Dr. Carter states, "There are three main mitochondrial DNA lineages found across the world. The evolutionists have labeled these lines "M", "N", and "R"…"[61]

Thermodynamics

Engineers can earn a PhD in many subcategories of the massive field of thermodynamics. The dynamics of heat affects all other aspects of engineering. The first two laws of thermodynamics are well-tested and well-proved. While the implications are massive, the first two laws are simple. The first law of thermodynamics: The conservation of energy. Energy can be changed from one form to another, but it cannot be created or destroyed. The total amount of energy and matter in the universe remains constant, merely changing from one form to another.

Albert Einstein popularized the first law of thermodynamics with his famous proposition "If a body at rest emits a total energy of E while remaining at rest, then the mass of that body decreases by E/c^2."

This is oversimplified into $E=mc^2$. Though technically this only applies to a body at rest, it is a workable understanding of the concept that matter and energy are interchangeable. In this formula, "c" represents the speed of light, in a vacuum, 299, 792, 458 meters per second or 186,300 miles per second.

Here is a link to a blog which works through the Lorentz transformation to explain how Albert Einstein arrived at his final formula. [62]

According to the first law of thermodynamics the universe is either 1) eternal, 2) created out of nothing, or 3) came into existence through some process that we know nothing about.

The Second Law of Thermodynamics states “in all energy exchanges, if no energy enters or leaves the system, the potential energy of the state will always be less than that of the initial state.” This is also commonly referred to as entropy. Another way of stating entropy is that all energy changes are in a downward direction.[63] Without a belief in the religious dogma that the universe is infinite and can therefore obtain energy from “outside” the system (which is scientifically unprovable), entropy will eventually lead to a “heat death” for the entire universe. Everything in the universe will be motionless, at a uniform temperature near absolute zero, broken down into subatomic particles.

Thermodynamics

First Law: Energy changes form,
cannot be created or destroyed.
Amount of energy and matter
constant, only changes form.
The universe is either 1) eternal,
2) created out of nothing, or
3) came into existence through some
unknown process.

Second Law:
Potential energy always less
than initial state.
Entropy = "heat death" for the
entire universe. Motionless,
at a uniform temperature
near absolute zero, broken down into
subatomic particles.

Caption: Aerodynamic First Law: Energy changes form, cannot be created or destroyed. Amount of energy and matter constant, only changes form. The universe is either 1) eternal, 2) created out of nothing, or 3) came into existence through some unknown process.
Second law: Potential energy always less than initial state. Entropy = "heat death" for the entire universe. Motionless, at a uniform temperature near absolute zero, broken down into subatomic particles.

Each one of these examples of physical evidence has the same message. To repeat a quote from Dr. Danny R. Faulkner at the beginning of this chapter:

"*While the early faint Sun paradox does not tell us that the Solar System is only thousands of years old, it does seem to rule out the age being billions of years.*"

Dr. Danny R. Faulkner

(Caption for the image, which includes an orange sun.) "While the early faint Sun paradox does not tell us that the Solar System is only thousands of years old, it does seem to rule out the age being billions of years."[64]

We can rephrase this statement to make it more inclusive. While none of these points in this chapter tell us that the earth is only thousands of years old, each one individually and all of them collectively seem to rule out the age being billions of years.

We close with the words of the committed Secular Humanist, Isaac Asimov, as he condemns not only his own belief system, but also the belief systems of everyone who rejects the evidence for the Word of God.

"I believe in evidence. I believe in observation, measurement, and reasoning, confirmed by independent observers. I'll believe anything, no matter how wild and ridiculous, if there is evidence for it. The wilder and more ridiculous something is, however, the firmer and more solid the evidence will have to be."[65]

"We can make inspired guesses, but we don't know for certain what physical and chemical properties of the planet's crust, its ocean, and its atmosphere made it so conducive to such a sudden appearance of life..."

Isaac Asimov

"I believe in evidence. I believe in observation, measurement, and reasoning, confirmed by independent observers. I'll believe anything, no matter how wild and ridiculous, if there is evidence for it. The wilder and more ridiculous something is, however, the firmer and more solid the evidence will have to be."

Isaac Asimov

"We can make inspired guesses, but we don't know for certain what physical and chemical properties of the planet's crust, its ocean, and its atmosphere made it so conducive to such a sudden appearance of life..."

(This image contains the quotes by Asimov on the previous page, with an image of the author.)

1 Charles Darwin, "Letter to Asa Gray," (Harvard Professor of Biology), 18 June, 1857.

2 John Adams, "Argument in defence of the [English] soldiers in the Boston Massacre trial," December 1770.

3 Mark Twain, *Life on the Mississippi,* first edition published by Osgood and Company, 1883.

4 Samuel Johnson, *The History of Rasselas, Prince of Abissinia,* 1759.

5 Dennis Prager, "Breastfeeding as a Religion," World Net Daily, http://wnd.com/, posted November 11, 2003 1:00 am Eastern.

6 Richard W. Pogge, Astronomy 162: Introduction to Stars, Galaxies, & the Universe, 2006, http://www.astronomy.ohio-state.edu/-pogge/Ast162/Unit2/sunshine.html

7 "Fusion", *Nobelprize.org* updated 9 Mar 2013 http://nobelprize.org/nobel_prizes/physics/articles/fusion/sun_4.html

8 Ian T Durham, "Hans Bethe" (Biographic article about Hans Bethe), Saint Anselm College, Goffstown, NH, http://www-history.mcs.st-and.ac.uk/Biographies/Bethe.html

9 Akridge, R. 1980. "The Sun Is Shrinking." *Acts & Facts.* 9 (4) and Faulkner, D. 1998. "The Young Faint Sun Paradox and the Age of the Solar System." *Acts & Facts.* 27 (6). [these two articles are quoted and paraphrased from throughout this section]

10 Roger Freedman, Robert Geller, William J. Kaufmann, *Universe: The Solar System,* Macmillan, New York, NY, 2010.

11 Two links to articles which examine the early faint sun paradox problem in more detail:

http://creation.com/our-steady-sun-a-problem-for-billions-of-years

http://creation.com/the-young-faint-sun-paradox-and-the-age-of-the-solar-system

12 Daily Mail online, October 3, 2011 http://www.dailymail.co.uk/sciencetech/article-2044480/NASAs-SDO-satellite-shows-boiling-sun-stunning-detail.html#ixzz2MnMZZ5lS

13 Ethan Siegal PhD in theoretical astrophysics at the University of Florida *Starts with a Bang*. "How the Sun works, from the inside out", originally posted August 12, 2011.

14 D. Russell Humphreys, Steven A. Austin, John R. Baumgardner, and Andrew A. Snelling, "Helium Diffusion Age of 6000 Years Supports Accelerated Nuclear Decay," *Creation Research Society Quarterly Journal. (CRSQ)* Vol 41 No 1 June 2004, *Creation Research.org,* Copyright © 2004 by Creation Research Society. Also Dr. Don DeYoung, *Thousands, Not Billions: Challenging an Icon of Evolution Questioning the Age of the Earth,* Green Forest, AR: Master Books, Inc., 2005.

15 Utah Geological Survey, *Utah.gov*.

16 Radiometric Dating background from the position of those who believe it to be valid can be studied on *TalkOrigins.org.,* especially the article *Radiometric Dating and the Geological Time Scale: Circular Reasoning or Reliable Tools?* Andrew MacRae Copyright 1997-2004 [Text last updated: October 2, 1998] and also these two books: G. Brent Dalrymple, *The Age of the Earth*. Stanford University Press: Stanford, CA, 1991. G. Faure, *Principles of Isotope Geology,* 2nd. edition. John Wiley and Sons: New York, NY, 1986.

17 John Michael Fischer, *Dinosaur bones have been Carbon-14 dated to less than 40,000 years,* http://newgeology.us/presentation48.html, 2012-2014.

18 Press release, Public Information Office, Jet Propulsion Laboratory, California Institute of Technology, *NASA,* July 21, 1994.

19 Andrew A. Snelling, "The Earth's magnetic field and the age of the Earth," first published: *Creation (Creation Ministries International),* 13(4):44-48 September 1991.

20 D. Russell Humphreys, *Earth's Magnetic Field is Decaying Steadily –with a Little Rhythm,* CRSQ (Creation Research Society Quarterly) July 1, 2010. http://www.creationresearch.org/crsq/articles/47/47_3/CRSQ%20Winter%202011%20Humphreys.pdf

21 Jonathan Sarfati, *The Earth's Magnetic Field: Evidence That the Earth Is Young* http://creation.com/the-earths-magnetic-field-evidence-that-the-earth-is-young

22 Alexandra Witze, "Geomagnetic Flip-Flops in a Flash," *Science News,* September 25, 210 Vol. 178, Number 7, and R.S. Coe, and M. Prevot, 1989. "Evidence suggesting extremely rapid field variation during a geomagnetic reversal," *Earth and Planetary Science Letters, Elsevier*, Amsterdam, Netherlands, vol. 92, pp. 296-297.

23 http://www.answersingenesis.org/home/area/cfol/ch3-grand-canyon.asp

24 Type/Process: Pyroclastic Flow
Volcanic Status: Historical
Image Number: 029-008
Photographer: Norm Banks, 1980 (U.S. Geological Survey)
Summit Elevation: 2549 meters

Latitude/Longitude: 46.20 N / 122.18 W
Timeframe: Last known eruption 1964 or later
Region: Canada and Western USA

25 G.R. Morton, (An old-earth supporter who calls himself a creationist apologist) "Young-Earth Arguments: A Second Look," 1998, *home.entouch.net*.

26 J.B. Delair and E.F. Oppe, "The Lost Sea of Andes," in Charles Hapgood's *The Path of the Pole*, Chilton Book Company, Philadelphia, PA, 1970.

27 Donald W. Patten and Samuel R. Windsor, "Catastrophic Theory of Mountain Uplifts (A Crustal Deformation Theory)," *Catastrophism and Ancient History* Vol. XIII Part 1 January 1991.

28 "Ancient temple found under Lake Titicaca," *BBC News, UK*, Wednesday, 23 August, 2000, 11:04 GMT 12:04.

29 J. P. Davidson, W. E. Reed, and P. M. Davis, "The Rise and Fall of Mountain Ranges," in *Exploring Earth: An Introduction to Physical Geology*, Upper Saddle River, New Jersey, Prentice Hall, 1997.

30 Erich A. Von Fange, "Time Upside Down," *Creation Research Quarterly*, June 1974.

31 *National Geographic*, July 26, 2008, "Tiny Fossils reveal Warm Antarctic Past," and *AntarcticConnection.com* reports on the Antarctic research stations.

32 Sean Pitman, M.D., in a PowerPoint presentation titled "Ancient Ice," created in Jan 2006, including testimony from a phone interview with Bob Cardin, project manager to recover one of the P38s lost on the glacier.

33 Fred Hall, "Ice Cores Not All That Simple," *AEON II: 1*, 1989:199.

34 "Superbridge," *NOVA*, PBS, November 12, 1997.

35 Dr. Nathan Green, online course overview for GEO.101, "Introduction to Geology," Spring 2006, University of Alabama.

36 Jonathan Sarfati, *Salty Seas: Evidence for a Young Earth, Creation* 21(1):16-17, December 1998, http://creation.com/salty-seas-evidence-for-a-young-earth

37 *GeorgiaEncyclopedia.org* gives background on the canyon but attributes its underlying geology to the "millions of years" formation theory. See also "Canyon Creation," by Rebecca Gibson, *Answers in Genesis,* September 2000.

38 National Park Service report on Wall Arch collapse with before and after photos, August 4-5, 2008.

39 Photo of recently-formed stalactites courtesy of Creation Ministries International (see footnote 44 for commentary on the Australian Mine photo). Lincoln Memorial Photo from National Parks services website.

40. National Park Services Website.

41 Dave E. Matson, "How Good Are Those Young-Earth Arguments?" on *Infidels.org*. copyright 1995.

42 *GORP.com* (Great Outdoor Recreation Page.)

43 "Cave Reveals Southwest's Abrupt Climate Swings During Ice Age," *Science Daily.com,* January 25, 2010.

44 http://creation.com/stalactites-do-not-take-millions-of-years

45 American Museum of Natural History website, "How Old are Kimberlites and Diamonds?" see also *Novori.com* for history and manufacture of laboratory produced diamonds.

46 Andrew Snelling (Dr.), "Radiocarbon in Diamonds Confirmed," *Answers in Genesis,* November 7, 2007.

(This study was conducted during the *RATE (Radioisotopes and the Age of The Earth)* research project at the Institute for Creation Research.)

47 "Coal, Volcanism and Noah's Flood," *TJ (Technical Journal)* 1(1): *Creation Ministries International*, 11-29 April 1984.

48 A.A. Snelling, "The Recent Origin of Bass Strait Oil and Gas," Creation, 5 (2):43-46 March 1982.5

49 Phil McCafferty, "Instant petrified wood?" *Popular Science,* October 1992, pp. 56-57. also Hamilton Hicks, 'Mineralized sodium silicate solutions for artificial petrification of wood,' United States Patent Number 4,612,050, September 16,1986, pp. 1-3. As cited by: Steven Austin, *CatastroRef*—"Catastrophe Reference Database: Catastrophes in Earth History, Geologic Evidence, Speculation and Theory," *Institute for Creation Research,* San Diego. Entry no. 267.

50 *Petrified Wood: Fast or Slow?* http://creation.com/petrified-wood-fast-or-slow

51 Michael Oard, *Frozen in Time: The Wooly Mammoth, The Ice Age and the Bible,* Green Forest, AR: Master Books, Inc., 2004.

52 http://creation.com/dino-dna-bone-cells#endRef5

53 http://www.nature.com/news/can-a-mammoth-carcass-really-preserve-flowing-blood-and-possibly-live-cells-1.13103

54 Schweitzer, Mary H. and Jennifer L. Wittmeyer, North Carolina State University; John R. Horner, Montana State University; Jan B. Toporski, Carnegie Institution of Washington Geophysical Laboratory. "Soft-Tissue Vessels and Cellular Preservation in Tyrannosaurus Rex." *Science,* March 25, 2005. (NC State, the N.C. Museum of Natural Sciences and the National Science Foundation funded the research.)

55 Kevin Miller, Ben Stein, writers, Producers Logan Craft, Walt Ruloff and John Sullivan, Director Nathan Frankowski. Assoc. Prod. Mark Mathis. Ed. Simon Tondeur. *Expelled: No Intelligence Allowed.* © 2008 Premise Media Corporation, Rampart Films Production.

56 Bryan Sykes, *The Seven Daughters of Eve: The Science That Reveals Our Genetic Ancestry.* W.W. Norton, New York, N.Y., 2001.

57 Richard Dawkins, *The Greatest Show on Earth,* Free Press, Simon and Schuster, New York, NY, also by Bantam Press Transworld Publishers in Great Britain, 2009.

58 Randolph E. Schmid (Associated Press), "Skull Suggests Interbreeding of Neanderthal and Modern Man," *The Denver Post,* January 15, 2007.

59 Parsons, Thomas J., et. al. "A high observed substitution rate in the human mitochondrial DNA control region." Nature Genetics 15, 363 - 368 (1997).

60 http://creation.com/refuting-evolution-chapter-6-humans-images-of-god-or-advanced-apes#r25

61 http://creation.com/noah-and-genetics

62
http://terrytao.wordpress.com/2007/12/28/einsteins-derivation-of-emc2/

63 M.J. Farabee, *The Online Biology Book* (Farabee is a member of the Biology faculty at Estrella Mountain Community College, Avondale, Arizona. *emc.maricopa.edu*

64 Faulkner, D. 1998. "The Young Faint Sun Paradox and the Age of the Solar System. " Acts & Facts. 27 (6).

65 Isaac Asimov, *The Roving Mind.* Prometheus Books, 1997.

The best gift you can give an author

is an honest, thoughtful review. Please consider leaving one online. Help us understand what you liked and didn't like about the book and why. Help authors reach more readers and spread your influence and ours. If you liked the book, please recommend it to your spouse, friends, pastors, teachers, cashiers, employers, – anybody and everybody you see each day. If you don't know what to say, remember Proverb 16:3 – Commit thy works unto the Lord and thy thoughts shall be established. Thank you!

OTHER BOOKS AND PRODUCTS FROM FINDLEY FAMILY VIDEO PUBLICATIONS

All our books (including Historical Fiction, SciFi, contemporary relationships short stories, and an Archaeological Mystery serial) are linked on our blog.

Elk Jerky for the Soul includes posts on current issues, excerpts from our fiction and nonfiction works, Bible teaching, travel and everyday observations, and more.

http://findleyfamilyvideopublications.com/

Visit our YouTube Channel

https://www.youtube.com/channel/UCGhwNpU115ARMwgYwTIJBrA/featured. Book trailers, video excerpts, project teasers, and more. Science, History, Literature, and biblical worldview studies are the focus of our book and video projects.

Historical Fiction

by Michael J. Findley

The Ephron the Hittite Series (Including boxed set of all titles)

Ephron Son of Zohar

Tawananna Daughter of Zohar

Heth Son of Canaan Son of Ham, Noah

Shelometh Daughter of Yovov Wife of Ephron

Zita Son of Ephron and Shelometh

Adult Romantic Suspense

by Mary C. Findley

The Men of the Realmlands series

Book One: The Baron's Ring

Book Two: The Captain's Blade

Send a White Rose

Chasing the Texas Wind

Carrie's Hired Hand (novella)

Young Adult Historical Adventure

by Mary C. Findley

Hope and the Knight of the Black Lion (plus illustrated version)

The Benny and the Bank Robber Series

Benny and the Bank Robber (Plus homeschool editions for student and teacher with review and vocabulary)

Doctor Dad

The Oregon Sentinel

Lines in Pleasant Places

Science Fiction and Fantasy

by Michael J. Findley

The Empire Saga (all six of the following books in one volume)

City on a Hill and Sojourner (Combined Novella and Short Story)

Nehemiah LLC (Full-length novel available as a standalone ebook, paperback, and hardcover versions)

Empire One: Humiliation

Empire Two: Repentance

Empire Three: Sanctification

Steampunk

by Sophronia Belle Lyon (pen name for Mary C. Findley)

The Alexander Legacy Steampunk Literary Tribute Series

Book One: A Dodge, a Twist, and a Tobacconist (including illustrated version)

Book Two: The Pinocchio Factor

Book Three: The Most Dangerous Game

Book Four: Beware the Bustle

Fantasy/Allegory

by Mary C. Findley

Allegorical clockwork novella inspired by Little Red Riding Hood

The Acolyte's Education

A Paranormal Urban Fantasy serial

His Sign: The Wait Is Over

His Sign 2: The Ezra Solution

Contemporary Fiction

by Mary C. Findley

Romantic Suspense Novella

Fall On Your Knees

Relationships Short Stories

Fifty Shades of Faithful

Fifty Shades of Faithful 2: In Living Color

The Great Thirst Serial Archaeological Mystery (including boxed set of all titles)

Part One: Prepared

Part Two: Purified

Part Three: Pursued

Part Four: Persecuted

Part Five: Persevering

Part Six: Protected

Part Seven: Prevailing

Murder Mystery

Mapped Out Murders

Nonfiction

by Mary C. Findley

Write for the King of Glory, 2nd Edition (updated, with tips on indie writing and publishing)

by Michael J. and Mary C. Findley

The Good, the Bad, and the Ugly: A Readers' and Writers' Guide for Believers

Biblical Studies (Teacher and student editions plus excerpts in OT and NT Manuscript History)

Antidisestablishmentarianism (illustrated and plain versions)

Serial versions, illustrated and plain

What Is an Establishment of Religion?

What Is Secular Humanism?

What Is Science?

What Are the Results of the Establishment of Secular Humanism?

The Conflict of the Ages series (All have teacher and student editions)

I. The Scientific History of Origins

II. The Origin of Evil in the World that Was

III. They Deliberately Forgot: The Flood and the Ice Age

IV. Ice Age Civilizations

V. The Ancient World

by Michael J. Findley

Short Recaps of longer nonfiction works *(Antidisestablishmentarianism* and *Conflict of the Ages)*

Disestablish: An Overview from Creation to the Ice Age

Under the Sun: The Truth about History from the Beginning

*****

Christian Books in Multiple Genres. Join Christian Indie Author ~ Readers Group on Facebook. https://www.facebook.com/groups/291215317668431/

www.ingramcontent.com/pod-product-compliance
Lightning Source LLC
LaVergne TN
LVHW050527160826
845677LV00011B/1971

* 9 7 9 8 2 3 0 3 1 7 5 7 9 *